# PRENTICE HALL
# WORLD STUDIES
## FOUNDATIONS of GEOGRAPHY

In association with
**DK**

**Discovery** CHANNEL
**SCHOOL**

PEARSON

Prentice
Hall

Boston, Massachusetts
Upper Saddle River, New Jersey

## Program Consultants

### Heidi Hayes Jacobs

Heidi Hayes Jacobs, Ed.D., has served as an education consultant to more than 1,000 schools across the nation and abroad. Dr. Jacobs serves as an adjunct professor in the Department of Curriculum on Teaching at Teachers College, Columbia University. She has written two best-selling books and numerous articles on curriculum reform. She received an M.A. from the University of Massachusetts, Amherst, and completed her doctoral work at Columbia University's Teachers College in 1981. The core of Dr. Jacobs' experience comes from her years teaching high school, middle school, and elementary school students. As an educational consultant, she works with K–12 schools and districts on curriculum reform and strategic planning.

### Michal L. LeVasseur

Michal LeVasseur is the Executive Director of the National Council for Geographic Education. She is an instructor in the College of Education at Jacksonville State University and works with the Alabama Geographic Alliance. Her undergraduate and graduate work were in the fields of anthropology (B.A.), geography (M.A.), and science education (Ph.D.). Dr. LeVasseur's specialization has moved increasingly into the area of geography education. Since 1996 she has served as the Director of the National Geographic Society's Summer Geography Workshops. As an educational consultant, she has worked with the National Geographic Society as well as with schools and organizations to develop programs and curricula for geography.

## Senior Reading Consultants

### Kate Kinsella

Kate Kinsella, Ed.D., is a faculty member in the Department of Secondary Education at San Francisco State University. A specialist in second-language acquisition and content area literacy, she consults nationally on school-wide practices that support adolescent English learners and striving readers to make academic gains. Dr. Kinsella earned her M.A. in TESOL from San Francisco State University, and her Ed.D. in Second Language Acquisition from the University of San Francisco.

### Kevin Feldman

Kevin Feldman, Ed.D., is the Director of Reading and Early Intervention with the Sonoma County Office of Education (SCOE) and an independent educational consultant. At the SCOE, he develops, organizes, and monitors programs related to K–12 literacy. Dr. Feldman has an M.A. from the University of California, Riverside in Special Education, Learning Disabilities and Instructional Design. He earned his Ed.D. in Curriculum and Instruction from the University of San Francisco.

Acknowledgments appear on page 186, which constitutes an extension of this copyright page.

ISBN 0-13-204147-2
78910  V057  11 10

## Cartography Consultant

### DK Andrew Heritage

Andrew Heritage has been publishing atlases and maps for more than 25 years. In 1991, he joined the leading illustrated nonfiction publisher Dorling Kindersley (DK) with the task of building an international atlas list from scratch. The DK atlas list now includes some 10 titles, which are constantly updated and appear in new editions either annually or every other year.

# Academic Reviewers

### Africa
**Barbara B. Brown, Ph.D.**
African Studies Center
Boston University
Boston, Massachusetts

### Ancient World
**Evelyn DeLong Mangie, Ph.D.**
Department of History
University of South Florida
Tampa, Florida

### Central Asia and the Middle East
**Pamela G. Sayre**
History Department,
    Social Sciences Division
Henry Ford Community College
Dearborn, Michigan

### East Asia
**Huping Ling, Ph.D.**
History Department
Truman State University
Kirksville, Missouri

### Eastern Europe
**Robert M. Jenkins, Ph.D.**
Center for Slavic, Eurasian and
    East European Studies
University of North Carolina
Chapel Hill, North Carolina

### Latin America
**Dan La Botz**
Professor, History Department
Miami University
Oxford, Ohio

### Medieval Times
**James M. Murray**
History Department
University of Cincinnati
Cincinnati, Ohio

### North Africa
**Barbara E. Petzen**
Center for Middle Eastern Studies
Harvard University
Cambridge, Massachusetts

### Religion
**Charles H. Lippy, Ph.D.**
Department of Philosophy
    and Religion
University of Tennessee
    at Chattanooga
Chattanooga, Tennessee

### Russia
**Janet Vaillant**
Davis Center for Russian
    and Eurasian Studies
Harvard University
Cambridge, Massachusetts

### United States and Canada
**Victoria Randlett**
Geography Department
University of Nevada, Reno
Reno, Nevada

### Western Europe
**Ruth Mitchell-Pitts**
Center for European Studies
University of North Carolina
    at Chapel Hill
Chapel Hill, North Carolina

# Reviewers

**Sean Brennan**
Brecksville-Broadview Heights
    City School District
Broadview Heights, Ohio

**Stephen Bullick**
Mt. Lebanon School District
Pittsburgh, Pennsylvania

**Louis P. De Angelo, Ed.D.**
Archdiocese of Philadelphia
Philadelphia, Pennsylvania

**Paul Francis Durietz**
Social Studies
    Curriculum Coordinator
Woodland District #50
Gurnee, Illinois

**Gail Dwyer**
Dickerson Middle School,
    Cobb County
Marietta, Georgia

**Michal Howden**
Social Studies Consultant
Zionsville, Indiana

**Rosemary Kalloch**
Springfield Public Schools
Springfield, Massachusetts

**Deborah J. Miller**
Office of Social Studies,
    Detroit Public Schools
Detroit, Michigan

**Steven P. Missal**
Plainfield Public Schools
Plainfield, New Jersey

**Catherine Fish Petersen**
Social Studies Consultant
Saint James, Long Island, New York

**Joe Wieczorek**
Social Studies Consultant
Baltimore, Maryland

# FOUNDATIONS of GEOGRAPHY

## Develop Skills

Use these pages to develop your reading, writing, and geography skills.

# Focus on Geography

Learn the basic tools and concepts of geography.

- Practice your skills with every map in this book.
- Interact with every map online and on CD-ROM.

Maps and illustrations created by DK help build your understanding of the world. The DK World Desk Reference Online keeps you up to date.

The World Studies Video Program takes you on field trips to study countries around the world.

The *World Studies* Interactive Textbook online and on CD-ROM uses interactive maps and other activities to help you learn.

# Special Features

## COUNTRY DATABANK

Read about the countries that make up the regions of the world.

## Literature

A selection by a noted author brings geography to life.

### *My Side of the Mountain*

## DIAGRAPHICS

Investigate geographic concepts using diagrams, maps, and photographs.

23.5°

Earth's axis tilts at a 23.5°-angle from its orbit. This accounts for the seasons.

The sun, at the center of Earth's orbit, gives our planet light and warmth.

# Maps and Charts

## MAP MASTER™

## MAP MASTER™ Interactive

Go online to find an interactive version of every MapMaster Skills Activity map in this book. Use the Web Code provided to gain direct access to these maps.

### How to Use Web Codes:

1. Go to **www.PHSchool.com.**
2. Enter the Web Code.
3. Click Go!

# Building Geographic Literacy

Learning about a country often starts with finding it on a map. The MapMaster™ system in *World Studies* helps you develop map skills you will use throughout your life. These three steps can help you become a MapMaster!

## The MAP✦MASTER™ System

### 1 Learn

You need to learn geography tools and concepts before you explore the world. Get started by using the MapMaster Skills Handbook to learn the skills you need for success.

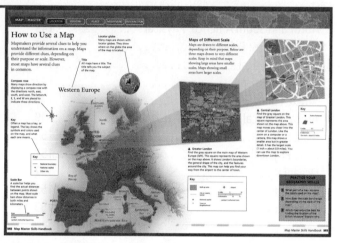

**Location** The Equator runs through parts of Latin America, but it is far from other parts of the region.

**Locate** Find the Equator on the map. Which climates are most common in Latin America, and how far is each climate region from the Equator?

**Draw Conclusions** How do climates change as you move away from the Equator?

Go Online
PHSchool.com Use Web Code
lfp-1142 for step-by-step map skills practice.

### 2 Practice

You need to practice and apply your geography skills frequently to be a MapMaster. The maps in *World Studies* give you the practice you need to develop geographic literacy.

### 3 Interact

Using maps is more than just finding places. Maps can teach you many things about a region, such as its climate, its vegetation, and the languages that the people who live there speak. Every MapMaster map is online at **PHSchool.com,** with interactive activities to help you learn the most from every map.

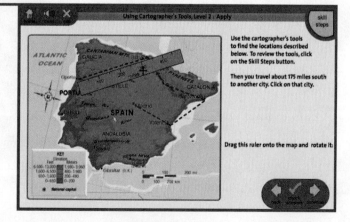

# Learning With Technology

You will be making many exciting journeys across time and place in *World Studies*. Technology will help make what you learn come alive.

**For:** An activity on the five themes of geography
**Visit:** PHSchool.com
**Web Code:** led-3101

For a complete list of features for this book, use Web Code lek-1000.

## Go Online at PHSchool.com

Use the Web Codes listed below and in each Go Online box to access exciting information or activities.

**How to Use the Web Code:**
1. Go to **www.PHSchool.com**.
2. Enter the Web Code.
3. Click Go!

## Foundations of Geography Activities

| Web Code | Activity |
|----------|----------|
| lep-3700 | Composite Volcano Eruption |
| lep-3701 | Water Cycle |
| lep-3702 | The Seasons |
| lep-3703 | Earth's Biomes |
| lep-3704 | Seismic Waves |
| lep-3705 | Topographic Map |
| lep-3706 | Weather Fronts |
| lep-3707 | Continental Drift |

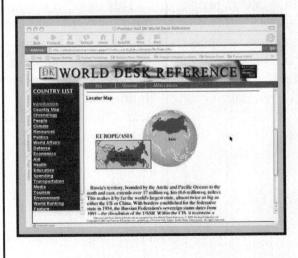

## World Desk Reference Online

There are more than 190 countries in the world. To learn about them, you need the most up-to-date information and statistics.
The **DK World Desk Reference Online** gives you instant access to the information you need to explore each country.

# Reading Informational Texts

Reading a magazine, an Internet page, or a textbook is not the same as reading a novel. The purpose of reading nonfiction texts is to acquire new information. On page RW6 you'll read about some 🔵 **Target Reading Skills** that you'll have a chance to practice as you read this textbook. Here we'll focus on a few skills that will help you read nonfiction with a more critical eye.

## Analyze the Author's Purpose

Different types of materials are written with different purposes in mind. For example, a textbook is written to teach students information about a subject. The purpose of a technical manual is to teach someone how to use something, such as a computer. A newspaper editorial might be written to persuade the reader to accept a particular point of view. A writer's purpose influences how the material is presented. Sometimes an author states his or her purpose directly. More often, the purpose is only suggested, and you must use clues to identify the author's purpose.

## Distinguish Between Facts and Opinions

It's important when reading informational texts to read actively and to distinguish between fact and opinion. A fact can be proven or disproven. An opinion cannot—it is someone's personal viewpoint or evaluation.

For example, the editorial pages in a newspaper offer opinions on topics that are currently in the news. You need to read newspaper editorials with an eye for bias and faulty logic. For example, the newspaper editorial at the right shows factual statements in blue and opinion statements in red. The underlined words are examples of highly charged words. They reveal bias on the part of the writer.

More than 5,000 people voted last week in favor of building a new shopping center, but the opposition won out. The margin of victory is irrelevant. Those <u>radical</u> voters who opposed the center are obviously <u>self-serving elitists</u> who do not care about anyone but themselves.

This month's unemployment figure for our area is 10 percent, which represents an increase of about 5 percent over the figure for this time last year. These figures mean unemployment is getting worse. But the people who voted against the mall probably do not care about creating new jobs.

## Identify Evidence

Before you accept an author's conclusion, you need to make sure that the author has based the conclusion on enough evidence and on the right kind of evidence. An author may present a series of facts to support a claim, but the facts may not tell the whole story. For example, what evidence does the author of the newspaper editorial on the previous page provide to support his claim that the new shopping center would create more jobs? Is it possible that the shopping center might have put many small local businesses out of business, thus increasing unemployment rather than decreasing it?

## Evaluate Credibility

Whenever you read informational texts, you need to assess the credibility of the author. This is especially true of sites you may visit on the Internet. All Internet sources are not equally reliable. Here are some questions to ask yourself when evaluating the credibility of a Web site.

❏ Is the Web site created by a respected organization, a discussion group, or an individual?

❏ Does the Web site creator include his or her name as well as credentials and the sources he or she used to write the material?

❏ Is the information on the site balanced or biased?

❏ Can you verify the information using two other sources?

❏ Is there a date telling when the Web site was created or last updated?

# Writing for Social Studies

Writing is one of the most powerful communication tools you will ever use. You will use it to share your thoughts and ideas with others. Research shows that writing about what you read actually helps you learn new information and ideas. A systematic approach to writing—including prewriting, drafting, revising, and proofing—can help you write better, whether you're writing an essay or a research report.

## Narrative Essays

Writing that tells a story about a personal experience

### 1 Select and Narrow Your Topic

A narrative is a story. In social studies, it might be a narrative essay about how an event affected you or your family.

### 2 Gather Details

Brainstorm a list of details you'd like to include in your narrative.

### 3 Write a First Draft

Start by writing a simple opening sentence that conveys the main idea of your essay. Continue by writing a colorful story that has interesting details. Write a conclusion that sums up the significance of the event or situation described in your essay.

### 4 Revise and Proofread

Check to make sure you have not begun too many sentences with the word *I*. Replace general words with more colorful ones.

Main idea

Details

Significance of narrative

In my last year of college, I volunteered for an organization called Amigos De Las Americas (Friends of the Americas). I was sent to a remote village in Brazil and worked with villagers to improve the community's water supply and sanitation systems. The experience made me realize I wanted to work in the field of public health. When I went to Brazil, I never imagined what an incredible sense of purpose it would add to my life.

# Persuasive Essays

Writing that supports an opinion or position

## 1 Select and Narrow Your Topic

Choose a topic that provokes an argument and has at least two sides. Choose a side. Decide which argument will appeal most to your audience and persuade them to understand your point of view.

## 2 Gather Evidence

Create a chart that states your position at the top and then lists the pros and cons for your position below, in two columns. Predict and address the strongest arguments against your stand.

## 3 Write a First Draft

Write a strong thesis statement that clearly states your position. Continue by presenting the strongest arguments in favor of your position and acknowledging and refuting opposing arguments.

## 4 Revise and Proofread

Check to make sure you have made a logical argument and that you have not oversimplified the argument.

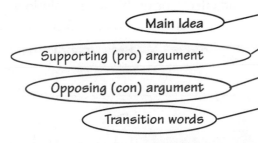

- Main Idea
- Supporting (pro) argument
- Opposing (con) argument
- Transition words

It is vital to vote in elections. When people vote, they tell public officials how to run the government. Not every proposal is carried out; however, politicians do their best to listen to what the majority of people want. Therefore, every vote is important.

## Expository Essays

Writing that explains a process, compares and contrasts, explains causes and effects, or explores solutions to a problem

### ❶ Identify and Narrow Your Topic

Expository writing is writing that explains something in detail. It might explain the similarities and differences between two or more subjects (compare and contrast). It might explain how one event causes another (cause and effect). Or it might explain a problem and describe a solution.

### ❷ Gather Evidence

Create a graphic organizer that identifies details to include in your essay.

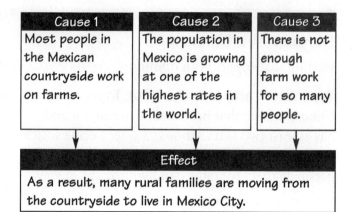

| Cause 1 | Cause 2 | Cause 3 |
|---|---|---|
| Most people in the Mexican countryside work on farms. | The population in Mexico is growing at one of the highest rates in the world. | There is not enough farm work for so many people. |

**Effect**

As a result, many rural families are moving from the countryside to live in Mexico City.

### ❸ Write Your First Draft

Write a topic sentence and then organize the essay around your similarities and differences, causes and effects, or problem and solutions. Be sure to include convincing details, facts, and examples.

### ❹ Revise and Proofread

## Research Papers

Writing that presents research about a topic

### ❶ Narrow Your Topic

Choose a topic you're interested in and make sure that it is not too broad. For example, instead of writing a report on Panama, write about the construction of the Panama Canal.

### ❷ Acquire Information

Locate several sources of information about the topic from the library or the Internet. For each resource, create a source index card like the one at the right. Then take notes using an index card for each detail or subtopic. On the card, note which source the information was taken from. Use quotation marks when you copy the exact words from a source.

Source #1
McCullough, David. *The Path Between the Seas: The Creation of the Panama Canal, 1870-1914.* N.Y., Simon and Schuster, 1977.

### ❸ Make an Outline

Use an outline to decide how to organize your report. Sort your index cards into the same order.

Outline
I. Introduction
II. Why the canal was built
III. How the canal was built
   A. Physical challenges
   B. Medical challenges
IV. Conclusion

> **Introduction**
>
> Building the Panama Canal
>
> Ever since Christopher Columbus first explored the Isthmus of Panama, the Spanish had been looking for a water route through it. They wanted to be able to sail west from Spain to Asia without sailing around South America. However, it was not until 1914 that the dream became a reality.

> **Conclusion**
>
> It took eight years and more than 70,000 workers to build the Panama Canal. It remains one of the greatest engineering feats of modern times.

### ❹ Write a First Draft

Write an introduction, a body, and a conclusion. Leave plenty of space between lines so you can go back and add details that you may have left out.

### ❺ Revise and Proofread

Be sure to include transition words between sentences and paragraphs. Here are some examples:

To show a contrast—*however, although, despite.*

To point out a reason—*since, because, if.*

To signal a conclusion—*therefore, consequently, so, then.*

## Evaluating Your Writing

Use this table to help you evaluate your writing.

|  | Excellent | Good | Acceptable | Unacceptable |
|---|---|---|---|---|
| **Purpose** | Achieves purpose—to inform, persuade, or provide historical interpretation—very well | Informs, persuades, or provides historical interpretation reasonably well | Reader cannot easily tell if the purpose is to inform, persuade, or provide historical interpretation | Purpose is not clear |
| **Organization** | Develops ideas in a very clear and logical way | Presents ideas in a reasonably well-organized way | Reader has difficulty following the organization | Lacks organization |
| **Elaboration** | Explains all ideas with facts and details | Explains most ideas with facts and details | Includes some supporting facts and details | Lacks supporting details |
| **Use of Language** | Uses excellent vocabulary and sentence structure with no errors in spelling, grammar, or punctuation | Uses good vocabulary and sentence structure with very few errors in spelling, grammar, or punctuation | Includes some errors in grammar, punctuation, and spelling | Includes many errors in grammar, punctuation, and spelling |

# How to Read Social Studies

## Target Reading Skills

The Target Reading Skills introduced on this page will help you understand the words and ideas in this book and in other social studies reading you do. Each chapter focuses on one of these reading skills. Good readers develop a bank of reading strategies, or skills. Then they draw on the particular strategies that will help them understand the text they are reading.

### Chapter 1 Target Reading Skill

**Clarifying Meaning** If you do not understand something you are reading right away, you can use several skills to help clarify the meaning of the word or idea. In this chapter you will practice these strategies for clarifying meaning: rereading, reading ahead, and paraphrasing.

### Chapter 2 Target Reading Skill

**Using Context** Using the context of an unfamiliar word can help you understand its meaning. Context includes the words, phrases, and sentences surrounding a word. In this chapter you will practice using these context clues: descriptions, definitions, comparisons, and examples.

### Chapter 3 Target Reading Skill

**Comparing and Contrasting** You can use comparison and contrast to sort out and analyze information you are reading. Comparing means examining the similarities between things. Contrasting is looking at differences. In this chapter you will practice these skills: comparing and contrasting, identifying contrasts, making comparisons, and recognizing contrast signal words.

### Chapter 4 Target Reading Skill

**Using Sequence** Noting the order in which significant events take place can help you understand and remember them. In this chapter you will practice these sequence skills: sequencing, or finding the order of events, sequencing important changes, and recognizing sequence signal words.

### Chapter 5 Target Reading Skill

**Identifying the Main Idea** Since you cannot remember every detail of what you read, it is important that you identify the main ideas. The main idea of a section or paragraph is the most important point and the one you want to remember. In this chapter you will practice these skills: identifying stated and implied main ideas and identifying supporting details.

# FOUNDATIONS of GEOGRAPHY

Are you curious about our world? Do you want to know why winters are cold and summers are hot? Have you wondered why some people live and work in cities and others work on farms in the countryside? If you answered yes to any of these questions, you want to know more about geography.

## Guiding Questions

The text, photographs, maps, and charts in this book will help you discover answers to these Guiding Questions.

1. **Geography** What are Earth's major physical features?

2. **History** How have people's ways of life changed over time?

3. **Culture** What is a culture?

4. **Government** What types of government exist in the world today?

5. **Economics** How do people use the world's natural resources?

## Project Preview

You can also discover answers to the Guiding Questions by working on projects. Project possibilities are listed on page 136 of this book.

# Investigate the Political World

There are more than 190 independent countries in the world. Some of those countries have dependencies, or areas outside of those countries that belong to them. Every land area where people live belongs to some country. The blue areas on maps in this book show the world's oceans, seas, and lakes. The other colors on this map show the areas of the world's countries and dependencies.

**Go Online** PHSchool.com Use Web Code **nfp-3020** for the **interactive maps** on these pages.

▲ **Denmark**
Denmark is one of the oldest continuously existing states. Christiansborg Palace is the seat of the Danish Parliament.

◄ **Niagara Falls**
The border between the United States and Canada runs through the falls. Both countries share its tourist and power-generating benefits.

## LOCATION

### 1 Examine Country Borders

Governments have drawn the borders between countries. Some borders follow mountains or rivers. Others are straight lines. On the map, look at the United States and Canada. These are the large yellow and pink countries in North America. Parts of their borders are straight, but others are crooked. Why might this be? What might explain the location of other borders on this map?

**ARCTIC OCEAN**

Arctic Circle
60° N
150° W  120° W  90° W  60° W

**NORTH AMERICA**

**ATLANTIC OCEAN**

30° N
Tropic of Cancer

150° W

120° W **PACIFIC OCEAN**

Equator 0°

90° W

**SOUTH AMERICA**

Tropic of Capricorn
30° S

**ATLANTIC OCEAN**

30° W

60° S
Antarctic Circle **SOUTHERN OCEAN**
60° W

**The World: Political Key**

— National border
- - - Disputed border

## PLACE

# 2 Analyze the Continents

Notice the six black labels on the world map. These labels name continents. Which continent's name is also the name of a country? You can see that some continents have more countries than others. Which continent is made up mostly of small countries?

▲ **Russia**
St. Basil's Cathedral was built in the 1500s in Moscow, the Russian capital. At that time, the Russian church had great political power.

ARCTIC OCEAN

Arctic Circle

60° N

EUROPE

ASIA

180°

30° N

Tropic of Cancer

PACIFIC OCEAN

AFRICA

Equator

INDIAN OCEAN

AUSTRALIA

Tropic of Capricorn

0° 30° E 60° E 90° E 120° E 150° E 180°

0°

30° E 60° E 90° E

0 miles 3,000
0 kilometers 3,000
Robinson

120° E

150° E

60° S

180°

180°

0°

◀ **Ghana**
The traditional leader of the Asante people in Ghana is called the Asantehene. Otumfuo Opoku Ware II held this position for thirty years.

▲ **East Timor**
These people are celebrating the independence of East Timor, which became a nation in 2002.

# Investigate the Physical World

People's lives are constantly shaped by their physical environment. The physical features of a place often determine where and how people live. Yet the physical world is always changing, too. Some changes come very slowly. For example, it took millions of years for Earth's crust to lift and form mountains. Other changes are fast and dramatic, such as when a volcano erupts or an earthquake hits.

▲ **Alaska**
Glaciers like this one at Portage, Alaska, have shaped the land for thousands of years.

## PLACE

## 3 Infer From a Map

Notice the bumpy texture and brownish colors on the map. These indicate a mountainous landscape. Now find the continent of South America. Look for the Amazon Basin. What does the key tell you about its elevation? Notice the photograph of the Tigre River as it weaves through the basin. Describe that landscape. Now find the Andes on the map, and describe what you would expect to see there.

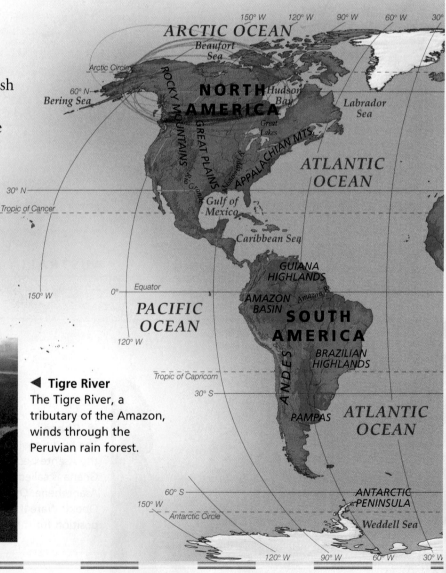

◀ **Tigre River**
The Tigre River, a tributary of the Amazon, winds through the Peruvian rain forest.

# HUMAN-ENVIRONMENT INTERACTION

## 4 Examine Landforms as Barriers

Physical barriers can make movement between areas difficult. For example, take a look at the continents in the map below. Some of them are separated from one another by vast areas of water. Examine the elevation key. Look closely at the map's labels. What other physical landforms might have acted as barriers to movement?

▲ **Mount Fuji, Japan**
Volcanoes such as this one have created islands along the rim of the Pacific Ocean.

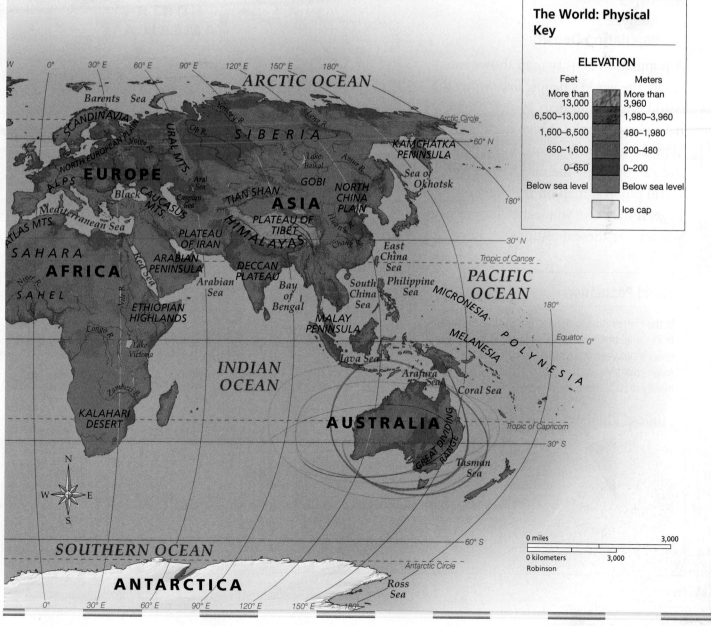

**The World: Physical Key**

**ELEVATION**

| Feet | | Meters |
|---|---|---|
| More than 13,000 | | More than 3,960 |
| 6,500–13,000 | | 1,980–3,960 |
| 1,600–6,500 | | 480–1,980 |
| 650–1,600 | | 200–480 |
| 0–650 | | 0–200 |
| Below sea level | | Below sea level |
| | | Ice cap |

# Investigate Population

For thousands of years, the world's population grew slowly. In the past 200 years, however, health care, living conditions, and food production have greatly improved. This has led to a huge population burst. In 1800, the world's population numbered less than 1 billion people. Today, it is more than 6 billion, and growing quickly.

▲ **China**
A crowd of people walk through a park in the capital city of Beijing. China has the largest population of any country in the world.

## REGIONS

**5 Analyze Population Density**

A population density map shows you where the world's people live. Study the world population map. Which places have many people? Which have few? Why do you think people live where they do? As you study the map, refer to the world physical map on the previous page. It may give you some clues to help you answer these questions.

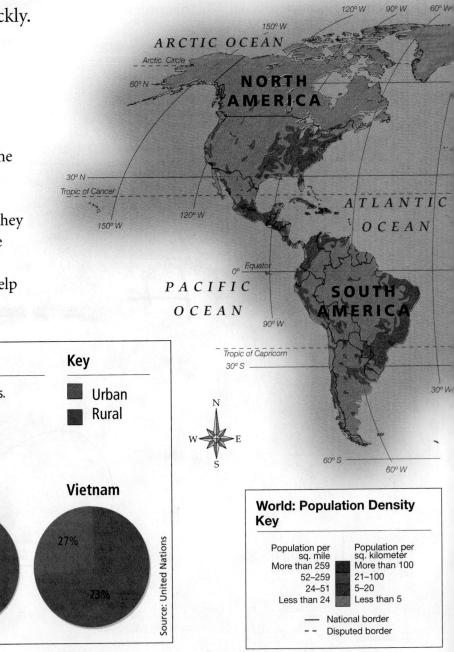

### World Population

In the United Kingdom, most people live in cities. In Panama, the population is almost equally divided between urban and rural areas. In some Asian countries, such as Vietnam, people live mainly in rural areas.

**Key**

■ Urban
■ Rural

Source: United Nations

**United Kingdom**

11%
89%

**Panama**

58%  42%

**Vietnam**

27%
73%

### World: Population Density Key

| Population per sq. mile | Population per sq. kilometer |
|---|---|
| More than 259 | More than 100 |
| 52–259 | 21–100 |
| 24–51 | 5–20 |
| Less than 24 | Less than 5 |

— National border
-- Disputed border

## MOVEMENT

### 6 Compare Continents

When high population densities cover large areas, those areas have large populations. Look at the continents on the map. Which continent do you think has the largest population, based on the size of its areas of high population density? Which continent do you think has the lowest population? Compare North America and South America on the map. Which continent do you think has the larger population?

**▲ New Zealand**
The Whanganui River flows through a New Zealand national park. New Zealand has a low population density.

EUROPE

ASIA

AFRICA

PACIFIC OCEAN

INDIAN OCEAN

AUSTRALIA

30° W | 0° | 30° E | 60° E | 90° E | 120° E | 150° E | 180°

60° N

30° N
Tropic of Cancer

Equator          0°

Tropic of Capricorn
30° S

0°   30° E   60° E   90° E   120° E   150° E   180°

N W E S

0 miles          3,000
0 kilometers   3,000
Robinson

### PRACTICE YOUR GEOGRAPHY SKILLS

1. In Asia there is a ring of dense population next to an area with low population. Look at the physical map of the world on pages 4 and 5. What landform may explain this difference?

2. Look at Northern Africa. Find the area of heavy population that forms a curving line on the map. How does the physical map on pages 4 and 5 explain this?

**Monaco is the most densely populated European nation. ▶**

# The World of Geography

## Chapter Preview

This chapter will introduce you to the study of Earth, the planet where we live.

### Section 1
**The Five Themes of Geography**

### Section 2
**The Geographer's Tools**

### Target Reading Skill

**Clarifying Meaning** In this chapter you will focus on clarifying meaning by learning how to read ahead and how to paraphrase.

▶ A satellite launched from the space shuttle *Discovery* orbits Earth.

# The Five Themes of Geography

## Prepare to Read

### Objectives

In this section you will
1. Learn about the study of Earth.
2. Discover five ways to look at Earth.

### Taking Notes

As you read the section, look for details about each of the five themes of geography. Copy the web diagram below and write down details related to each theme. Add ovals as needed for additional themes or details.

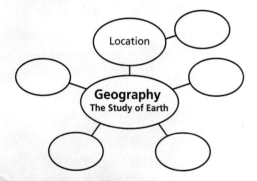

### Target Reading Skill

**Reread or Read Ahead** If you do not understand a passage, reread it to look for connections among the words and sentences. Reading ahead can also help. Words and ideas may be clarified further on.

### Key Terms

- **geography** (jee AHG ru fee) *n.* the study of Earth
- **cardinal directions** (KAHR duh nul duh REK shunz) *n.* the directions north, east, south, and west
- **latitude** (LAT uh tood) *n.* the distance north or south of Earth's Equator, in degrees
- **longitude** (LAHN juh tood) *n.* the distance east or west of the Prime Meridian, in degrees
- **hemisphere** (HEM ih sfeer) *n.* a half of Earth
- **parallel** (PA ruh lel) *n.* a line of latitude
- **meridian** (muh RID ee un) *n.* a line of longitude

**Geographers use maps and other tools to understand Earth.**

## The Study of Earth

**Geography** is the study of Earth, our home planet. Geographers try to answer two basic questions: Where are things located? and, Why are they there? To find answers to these questions, geographers consider Earth from many points of view.

✓ **Reading Check** What questions do geographers try to answer?

## Five Ways to Look at Earth

Five themes can help you organize information about Earth and its people. These themes are location, regions, place, movement, and human-environment interaction. They can help you understand where things are located, and why they are there.

**Location** Geographers begin to study a place by finding where it is, or its location. Geographers use both cardinal and intermediate directions to describe location. The **cardinal directions** are north, east, south, and west. Intermediate directions lie between the cardinal directions. For example, northwest is halfway between north and west.

Geographers also use two special measurements of Earth to describe location. **Latitude** is the distance north or south of the Equator, measured in units called degrees. Degrees are units that measure angles. **Longitude** is the distance east or west of the Prime Meridian, measured in degrees.

Lines of latitude are east-west circles around the globe. All points on the circle have the same latitude. The line of latitude around the middle of the globe, at 0 degrees (0°) of latitude, is the Equator. Lines of longitude run north and south. The Prime Meridian is the line of longitude that marks 0° of longitude.

# The Hemispheres

The Equator and the Prime Meridian both divide Earth in two. Each half of Earth is called a **hemisphere.** The Equator divides Earth into Northern and Southern hemispheres. The Prime Meridian divides Earth into Eastern and Western hemispheres.

The Western Hemisphere includes the area from the Prime Meridian west to 180° of longitude.

The Eastern Hemisphere includes the area from the Prime Meridian east to 180° of longitude.

The North Pole is 90° north of the Equator.

The Prime Meridian marks 0° longitude.

The Northern Hemisphere includes all lines of latitude north of the Equator.

The Equator marks 0° latitude.

The Southern Hemisphere contains all lines of latitude south of the Equator.

### GEOGRAPHY SKILLS PRACTICE

**Location** Geographers can pinpoint the location of any place on Earth using lines of latitude and longitude. **Use Latitude and Longitude** What place on Earth is located at 0° longitude and 90° north latitude?

# The Global Grid

Lines of longitude and latitude form a global grid. Geographers can identify the absolute location of any point on Earth by finding the latitude and longitude lines that intersect at that point. Lines of latitude are also called **parallels,** because they run east and west and are parallel to one another. This means that they never cross. Lines of longitude are also called **meridians.** Meridians run north and south, from the North Pole to the South Pole.

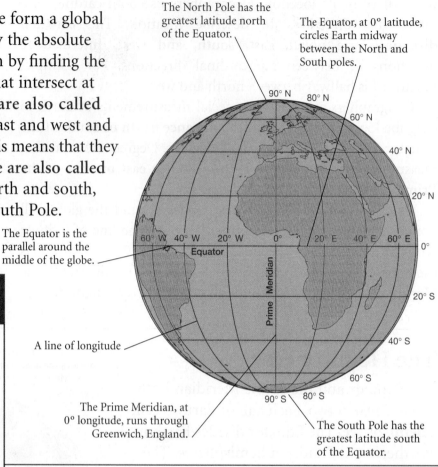

The North Pole has the greatest latitude north of the Equator.

The Equator, at 0° latitude, circles Earth midway between the North and South poles.

The Equator is the parallel around the middle of the globe.

A line of longitude

The Prime Meridian, at 0° longitude, runs through Greenwich, England.

The South Pole has the greatest latitude south of the Equator.

## GEOGRAPHY SKILLS PRACTICE

**Location** Latitude and longitude are measured in degrees from imaginary lines on Earth's surface. **Compare and Contrast** From which line is latitude measured? Where do degrees of longitude start?

**Read Ahead**
Read ahead to see how physical features may define regions.

Lines of longitude and latitude form a global grid. This grid allows geographers to state the absolute location, or exact address, of any place on Earth. For example, Savannah, Georgia, is located at 32° north latitude and 81° west longitude.

Geographers also discuss relative location, or the location of a place relative to another place. A geographer might give the relative location of Tallahassee, Florida, by saying, "Tallahassee is about 400 miles northwest of Miami."

**Regions** Geographers use the theme of regions to group places that have something in common. A region has a unifying human or physical feature such as population, history, climate, or landforms. For example, a country is a region with a common national government, and a city is a region with a common local government. A school district is a region defined by a common school system. Land areas can also be divided into regions that share physical features, such as mountains or a dry climate. Physical regions of the western United States include the Rocky Mountains and the Mojave (mo HAH vee) Desert.

**Place** Geographers also study place. Place includes the human and physical features at a specific location. To describe physical features, you might say the climate is hot or cold. Or you might say that the land is hilly. To discuss human features, you might talk about how many people live in a place and the kinds of work they do. You might also describe their religions or the languages they speak.

**Movement** The theme of movement helps explain how people, goods, and ideas get from one place to another. For example, when people from other countries came to the United States, they brought traditional foods that enriched the American way of life. The theme of movement helps you understand such cultural changes. Movement helps you understand many other facts about the world. For example, radios and computers have helped music from the United States to spread and become popular around the world.

**Human-Environment Interaction** This theme explores how people affect their environment, or their natural surroundings, and how their environment affects them. Perhaps they have cut trails into the mountainside. Or they may have learned how to survive with little water.

**Farmers in India**
These women are using the wind to separate grain for flour from chaff, or husks. Farming is an example of human-environment interaction. **Infer** *Do you think that these farmers use much modern machinery?*

✓ **Reading Check** **What is the purpose of the five themes of geography?**

---

## Section 1 Assessment

**Key Terms**
Review the key terms at the beginning of this section. Use each term in a sentence that explains its meaning.

**Target Reading Skill**
What did you learn about physical features and regions by reading ahead?

**Comprehension and Critical Thinking**
**1. (a) Recall** What do geographers study?

**(b) Explain** What basic questions guide geographers?
**2. (a) Explain** How can the five themes help geographers?
**(b) Predict** How might a geographer use the theme of movement to describe the area where you live?
**3. (a) Define** What does the theme of location cover?
**(b) Contrast** How would a description of your home town as a place be different from a description of your home town's location?

**Writing Activity**
Read the passage above on human-environment interaction. Then write a paragraph describing ways that people in your area interact with their natural environment.

Go Online
PHSchool.com

**For:** An activity on the five themes of geography
**Visit:** PHSchool.com
**Web Code:** led-3101

**W**ould you seek medical advice from a plumber? Would you go to an encyclopedia to keep track of this season's basketball scores? Of course you wouldn't. Information is only as good as its source. To get reliable information, you have to go to an appropriate, trustworthy, and knowledgeable source.

## Learn the Skill

Follow these steps to determine whether information is reliable.

**1** **Find out the source of the information.** If it comes from a printed source, find out the name of the source, the author, and the date of publication. If it appeared on television, find out the name, date, and type of program (news, drama, or documentary). Do not accept information from Internet sites that do not give a date and an author.

**2** **Find out if the information is recent enough for your purpose.** If you need current information, search for recent newspaper articles and up-to-date Web sites. Even if your topic is historic, researchers may have discovered new information about it. Seek the most current information.

**3** **Find out if the information is accurate.** On certain topics, nearly all sources agree. For other topics, try to find information on which several respected sources agree. To be clear, you might say, "Several sources agree that" or "According to." If reliable sources disagree, you might note that disagreement in your writing.

**4** **Look up the author's qualifications and methods.** When you check out an author's qualifications, always ask yourself whether he or she has a bias, or a one-sided view.

### Is it Reliable?

To see if a source is reliable, ask
- What is the source?
- Is it recent enough?
- Is it accurate?
- Is the author qualified or biased?

# Practice the Skill

Now use steps 1–4 to answer some questions about reliable information.

**1** Where might you go to find information on the location of the capital of Japan? On the population of North Carolina? On the major industries of Cuba? On presidential election results in Russia?

**2** Would a 20-year-old encyclopedia be a reliable source of information on active volcanoes in Hawaii? On the type of money used in Europe? On the longest river in the world? Explain your answers.

**3** If you heard in a television documentary that most of the world's diamonds are mined in southern Africa, how could you check the accuracy of that statement?

**4** Suppose you do an Internet search for information on the amount of beef produced in the United States last year. The search leads you to articles by three authors. Who would be the best source of information: an economist for the U.S. Department of Agriculture, the largest cattle rancher in Texas, or a leading university expert on beef production? Explain your answer.

## Apply the Skill

If you had to research a report on the health of children in India, what kinds of sources would you search for reliable information? Name at least two sources, and explain why they would be reliable.

**These boys are playing ball in front of the famed Taj Mahal, in India.**

# The Geographer's Tools

## Prepare to Read

### Objectives

In this section you will

1. Find out how maps and globes show information about Earth's surface.
2. See how mapmakers show Earth's round surface on flat maps.
3. Learn how to read maps.

### Taking Notes

As you read this section, look for details about each of the following map topics: comparing maps with globes, map projections, and parts of a map. Copy the outline below and write each detail under the correct topic.

I. Maps and globes
   A. Globes
   B.
      1.
      2.
II. Projections
   A.

### Target Reading Skill

**Paraphrase** When you paraphrase, you restate what you have read in your own words. For example, you could paraphrase the first paragraph after the heading Globes and Their Weaknesses this way:

"Mapmakers found that globes are the best way to show the shapes of continents, but at a different size."

As you read this section, paraphrase or restate the information after each red or blue heading.

### Key Terms

- **scale** (skayl) *n.* relative size
- **distortion** (dih STAWR shun) *n.* loss of accuracy
- **geographic information systems** (jee uh GRAF ik in fur MAY shun SIS tumz) *n.* computer-based systems that provide information about locations
- **projection** (proh JEK shun) *n.* a way to map Earth on a flat surface
- **compass rose** (KUM pus rohz) *n.* a diagram of a compass showing direction
- **key** (kee) *n.* the section of a map that explains the symbols and colors on the map

A map can help you find directions.

## Globes and Maps

As people explored Earth, they collected information about the shapes and sizes of islands, continents, and bodies of water. Map makers wanted to present this information accurately.

**Globes and Their Weaknesses** The best way was to put the information on a globe, or a model with the same round shape as Earth itself. By using an accurate shape for Earth, mapmakers could show the continents and oceans of Earth much as they really are. The only difference would be the **scale,** or relative size.

But there is a problem with globes. Try making a globe large enough to show the streets in your town. The globe might have to be larger than your school building. Imagine putting a globe that big in your pocket every morning! A globe just cannot be complete enough to be useful for finding directions and at the same time small enough to be convenient for everyday use.

**Maps and Mapping** People, therefore, use flat maps. Flat maps, however, present another problem. Earth is round. A map is flat. Can you flatten an orange peel without stretching or tearing it? There will be sections that are stretched or bent out of shape. The same thing happens when mapmakers create flat maps. It is impossible to show Earth on a flat surface without some **distortion,** or loss of accuracy. Something will look too large, too small, or out of place. Mapmakers have found ways to limit distortion of shape, size, distance, and direction.

Mapmakers rely on ground surveys, or measurements made on the ground, to make maps. They also use aerial photographs and satellite images.

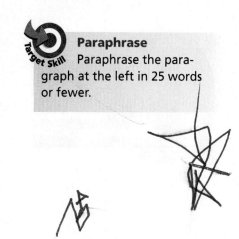

**Paraphrase**
Paraphrase the paragraph at the left in 25 words or fewer.

### Aerial Photographs and Satellite Images

Aerial photographs are photographs of Earth's surface taken from the air. Satellite images are pictures of Earth's surface taken from a satellite in orbit. Both types of image are valuable sources of information for mapmakers because they provide current information about Earth's surface in great detail. But they are not useful for finding objects that are hidden, such as underground transit lines, or features such as streams that may be covered by vegetation. Also, like any map, flat aerial photographs and satellite images give a distorted view of Earth's surface.

### Geographic Information Systems A geographic information system, or GIS, is a computer-based system that links information to locations. A GIS is useful not only to geographers but also to governments and businesses. A GIS connects information with places. For example, if a business needs to decide where to open an office, it can use a GIS to choose a location where it will reach the most customers. Military planners may use a GIS to improve their knowledge of the places where troops will operate. A GIS also may be used to produce maps.

✓ Reading Check **What are the advantages and disadvantages of each way of showing Earth's surface?**

**Satellite Image of North and South America**
This satellite view shows parts of North and South America. A storm system covers part of the southeastern United States. **Analyze Images** *How might this image pose problems as a source for making maps?*

Improve your map skills.

# Getting It All on the Map

In 1569, a mapmaker named Gerardus Mercator (juh RAHR dus mur KAY tur) created a flat map to help sailors navigate, or plan journeys, around the globe. To make his map flat and to keep his grid rectangular, Mercator expanded the area between lines of longitude near the poles. Mercator's map was very useful to sailors because it showed directions accurately, even though sizes and distances were distorted. More than 400 years later, nearly all seagoing navigators still use the Mercator **projection,** or method of mapping Earth on a flat surface.

**The Mercator Projection**  Mercator maps make areas near the poles look bigger than they are. This is because on a globe, the lines of longitude meet at the poles. To keep lines of longitude straight up and down, Mercator had to stretch the spaces between them north and south of the Equator. Land near the Equator was about the right size, but land areas near the poles became much larger. For example, on Mercator's map, Greenland looks bigger than South America. Greenland is actually only about one eighth as big as South America. Geographers call a Mercator projection a conformal map. It shows correct shapes but not true distances or sizes. What other areas, besides Greenland, do you think might look larger than they should?

## Making a Mercator Map

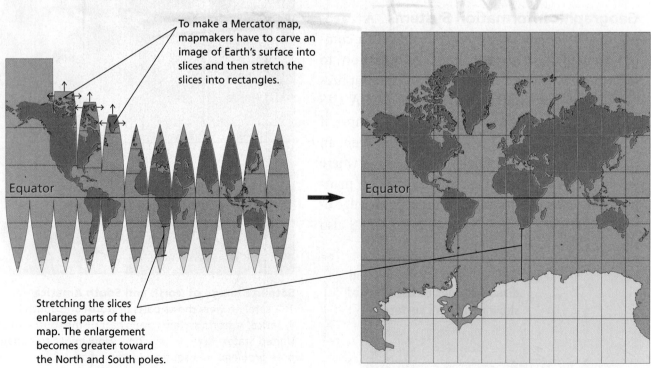

To make a Mercator map, mapmakers have to carve an image of Earth's surface into slices and then stretch the slices into rectangles.

Equator

Stretching the slices enlarges parts of the map. The enlargement becomes greater toward the North and South poles.

Equator

**Equal-Area Projections** An equal-area map shows the correct size of landmasses, but their shapes are altered. Lines that would be straight on Earth may be forced into curves to fit on the map's flat surface.

**The Robinson Projection** This projection is named for its designer, Arthur Robinson. Today, many geographers believe that the Robinson projection is the best world map available. It is used for most of the world maps in this book. This projection shows most distances, sizes, and shapes quite accurately. However, even a Robinson projection has distortions, especially in areas around the edges of the map.

**Other Projections** There are many other types of projections besides the ones shown here. Some are useful for showing small areas but not for showing the whole world. Others are good for specific purposes, such as planning a plane's flight route.

√ **Reading Check** What are the strengths and weaknesses of the Mercator, equal-area, and Robinson projections?

## Making an Equal-Area Map

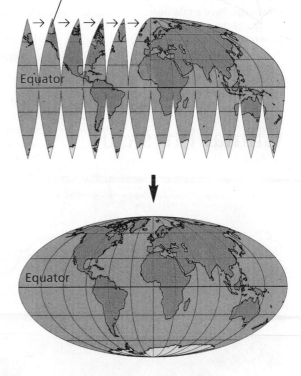

To make an equal-area map, the slices are squeezed into an oval.

Equator

Equator

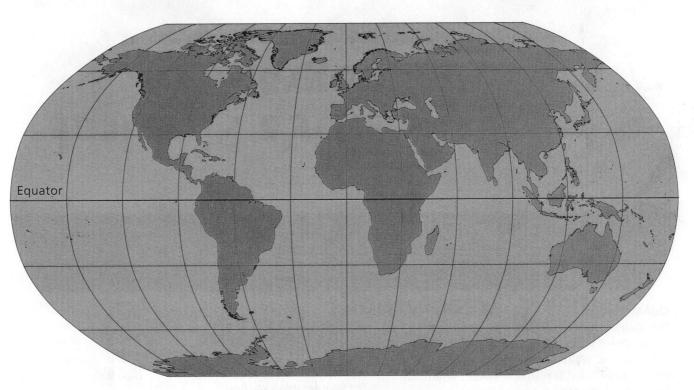

Equator

**The World: Robinson Projection**

# Reading Maps

Look at the maps shown on these two pages. One is a physical map of the country of China. The other is a highway map of the state of Georgia. These maps cover completely different areas and show different kinds of information. Despite their differences, both maps have all of the basic parts that you will find on most maps. Knowing how to use these parts will help you to read and understand any kind of map.

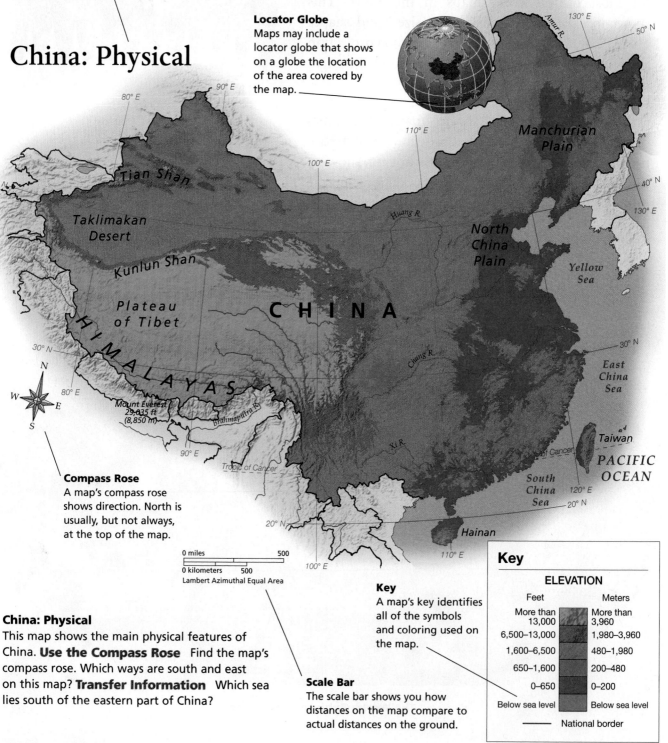

**Title**
Most maps have a title near the top of the map. The title generally tells you the type of information and the area covered on the map.

**Locator Globe**
Maps may include a locator globe that shows on a globe the location of the area covered by the map.

## China: Physical

**Compass Rose**
A map's compass rose shows direction. North is usually, but not always, at the top of the map.

**China: Physical**

This map shows the main physical features of China. **Use the Compass Rose** Find the map's compass rose. Which ways are south and east on this map? **Transfer Information** Which sea lies south of the eastern part of China?

**Key**
A map's key identifies all of the symbols and coloring used on the map.

**Scale Bar**
The scale bar shows you how distances on the map compare to actual distances on the ground.

### Key

**ELEVATION**

| Feet | | Meters |
|---|---|---|
| More than 13,000 | | More than 3,960 |
| 6,500–13,000 | | 1,980–3,960 |
| 1,600–6,500 | | 480–1,980 |
| 650–1,600 | | 200–480 |
| 0–650 | | 0–200 |
| Below sea level | | Below sea level |
| | ——— National border | |

# Georgia Highways

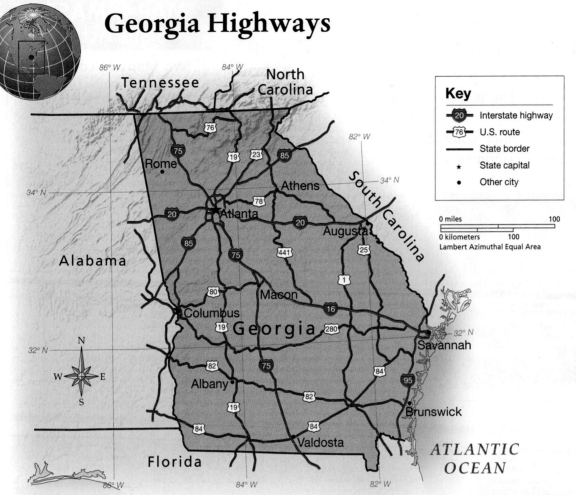

**Key**

- 🛡20 Interstate highway
- 🛡76 U.S. route
- ── State border
- ★ State capital
- • Other city

0 miles          100
0 kilometers     100
Lambert Azimuthal Equal Area

**The Parts of a Map**  Both maps on these pages have what geographers call a **compass rose,** a diagram of a compass showing direction. If you want to find directions such as north, south, east, or west, just look for the map's compass rose.

Both maps also have a scale bar. The scale bar shows how distances on the map compare to actual distances on the land. Scales vary, depending on the map. If you compare the scale bar on the map of China to the bar on the map of Georgia, you will see that the map of China covers much greater distances on the ground even though the map is not much bigger.

On any map, the **key,** or legend, is the part of the map that explains the symbols and shading on the map. For example, the key on the highway map of Georgia shows the colored lines that stand for different kinds of highways. While some maps use symbols, other maps, like the physical map of China, use coloring to present information. The key shows which colors stand for which elevations.

**Georgia Highways**
Notice that this map of Georgia has the same basic parts as the physical map of China: a title, a key, a locator globe, a compass rose, and a scale bar.
**Use Scale** *Using a ruler, measure the distance on the map between Atlanta and Macon. Then hold the ruler against the scale bar. How many miles is Atlanta from Macon?*

✔ Reading Check  **How do the different parts of a map help you to find information?**

# Maps of Different Scale

On the scale bar for the map of Greater London, a mile covers a small space. This map has a small scale. It gives a general picture of a large area. Maps with a larger scale, such as the map of Central London, show more detail and are useful for finding landmarks.

**Two Maps of London**
The map of Central London zooms in on the area inside the red box on the map of Greater London. **Analyze** Which map shows the city's size? Which shows tourist attractions?

**Go Online**
**PHSchool.com** Use Web Code **lep-3112** for step-by-step map skills practice.

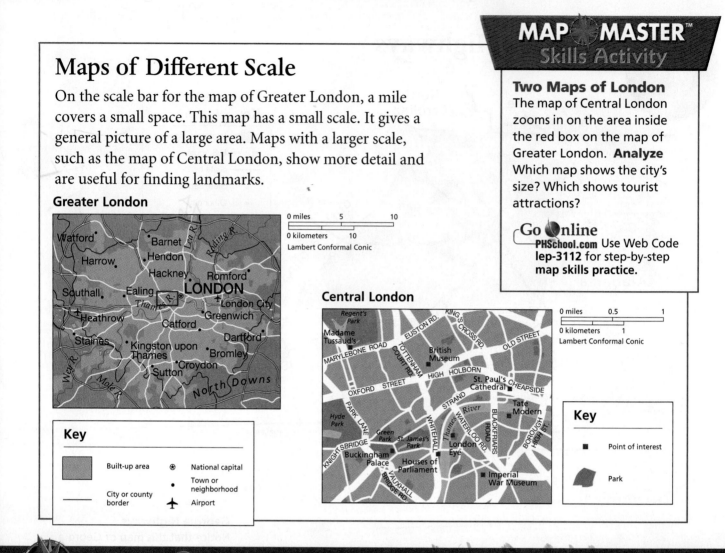

**Greater London**

0 miles  5  10
0 kilometers  10
Lambert Conformal Conic

**Central London**

0 miles  0.5  1
0 kilometers  1
Lambert Conformal Conic

**Key**

| | Built-up area |
| ⊛ | National capital |
| • | Town or neighborhood |
| ✈ | Airport |
| | City or county border |

**Key**

| ■ | Point of interest |
| | Park |

---

## Section 2 Assessment

### Key Terms
Review the key terms at the beginning of this section. Use each term in a sentence that explains its meaning.

### Target Reading Skill
Go back and find the paragraph under the heading The Mercator Projection. Paraphrase this paragraph, or rewrite it in your own words.

### Comprehension and Critical Thinking
**1. (a) Identify** What information sources do mapmakers use?
**(b) Evaluate** What are the advantages and disadvantages of each information source?

**(c) Predict** To make a map of small streams in an area of thick vegetation, what source would a mapmaker most likely use?
**2. (a) Recall** What are the advantages and disadvantages of a Mercator projection and of an equal-area projection?
**(b) Apply Information** Which projection would you use to plan a voyage by ship in a straight line across an ocean?
**3. (a) Define** On a map, what are the key, title, compass rose, and scale bar?
**(b) Synthesize Information** If you made a map of places to shop in your area, what might you put in the map's key?

### Writing Activity
Look at the physical map of China. Plan a route for a trip from its east coast to its western border. Using information from the map, describe the landscape that you will see along the way.

**Go Online**
**PHSchool.com**

**For:** An activity on maps
**Visit:** PHSchool.com
**Web Code:** led-3102

# Review and Assessment

## ◆ Chapter Summary

### Section 1: The Five Themes of Geography

- Geography is the study of Earth.
- Geographers can pinpoint any location on the surface of Earth using lines of latitude and longitude, which form an imaginary grid.
- There are five themes of geography—location, regions, place, movement, and human-environment interaction. They offer five ways to gather and understand information about places on Earth.

### Section 2: The Geographer's Tools

- Maps can show more details of Earth's surface than globes, but showing Earth's round surface on flat maps causes distortion.
- Projections are different ways of showing Earth's round surface on a flat map.
- Parts of the map such as the key, compass rose, and scale bar can help you to find and understand information on any map.

**Earth viewed from space**

## ◆ Key Terms

Each of the statements below contains a key term from the chapter. If the statement is true, write *true*. If it is false, rewrite the statement to make it true.

1. The **cardinal directions** are north, east, south, and west.

2. **Latitude** is a measure of the distance north or south of Earth's Equator.

3. **Longitude** is a measure of the distance north or south of the Equator.

4. A **hemisphere** is a half of Earth.

5. A **meridian** is a line of latitude.

6. The **scale** is the part of the map that shows cardinal directions.

7. A **projection** is a way of mapping the flat surface of Earth onto a round globe.

8. The **compass rose** is the part of a map that shows symbols and their meanings.

9. The **key** is the part of the map that shows relative distances.

# Review and Assessment (continued)

## ◆ Comprehension and Critical Thinking

**10. (a) List** What five themes can help you organize infomation about Earth?
**(b) Categorize** Under which theme would you discuss building a dam on a river in a desert?

**11. (a) Recall** How do geographers pinpoint the exact location of any place on Earth?
**(b) Infer** Why might it be useful to know the exact location of a place?

**12. (a) Identify** What unifying characteristics might be used to describe a region?
**(b) Draw Conclusions** Might a single place be part of more than one region? Explain.

**13. (a) Recall** What are the disadvantages of globes? What are the disadvantages of maps?
**(b) Apply Information** Which would be more helpful for studying the exact shapes of continents, a globe or a map?

**14. (a) Describe** What are the main features of the Mercator projection?
**(b) Infer** Why is the Mercator projection still used by navigators today?
**(c) Generalize** When might you want to use a projection other than the Mercator projection?

**15. (a) List** What are the basic parts that most maps have?
**(b) Synthesize Information** How can you use the parts of a new map to understand it?

## ◆ Skills Practice

**Using Reliable Information** In the Skills for Life activity in this chapter, you learned how to use reliable information. Review the steps for this skill. Then apply them to the text below. Suppose you found this text in a teen magazine. Decide whether you think the information is reliable. Write a sentence that explains why or why not.

"Japan is a very clean country. I spent a whole week in Japan. The buses and trains were very clean. I didn't go inside a Japanese home, but I bet they are very clean, too."

## ◆ Writing Activity: Geography

Write down the name of the place where you live. Below that name, list the five themes of geography. Next to each theme, describe how it applies to your city, town, or state.

---

## MAP MASTER™ Skills Activity

### The Globe

**Place Location** For each place listed below, write the letter from the map that shows its location.
1. Prime Meridian
2. Equator
3. North Pole
4. South Pole
5. Europe
6. Africa
7. South America
8. North America

**Go Online**
PHSchool.com Use Web Code lep-3113 for an interactive map.

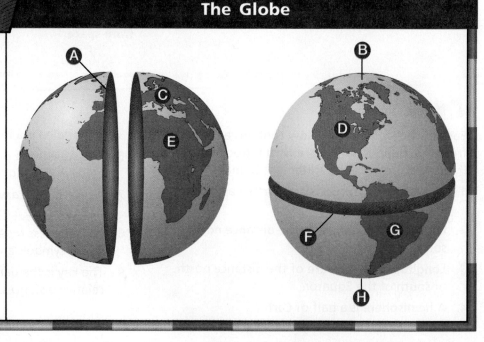

---

# Standardized Test Prep

## Test-Taking Tips

Some questions on standardized tests ask you to make mental maps. Do the exercise in the box below. Then follow the tips to answer the sample question.

> Draw a simple map of the world based on maps you have seen. Draw a rough shape for each landmass. Draw the Prime Meridian and the Equator across the map.

**TIP** Find the continents on your map. How is the world divided into hemispheres?

**Pick the letter that best answers the question.**

Which continent lies completely in both the Northern Hemisphere and the Western Hemisphere?

**A** Europe

**B** Greenland

**C** North America

**D** Australia

**TIP** Beware of careless errors. Read the question twice and think carefully about each answer choice.

**Think It Through** Australia is located completely in both the Southern Hemisphere and the Eastern Hemisphere. Europe is in the Northern Hemisphere but also mostly in the Eastern Hemisphere. Greenland is completely in both the Northern Hemisphere and the Western Hemisphere—as the question asks. But be careful! Greenland is not a continent. The answer is C.

## Practice Questions

**Use the tips above and other tips in this book to help you answer the following questions.**

1. Which of the following is NOT a tool a geographer would use to study absolute location?

   **A** cardinal directions

   **B** climate

   **C** lines of latitude

   **D** degrees

2. What disadvantage do all flat maps share?

   **A** They have some sort of distortion.

   **B** They are hard to carry.

   **C** There are few sources to create them.

   **D** They can only show areas at a small scale.

3. A map with cities and colored lines marked with numbers is probably a type of

   **A** climate map.

   **B** road map.

   **C** physical map.

   **D** vegetation map.

**Read the passage below and answer the question that follows.**

This area is located in the United States, west of the Mississippi River. It is mainly hot and dry, with little rainfall, so people have built many dams there. Its landforms include rivers, canyons, and deserts.

4. Which of the five themes are used to describe this area?

   **A** location, movement, regions

   **B** movement, place, regions, human-environment interaction

   **C** regions, location, movement

   **D** location, place, human-environment interaction

Go Online
PHSchool.com

Use Web Code **lea-3103**
for a **Chapter 1 self-test.**

# Earth's Physical Geography

## Chapter Preview

This chapter will introduce you to the physical geography of Earth, including the planet's structure, climate, and vegetation.

### Target Reading Skill

**Context** In this chapter you will focus on using context to help you understand unfamiliar words. Context includes the words, phrases, and sentences surrounding a word.

▶ Delicate Arch in Arches National Park, Utah

# Our Planet, Earth

## Prepare to Read

### Objectives

In this section you will
1. Learn about Earth's movement in relation to the sun.
2. Explore seasons and latitude.

### Taking Notes

Copy the table below. As you read this section, fill in the table with information about the movements of Earth relative to the sun, days and nights, seasons, and latitude. Add more lines as you need them.

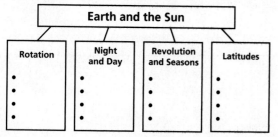

**Earth and the Sun**

| Rotation | Night and Day | Revolution and Seasons | Latitudes |
|----------|---------------|------------------------|-----------|
| • | • | • | • |
| • | • | • | • |
| • | • | • | • |
| • | • | • | • |

###  Target Reading Skill

**Use Context Clues** You can sometimes find the meaning of a word by using context—the words and sentences around that word. In some cases the context will describe the word. In this example, the phrase in italics describes a planet:

A planet is a *large object that circles a star.*

As you read, look at the context for the word *galaxy* in the paragraph below. What do you think *galaxy* means?

### Key Terms

* **orbit** (AWR bit) *n.* the path one body makes as it circles around another
* **revolution** (rev uh LOO shun) *n.* circular motion
* **axis** (AK sis) *n.* an imaginary line through Earth between the North and South poles, around which Earth turns
* **rotation** (roh TAY shun) *n.* a complete turn

**The Milky Way Galaxy**

## Earth and the Sun

Earth, the sun, the planets, and the stars in the sky are all part of a galaxy, or family of stars. Our galaxy is just one of the billions of galaxies in the universe. We call our galaxy the Milky Way because, in a dark night sky, away from city lights, its billions of stars look like a trail of spilled milk. Our sun is one of those stars. The sun is just a tiny speck compared to the rest of the Milky Way, but it is the center of everything for Earth and the other planets in the solar system. The solar system includes Earth, the other planets, and other objects that orbit the sun.

Even though the sun is about 93 million miles (150 million kilometers) away, it provides Earth with heat and light. Earth travels around the sun in a nearly circular **orbit,** which is the path one body makes as it circles around another. Earth takes $365\frac{1}{4}$ days, or one year, to complete one **revolution,** or circular motion, in its orbit around the sun.

**Understanding Days and Nights** As Earth circles the sun, it also spins in space. Earth turns around its **axis**—an imaginary line running through Earth between the North and South poles. Each complete turn, or **rotation,** takes about 24 hours. As Earth rotates, it is night on the side away from the sun. As Earth turns toward the sun, the sun appears to rise. When a side of Earth faces the sun, it is daytime. Then, as that side of Earth turns away from the sun, the sun appears to set.

**Time Zones** Earth rotates toward the east, so the day starts earlier in the east. The time difference is just a few seconds per mile. If every town had its own local time, it would be very confusing. So, governments have divided the world into standard time zones. Times in neighboring zones are one hour apart. There are also a few nonstandard time zones with times less than a full hour away from their neighbors.

✓ **Reading Check** **What is the connection between Earth's rotation and the change from day to night?**

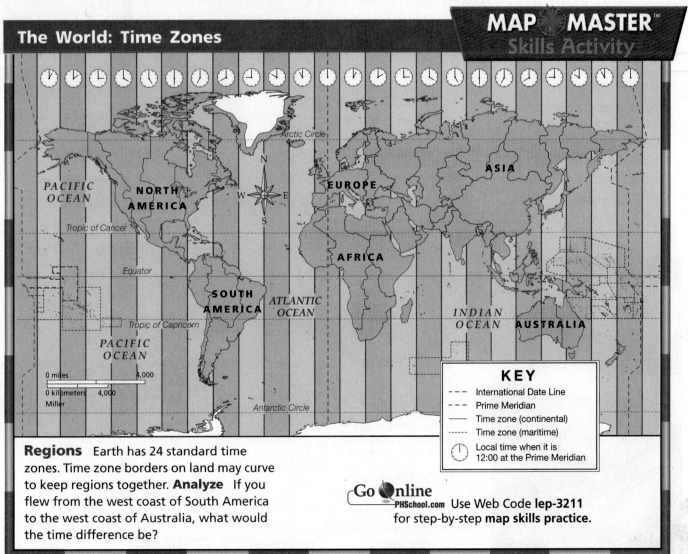

**The World: Time Zones**

**MAP MASTER™**
*Skills Activity*

**KEY**
- – – International Date Line
- - - - Prime Meridian
- —— Time zone (continental)
- · · · · Time zone (maritime)
- 🕐 Local time when it is 12:00 at the Prime Meridian

**Regions** Earth has 24 standard time zones. Time zone borders on land may curve to keep regions together. **Analyze** If you flew from the west coast of South America to the west coast of Australia, what would the time difference be?

**Go Online**
PHSchool.com Use Web Code **lep-3211** for step-by-step **map skills practice.**

## Seasons and Latitude

The axis of Earth is tilted relative to its orbit. At different points in Earth's orbit, the Northern Hemisphere may tilt toward or away from the sun. At other points in the orbit, neither hemisphere tilts toward or away from the sun. The revolution of the tilted planet Earth causes seasons.

At the summer solstice, the Northern Hemisphere is tilted farthest toward the sun. Places in this hemisphere have longer daylight and more direct sunlight at the solstice than at other times of the year. This direct sunlight causes the heat of summer.

**Use Context Clues** If you do not know what the summer solstice is, look at the words that follow this term in the text. They describe the summer solstice.

# The Revolution of Earth

As Earth travels around the sun, the tilt of its axis causes our seasons. Each hemisphere shifts from the long days and direct sun of summer to the short days and indirect sun of winter, and then back again. This diagram shows seasons in the Northern Hemisphere.

**Spring ▶**
At the spring equinox, about March 21, days and nights are nearly equal in length. Earth's axis tilts "sideways." The sun is directly over the Equator.

**Summer ▶**
At the summer solstice, about June 21, the sun is directly over the Tropic of Cancer. North of the Arctic Circle, the sun never sets, and there is continuous daylight.

June May April

Equator

Arctic Circle

Tropic of Cancer

Tropic of Capricorn

23.5°

Earth's axis tilts at a 23.5° angle from its orbit. This accounts for the seasons.

July

August

September

The sun, at the center of Earth's orbit, gives our planet light and warmth.

**◀ A Beach in Maine**
During the long, warm days of summer, green plants grow and people head for beaches.

Diagram not to scale

As Earth moves through its orbit, the Northern Hemisphere is tilted farther from the sun. Sunlight is less direct, and we have the chill of fall. When the Northern Hemisphere is tilted farthest from the sun at the winter solstice, days are short, the sun's rays reach us at a steep angle, and we have cold weather. Finally, Earth's revolution moves the Northern Hemisphere back toward the sun, and we have the warming trend of spring.

When the Northern Hemisphere is tilted toward the sun, the Southern Hemisphere is tilted away, and vice versa, so the seasons are reversed in the Southern Hemisphere.

**▲ Winter in the Arctic**
Iqaluit, Canada, is near the Arctic Circle. In winter, there is very little sun, and temperatures are bitterly cold.

**▼ Winter**
About December 21, at winter solstice, the sun is directly over the Tropic of Capricorn, and the area north of the Arctic Circle is in constant darkness.

March
February
January
*Arctic Circle*
*Tropic of Capricorn*

December
November
October

**◄ Fall**
By about September 23, the sun is again directly over the Equator. Less direct sunlight in the Northern Hemisphere brings cooler temperatures.

*Arctic Circle*
*Tropic of Cancer*
*Equator*
*Tropic of Capricorn*

### GEOGRAPHY SKILLS PRACTICE

**Regions** Earth's tilt means that the seasons are different in the Northern and Southern hemispheres. **Compare and Contrast** When it is spring in the Northern Hemisphere, what is the season in the Southern Hemisphere?

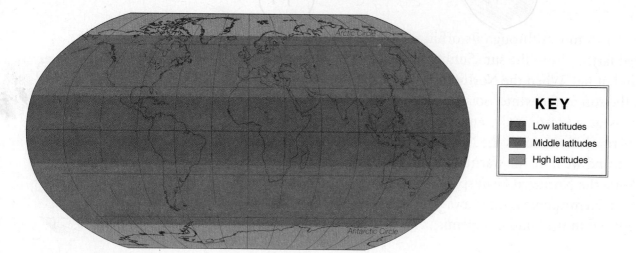

**Zones of Latitude**
The low latitudes, or tropics, are the single orange band around the Equator. The middle latitudes are the two yellow bands just to the north and south. The two green zones in the far north and south are the high latitudes, or polar zones.

**Latitudes**   The areas between the Tropic of Cancer and the Tropic of Capricorn are called the low latitudes, or the tropics. The tropics have fairly direct sunlight and hot weather all year.

The areas above the Arctic Circle and below the Antarctic Circle are the high latitudes, or the polar zones. Though the polar zones may receive long hours of sunlight during the summer, the sun is never directly overhead. They are cool or very cold all year.

The areas between the high and low latitudes are the middle latitudes, or the temperate zones. In summer, these areas receive fairly direct sunlight. In winter, they get very indirect sunlight. So, the middle latitudes have marked seasons: a hot summer, a cold winter, and a moderate spring and fall.

✓ **Reading Check**   **What is the relation between seasons and latitude?**

# Section 1 Assessment

## Key Terms
Review the key terms at the beginning of this section. Use each term in a sentence that explains its meaning.

## Target Reading Skill
Find the phrase *winter solstice* on page 31. Use context to figure out its meaning. What do you think it means? What clues helped you find a meaning?

## Comprehension and Critical Thinking
**1. (a) Define**   What is the rotation of Earth?

**(b) Synthesize Information**
How is Earth's rotation connected to the change from day to night?
**2. (a) Identify**   On the time zone map on page 29, find the time zone where you live.
**(b) Evaluate**   What is the time difference between your home and Greenwich, England?
**(c) Analyze**   How is this time difference related to Earth's rotation?
**3. (a) Recall**   What is Earth's tilt?
**(b) Describe**   How does Earth's orbit affect its tilted hemispheres?

**(c) Identify Cause and Effect**
How do Earth's tilt and orbit cause the seasons?

## Writing Activity
Write a short passage for a younger child, explaining the movements of Earth.

**For:** An activity on our planet, Earth
**Visit:** PHSchool.com
**Web Code:** led-3201

# Forces Shaping Earth

## Prepare to Read

### Objectives

In this section you will
1. Learn about the planet Earth.
2. Explore the forces inside Earth.
3. Explore the forces on Earth's surface.

### Taking Notes

As you read this section, look for details about Earth's structure, Earth's landforms, forces inside Earth, how continents move, and forces on Earth's surface. Copy the web diagram below, add more branches and ovals as needed, and write each detail in the correct oval.

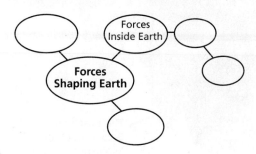

### Target Reading Skill

**Use Context Clues** You can sometimes find the meaning of a word or phrase by using context. Sometimes the context will define or restate the word. In this example, the phrase in italics defines *continent*:

> A continent, or *one of Earth's large land areas* . . .

As you read, look at the context for the phrase *Ring of Fire* in the paragraph below. What do you think the phrase *Ring of Fire* means?

### Key Terms

- **core** (kawr) *n.* the sphere of very hot metal at the center of Earth
- **mantle** (MAN tul) *n.* the thick layer around Earth's core
- **crust** (krust) *n.* the thin, rocky layer on Earth's surface
- **magma** (MAG muh) *n.* soft, nearly molten rock
- **plate** (playt) *n.* a huge block of Earth's crust
- **weathering** (WETH ur ing) *n.* a process that breaks rocks down into small pieces
- **erosion** (ee ROH zhun) *n.* the removal of small pieces of rock by water, ice, or wind

# Understanding Earth

Around the rim of the Pacific Ocean is a string of volcanoes and earthquake belts called the "Ring of Fire." About 80 percent of the world's earthquakes and many of the world's active volcanoes occur in that ring. Earthquakes and volcanoes are two forces that shape and reshape Earth. They are one reason why Earth's surface constantly changes. They also provide clues about Earth's structure.

**Hot rock from inside Earth flows into the Pacific Ocean to form new land in Hawaii.**

**What Is Earth Made Of?** To understand the forces that shape Earth, you must study Earth's structure. A sphere of very hot metal at the center of Earth is called the **core.** The **mantle** is a thick, hot, rocky layer around the core. The thin layer of rocks and minerals that surrounds the mantle is called the **crust.** In effect, the crust floats on top of the mantle. The heat of the core and mantle helps shape Earth's crust. The surface of the crust includes Earth's land areas as well as the ocean floors.

## Earth's Layers

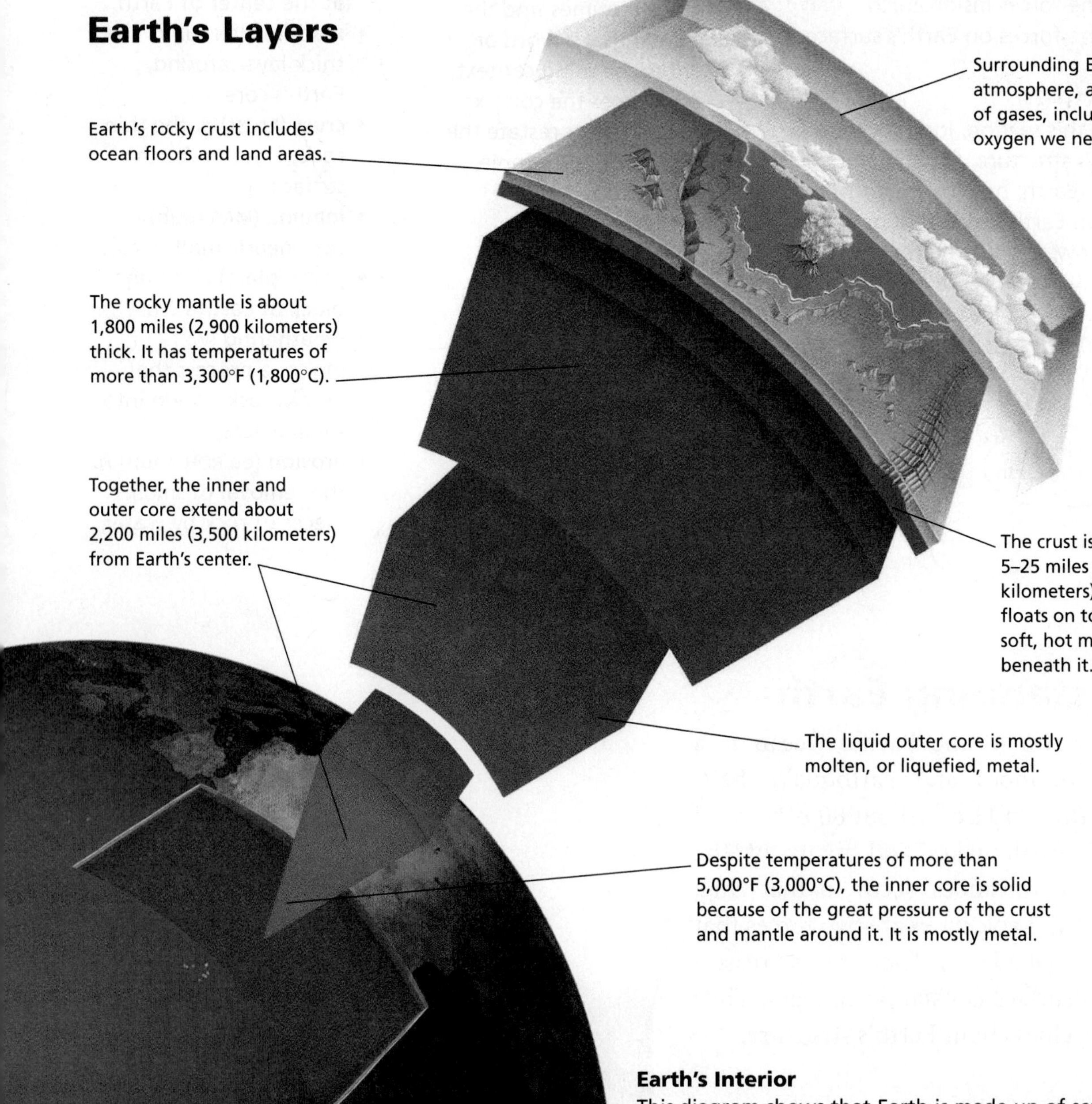

Earth's rocky crust includes ocean floors and land areas.

Surrounding Earth is the atmosphere, a layer of gases, including the oxygen we need to live.

The rocky mantle is about 1,800 miles (2,900 kilometers) thick. It has temperatures of more than 3,300°F (1,800°C).

Together, the inner and outer core extend about 2,200 miles (3,500 kilometers) from Earth's center.

The crust is only 5–25 miles (8–40 kilometers) thick. It floats on top of the soft, hot mantle beneath it.

The liquid outer core is mostly molten, or liquefied, metal.

Despite temperatures of more than 5,000°F (3,000°C), the inner core is solid because of the great pressure of the crust and mantle around it. It is mostly metal.

**Earth's Interior**
This diagram shows that Earth is made up of several layers, from the very hot inner core at its center to the much cooler crust on its outer surface. Above the crust, where people live, are the oceans and atmosphere.
**Analyze Images** *What difficulties might you have if you tried to dig beneath the crust to Earth's center?*

**Water and Air** Less than 30 percent of Earth's surface is land. Water covers more than 70 percent of Earth's surface in lakes, rivers, seas, and oceans. The oceans hold about 97 percent of Earth's water. This water is salty. Very little of Earth's water is fresh water, or water without salt. Most fresh water is frozen in ice sheets near the North and South poles. People can use only a small part of Earth's fresh water. This fresh water comes from lakes, rivers, and ground water, which are fed by rain.

Above Earth's surface is the atmosphere, a layer of gases a few miles thick. It provides life-giving oxygen to people and animals, and carbon dioxide to plants.

**Landforms** Many different landforms, or shapes and types of land, cover Earth's land surfaces. Mountains are landforms that rise more than 2,000 feet (610 meters) above sea level or the surrounding flatlands. They are wide at the bottom and rise steeply to a narrow peak or ridge. A volcano is a kind of mountain. Hills are landforms with rounded tops, which rise above the surrounding land but are lower and less steep than mountains. A plateau is a large, mostly flat area that rises above the surrounding land. At least one side of a plateau has a steep slope. Plains are large areas of flat or gently rolling land.

✔ **Reading Check** **Which layer of Earth contains all of its landforms?**

**Use Context Clues**
If you do not know what the atmosphere is, notice that a definition follows the phrase. The definition tells you what the word means.

**Land and Water**
Ice floes float near Alexander Island, off the coast of Antarctica. Salt water covers most of Earth's surface. Most fresh water is ice, frozen in polar regions such as Antarctica.
**Analyze Images** *What landforms can you see in this photograph?*

# Forces Inside Earth

Heat deep inside Earth is constantly reshaping the planet's surface. The intense heat causes rock to rise toward the surface. Where streams of this soft, nearly molten rock called **magma** reach Earth's crust, they push up the crust to form volcanoes. Volcanoes spew molten rock, or lava, from inside Earth. Streams of magma may also push the crust apart along seams. Huge blocks of Earth's crust called **plates** are separated by these seams. Plates may include continents or parts of continents. Each plate also includes part of the ocean floor. Along seams, mainly beneath oceans, streams of magma rise from inside Earth. As the magma cools, it forms new crust and pushes the old crust away from the seams.

# How Continents Move

Rising magma forms new crust along seams between Earth's plates. Beneath the surface, some scientists believe, magma moves like a conveyor belt. The belt drags the growing plates and the continents that they carry.

Where two plates push against each other, the pressure makes the crust bend and buckle to form steep mountains.

Plates move only an inch or two (a few centimeters) a year.

Crust

Mantle

Earthquakes occur when blocks of crust slide sideways against each other.

Some scientists think that sheets of mantle act like conveyor belts that move the plates of crust above them.

Sheets of magma rise to the surface from Earth's interior along a seam between plates of crust.

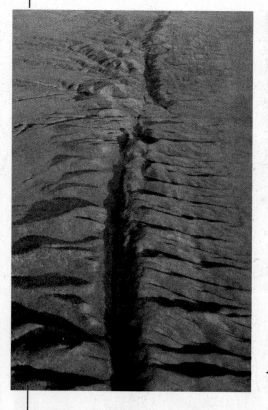

◄ **Two plates rub together along the San Andreas Fault in California.**

**Volcanoes and Earthquakes**   Where a plate of ocean crust collides with a plate of continental crust, the ocean crust plunges underneath the continental plate and melts. Molten rock surges upward, exploding onto the surface through a volcano. The Ring of Fire surrounds the plates that make up the Pacific Ocean. Streams of magma also form volcanoes at places other than plate boundaries. Such volcanoes have shaped the Hawaiian Islands, which are far from a plate boundary.

When two plates push together, the crust cracks and splinters from the pressure. The cracks in Earth's crust are called faults. When blocks of crust rub against each other along faults, they release huge amounts of energy in the form of earthquakes.

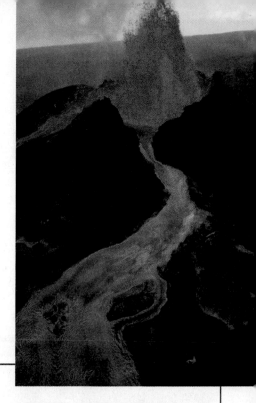

▲ **Molten rock pours from a volcano in Hawaii.**

Magma from inside Earth cools to form new crust in the form of rock. This rock piles up in underwater mountains called mid-ocean ridges.

As new ridges form, older crust is pushed away. Plates on either side of a seam move slowly apart.

**Ocean**

**Land**

Streams of rising magma form chains of volcanoes.

When ocean crust plunges beneath land, it melts into streams of magma that rise to the surface.

**GEOGRAPHY SKILLS PRACTICE**

**Movement**   The diagram shows how moving plates behave. **Predict**  If a plate of ocean crust plunged underneath a continental plate, what landforms would you expect to develop?

**A World of Moving Plates** For hundreds of years, geographers wondered how Earth's landmasses took their present shapes and positions. When they looked at the globe, they thought they saw matching shapes in continents that are very far apart. Now that they know how forces inside Earth move continents, they know that those continents were once close together.

✓ Reading Check **How do continents move apart?**

## Plate Movements

### Plates 250 million years ago

### Plates Shifting Through Time

Most geographers believe that long ago Earth had only one huge continent. They call it Pangaea (pan JEE uh). About 200 million years ago, they conclude, plate movement began to split Pangaea apart. They think that these pieces came to form the continents that we know today. **Analyze** *According to these maps, which present-day continents were once joined together?*

### Plates 150 million years ago

### Present-Day Plates

The map below shows Earth's modern plates and plate edges. It also shows how the plates are moving. Earthquakes and volcanoes cluster along plate edges. **Identify** *Which plate is colliding with the North American Plate?*

### Plates 75 million years ago

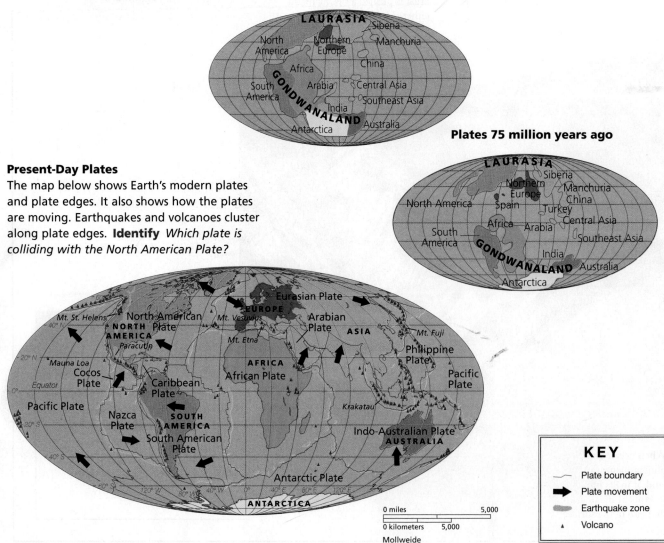

KEY

— Plate boundary
➤ Plate movement
Earthquake zone
▲ Volcano

0 miles 5,000
0 kilometers 5,000
Mollweide

# Forces on Earth's Surface

Forces inside Earth move plates apart, produce volcanoes, and slowly build up Earth's crust. Other forces slowly wear it down and reshape it. The forces that wear Earth down are not as dramatic as volcanoes, but over time they are just as effective.

**Weathering** is a process that breaks rocks down into tiny pieces. Water, ice, and living things like lichens on rocks all cause weathering. Weathering helps create soil, too. Tiny pieces of rock combine with decayed animal and plant material to form soil.

Once this breaking down has taken place, landforms are reshaped by **erosion,** or the removal of small pieces of rock by water, ice, or wind. Hundreds of millions of years ago, the Appalachian Mountains in the eastern United States were as high as the Rocky Mountains of the western United States now are. Rain, snow, and wind slowly wore them down into much lower peaks.

When water, ice, and wind remove material, they deposit it downstream or downwind to create new landforms. Plains are often made of material carried from upstream by rivers.

✓ **Reading Check** What landforms are products of weathering and erosion?

**Weathering and erosion formed this natural sandstone bridge in Jordan.**

# Section 2 Assessment

## Key Terms

Review the key terms at the beginning of this section. Use each term in a sentence that explains its meaning.

## Target Reading Skill

Find the word *landforms* in the last paragraph of page 35. Use the context to find its meaning. What does it mean? What clues did you use to find its meaning?

## Comprehension and Critical Thinking

**1. (a) List** What are Earth's three main layers?

**(b) Synthesize Information** How do those layers interact?

**2. (a) Recall** What forces inside Earth shape Earth's surface?

**(b) Explain** How do these forces explain the movement of the continents?

**(c) Predict** How might a continent split in two?

**3. (a) Identify** What forces cause weathering and erosion?

**(b) Compare and Contrast** How is erosion different from weathering?

## Writing Activity

Think about the region where you live. Does it have steep mountains or volcanoes, rounded hills, or plains? Write a paragraph describing some of the natural forces that are slowly reshaping your region.

**Go Online**
**PHSchool.com**

**For:** An activity on Pangaea
**Visit:** PHSchool.com
**Web Code:** led-3202

# Climate and Weather

## Prepare to Read

### Objectives

In this section you will
1. Learn about weather and climate.
2. Explore latitude, landforms, and precipitation.
3. Discover how oceans affect climate.

### Taking Notes

As you read this section, look for topics related to climate and weather, such as landforms, precipitation, oceans, and storms. Copy the outline below and add headings as needed to show the relationships among these topics.

```
  I.  Weather
 II.  Climate
      A.  Latitudes
      B.
          1.
          2.
III.  Storms
```

### Target Reading Skill

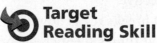

**Use Context Clues** You can sometimes learn the meaning of a word or phrase when the context gives a comparison. In this example, the word *cyclone* is compared to the phrase in italics.

A cyclone is like *a huge spiral escalator moving air upward.*

### Key Terms

- **weather** (WETH ur) *n.* the condition of the air and sky from day to day
- **precipitation** (pree sip uh TAY shun) *n.* water that falls to the ground as rain, sleet, hail, or snow
- **temperature** (TEM pur uh chur) *n.* how hot or cold the air is
- **climate** (KLY mut) *n.* the average weather over many years
- **tropical cyclone** (TRAHP ih kul SY klohn) *n.* an intense wind and rain storm that forms over oceans in the tropics.

**This Inuit woman and child are dressed for their cold climate.**

## Weather or Climate?

Every morning, most people check the weather before they get dressed. But in some parts of India, people have very serious reasons for watching the **weather,** or the condition of the air and sky from day to day. In parts of India, it rains only during one time of year. No one living there wants the rainy days to end too soon. That rain must fill the wells with enough fresh water to last for the entire year.

In India, people are concerned about **precipitation,** or water that falls to the ground as rain, sleet, hail, or snow. When you get dressed in the morning, you may want to know the **temperature,** or how hot or cold the air is. Weather is mainly measured by temperature and precipitation.

The **climate** of a place is the average weather over many years. Climate is not the same as weather. Weather is what people see from day to day. Climate is what usually happens from year to year.

✔ Reading Check **What is the difference between weather and climate?**

# Why Climates Vary

Earth has many climates. Some climates are so hot that people rarely need to wear a sweater. In some cold climates, snow stays on the ground most of the year. And there are places on Earth where more than 30 feet (9 meters) of rain falls in a single year.

Climate depends on location. Places in the low latitudes, or tropics, have hot climates, because they get direct sunlight. Places in the high latitudes, or polar regions, have cold climates, because their sunlight is indirect.

Air and water spread heat around the globe as they move. Without wind and water, places in the tropics would overheat. Oceans gain and lose heat slowly, so they keep temperatures mild near coasts. Mountains can also affect climates.

✔ **Reading Check** **How does latitude affect temperature?**

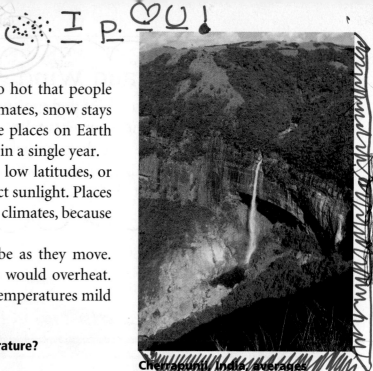

Cherrapunji, India, averages 37 feet (11 meters) of rain a year. The rain then flows into lakes, streams, and waterfalls.

## The Water Cycle

Water evaporates from bodies of water or land areas where rain has fallen and rises into the sky.

The heated water vapor condenses to form clouds made up of little drops of water.

As moist air rises, it cools and drops its moisture. This can happen when air is forced up a mountain slope or when air rises in a storm system.

Water seeps into the ground or runs into streams. It then flows to the sea or evaporates again.

**The Water Cycle**
Water evaporates from the surface and then falls back as precipitation. **Predict** *Which side of a mountain will get more rain, the side facing the wind, or the side facing away?*

# Air Circulation and Wind

Winds and air currents move heat and moisture between different parts of Earth. These currents follow regular patterns related to latitude. The diagram below shows these circular patterns of air movement, which form a series of belts, or cells, that circle Earth.

**A strong onshore wind blows in Miami Beach, Florida.**

Regions where air sinks, such as the poles, have dry climates.

In the temperate zones, warm winds from the southwest rise over cold polar air.

Dry air sinks, creating a band of deserts around the continents.

Warm, moist air rises at the Equator.

Wherever air rises, its moisture condenses and falls as precipitation.

The global belts of circulating air are called cells.

Very cold air sinks at the poles and flows outward. Earth's rotation bends these winds so that they blow from the east.

At the poles, the sun's rays reach Earth at a steep angle, and the air stays cold.

Direct sunlight at the Equator heats Earth's surface.

Over the tropics, warm air blows toward the Equator, where it rises. Because of Earth's rotation, these winds bend to blow from the southeast or east.

## GEOGRAPHY SKILLS PRACTICE

**Regions** Regions where air rises have heavier precipitation than regions where air sinks. **Compare and Contrast** How can this diagram explain the regions of heavy precipitation shown on the map on page 43 titled The World: Precipitation?

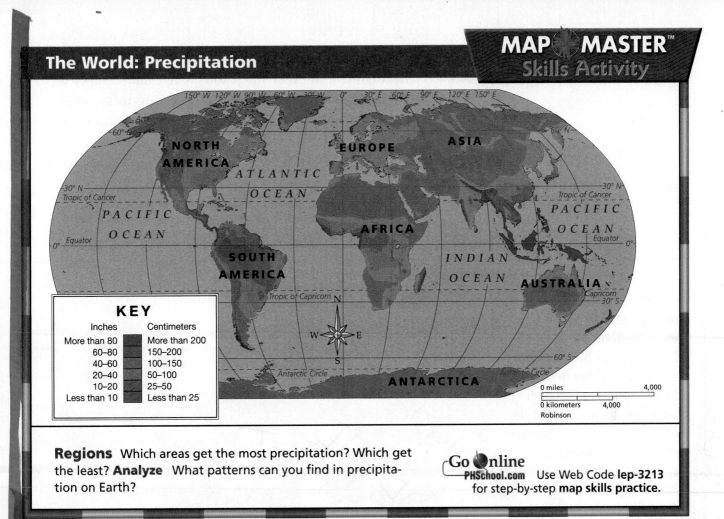

KEY

| Inches | | Centimeters |
|---|---|---|
| More than 80 | | More than 200 |
| 60–80 | | 150–200 |
| 40–60 | | 100–150 |
| 20–40 | | 50–100 |
| 10–20 | | 25–50 |
| Less than 10 | | Less than 25 |

0 miles        4,000
0 kilometers   4,000
Robinson

**Regions** Which areas get the most precipitation? Which get the least? **Analyze** What patterns can you find in precipitation on Earth?

Go Online
PHSchool.com Use Web Code **lep-3213**
for step-by-step **map skills practice.**

# Oceans and Climates

The oceans help distribute Earth's heat and shape climates. Global wind patterns help create ocean currents, which are like vast rivers in the oceans. Ocean currents move across great distances. Generally, warm water flows away from the Equator, while cold water moves toward the Equator.

**Oceans and Currents** In the Atlantic Ocean, the Gulf Stream, a warm current, travels northeast from the tropics. The Gulf Stream and the North Atlantic Current carry warm water all the way to western Europe. That warm water gives western Europe a milder climate than other regions at the same latitude.

The cold Peru Current moves north from Antarctica along the coast of South America. The city of Antofagasta (ahn toh fah GAHS tah) lies along that coast, in Chile. Even though Antofagasta is closer than Miami, Florida, is to the Equator, the average temperature in Antofagasta during the hottest month of summer is just 68°F (20°C).

**Using Prereading Strategies**
If you do not know what ocean currents are, notice that they are compared to vast rivers in the ocean. How does the comparison help you find the meaning?

**The Ocean's Cooling and Warming Effects** Bodies of water affect climate in other ways, too. Water takes longer to heat or cool than land. As the air and land heat up in summer, the water remains cooler. Wind blowing over the water cools the nearby land. So in summer, a region near an ocean or lake will be cooler than an inland area at the same latitude. In the winter, the water remains warmer than the land. So places near lakes or oceans are warmer in winter than inland areas.

# The World: Climate Regions

You can see patterns in a map of Earth's climate regions. Notice that tropical wet climate regions hug the Equator on several continents. Farther from the Equator are arid and semiarid climate regions. Elsewhere, regions where the wind blows off the ocean have wetter climates than regions farther inland. Each climate region on this map is described more fully in the next section.

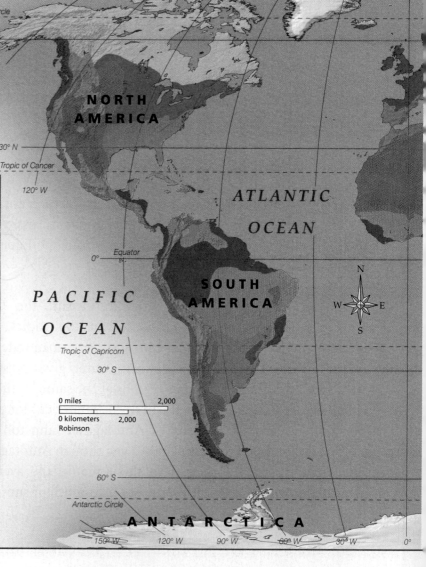

▲ **Arid** This view from the air shows the Colorado River winding through the Grand Canyon in Arizona.

Consider San Francisco, California, and St. Louis, Missouri. Both cities are near 38° north latitude. However, San Francisco borders the Pacific Ocean. In winter, the ocean is warmer than the air. The ocean keeps San Francisco much warmer than St. Louis in winter. In summer, the ocean is cooler than the air, so it keeps San Francisco cool.

**Reading Check** **During the summer, are places near the ocean warmer or cooler than places inland?**

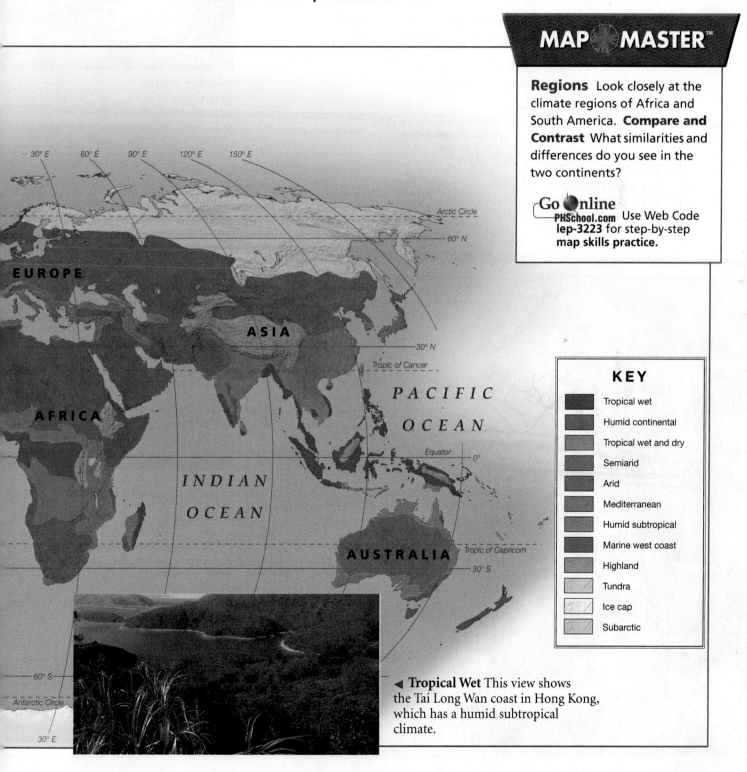

**MAP MASTER™**

**Regions** Look closely at the climate regions of Africa and South America. **Compare and Contrast** What similarities and differences do you see in the two continents?

**Go Online**
**PHSchool.com** Use Web Code **lep-3223** for step-by-step **map skills practice.**

EUROPE

ASIA

AFRICA

PACIFIC

OCEAN

INDIAN

OCEAN

AUSTRALIA

*30° E*   *60° E*   *90° E*   *120° E*   *150° E*

*Arctic Circle*

*60° N*

*30° N*

*Tropic of Cancer*

*Equator*   *0°*

*Tropic of Capricorn*

*30° S*

*60° S*

*Antarctic Circle*

*30° E*

**KEY**

- Tropical wet
- Humid continental
- Tropical wet and dry
- Semiarid
- Arid
- Mediterranean
- Humid subtropical
- Marine west coast
- Highland
- Tundra
- Ice cap
- Subarctic

◄ **Tropical Wet** This view shows the Tai Long Wan coast in Hong Kong, which has a humid subtropical climate.

# Weather Forecasting

Television weather forecasters rely on scientists and equipment from all over the world. Weather stations record local conditions. Satellites orbit overhead to photograph large weather systems. Weather balloons and radar provide still more data. The results, displayed on weather maps or presented in forecasts, can warn citizens of an approaching hurricane or simply remind people to carry an umbrella.

**Weather station**
This ranger is measuring rainfall at a weather station on the island of Madeira in the Atlantic Ocean. Stations like this send reports to forecasters.

Solar cell panels power the spacecraft.

**Weather satellites**
Scientists use satellites in space to record everything from wind patterns to the height of waves.

**GOES weather satellite**
U.S. weather satellites are called GOES (Geostationary Operational Environmental Satellites). They circle Earth in time with Earth's rotation, so they always stay above the same spot.

A hurricane

CURRENT TEMPERATURE

8 Portl
87 Minneapolis  79 Detroit
82  8 Washi D.C
86 Atlanta
96 Dallas  92 New Orleans  83

**Weather map**
Forecasters track weather patterns and storm systems, and display data on weather maps.

A gathering storm

**ANALYZING IMAGES**
How might a satellite help forecasters predict the weather?

# Raging Storms

Wind and water can make climates milder, but they also can create large and dangerous storms. **Tropical cyclones** are intense wind and rain storms that form over oceans in the tropics. Tropical cyclones that form over the Atlantic Ocean are called hurricanes. The winds near the center of a hurricane can reach speeds of more than 100 miles (160 kilometers) per hour. Hurricanes produce huge swells of water called storm surges, which flood over shorelines and can destroy buildings.

Tornadoes are like funnels of wind that can reach 200 miles (320 kilometers) per hour. The winds and the low air pressure they create in their centers can wreck almost anything in their path. They can be just as dangerous as hurricanes, but they affect much smaller areas.

Other storms are less dangerous. In winter, blizzards dump huge amounts of snow on parts of North America. And severe rainstorms and thunderstorms strike the continent most often in spring and summer.

✔ **Reading Check** **Which storms cover larger areas, hurrricanes or tornadoes?**

**Hurricane Katrina**
In 2005 Hurricane Katrina caused massive destruction along the south-eastern coast of the United States.
**Synthesizing Information**
*Is a hurricane more likely on a tropical coast or in a polar region far from the ocean?*

---

## Section 3 Assessment

### Key Terms
Review the key terms at the beginning of this section. Use each term in a sentence that explains its meaning.

### Target Reading Skill
Find the word *tornadoes* in the second paragraph on this page. Using the context, find out its meaning. What clues did you use to find its meaning?

### Comprehension and Critical Thinking
1. (a) **Identify** What is climate?
(b) **Explain** How is climate different from weather?
(c) **Analyze** Are hurricanes an example of climate or of weather?
2. (a) **Recall** What kind of climate occurs in most places near the Equator?
(b) **Contrast** Why are climates near the poles different from climates near the Equator?
3. (a) **Recall** How do bodies of water affect temperatures?
(b) **Predict** A city in the interior of a continent has very cold winters. How would you expect winter temperatures to differ in a coastal city at the same latitude as the interior city?

### Writing Activity
Write a paragraph describing your region's climate, or average weather. Are winters usually warm or cold? What can you say about summers? Do oceans affect your climate? How much precipitation does your region get? Is it mostly rain, or snow, or a mix?

**Writing Tip** Remember that every paragraph needs a main idea. Make a general statement about your climate in a topic sentence. Then add sentences with supporting details about your climate.

**Menghai, China, receives about 40 to 60 inches (100 to 150 centimeters) of rainfall each year.**

"**E**verybody talks about the weather, but nobody does anything about it," goes an old joke attributed to the humorist Mark Twain. It's still true, although today we track the weather so that we can predict and prepare for it. One way geographers track weather patterns is by making a climate graph. A climate graph usually presents information about average precipitation and average temperature. Often it shows a whole year of information, so you can see how conditions change with the seasons.

## Learn the Skill

To read a climate graph, follow the steps below.

**1** **Identify the elements of the graph.** A climate graph is actually two graphs in one: a line graph that shows temperature and a bar graph that shows rainfall. The scale on the left side goes with the line graph, and the scale on the right side goes with the bar graph. The scale along the bottom shows a time period.

**2** **Study the line graph.** Notice changes in temperature from month to month and from season to season. Draw a conclusion about the temperature of the place.

**3** **Study the bar graph.** Again, notice changes for months and for seasons. Draw a conclusion about rainfall.

**4** **Use your conclusions about both graphs to draw an overall conclusion about the climate of the location.** Does the location appear to have hot seasons and cold seasons? Or does it have a rainy season and a dry season? State your conclusion.

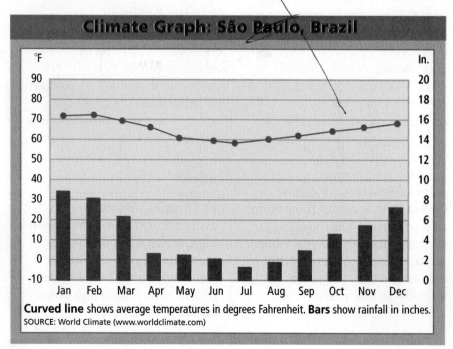

**Climate Graph: São Paulo, Brazil**

**Curved line** shows average temperatures in degrees Fahrenheit. **Bars** show rainfall in inches.
SOURCE: World Climate (www.worldclimate.com)

## Practice the Skill

Look at the graph of São Paulo, Brazil, on page 48.

**1** Read the labels on the sides and bottom of the graph. What do the numbers on the left side measure? What do the numbers on the right side measure? Look at the green bars. Which do they measure, temperature or rainfall? How do you know? Look at the line graph. What does it show? Now, look at the scale along the bottom of the graph. What period of time does it show?

**2** Describe the shape of the line graph—is it generally flat, or does it go up and down? What and when is São Paulo's highest average temperature? Its lowest temperature? Do you think São Paulo has a hot season and a cold season? Write a conclusion about temperatures in the city.

**3** What do the bars in the bar graph show? Are they generally the same height, or do they differ from month to month? What and when are São Paulo's highest and lowest average rainfall? Do you think São Paulo has a wet season and a dry season? Write a conclusion about rainfall in the city.

**4** Using your conclusions about São Paulo's climate, write a summary that includes answers to these questions: What kind of seasons does the city have? Does the weather change much during the year?

### Apply the Skill

To make your own climate graph, draw a large square on graph paper. Divide the square into 10 horizontal rows and 12 vertical columns. Title your graph "Climate Graph of Charleston, South Carolina." Then label the left side of your graph using one colored pencil and the right side with a different colored pencil. Write the months of the year along the bottom. Using the temperature and precipitation information in the table above, plot your line graph. Draw the lines with the same colored pencils you used to make the labels for temperature and precipitation.

### Charleston, South Carolina

| Month | Temperature (°Fahrenheit) | Precipitation (inches) |
|-------|---------------------------|------------------------|
| Jan | 48.4 | 2.9 |
| Feb | 50.9 | 3.0 |
| Mar | 57.7 | 3.6 |
| Apr | 65.3 | 2.4 |
| May | 72.7 | 3.2 |
| Jun | 78.8 | 4.7 |
| Jul | 81.7 | 6.8 |
| Aug | 81.0 | 6.4 |
| Sept | 76.6 | 5.1 |
| Oct | 67.8 | 2.9 |
| Nov | 59.5 | 2.1 |
| Dec | 52.2 | 2.7 |

## Prepare to Read

### Objectives

In this section you will
1. Investigate the relationship between climate and vegetation.
2. Explore Earth's vegetation regions.
3. Study vertical climate zones.

### Taking Notes

As you read, look for details about Earth's natural vegetation regions. Copy the chart below and list each type of climate in the first row of boxes. Add boxes as needed. In the box underneath each type of climate, list facts about each vegetation region that occurs in that type of climate.

```
           Climates and Vegetation
    ┌────────────────┬──────────────┬───────────────┐
 Tropical Climates    Dry Climates    Moderate Climates
    ┌────┐           ┌────┐          ┌────┐
    │ •  │           │ •  │          │ •  │
    │ •  │           │ •  │          │ •  │
    │ •  │           │ •  │          │ •  │
    └────┘           └────┘          └────┘
```

### Target Reading Skill

**Use Context Clues**
You can sometimes learn the meaning of a word or phrase when the context gives examples. In the passage below, the meaning of the word *scrub* is given by the examples in italics.

> Scrub includes *bushes, small trees, and low, woody undergrowth.*

### Key Terms

- **vegetation** (vej uh TAY shun) *n.* plants that grow in a region
- **tundra** (TUN druh) *n.* an area of cold climate and low-lying vegetation
- **canopy** (KAN uh pea) *n.* the layer formed by the uppermost branches of a rain forest
- **savanna** (suh VAN uh) *n.* a parklike combination of grasslands and scattered trees
- **desert scrub** (DEZ urt skrub) *n.* desert vegetation that needs little water
- **deciduous trees** (dee SIJ oo us treez) *n.* trees that lose their leaves seasonally
- **coniferous trees** (koh NIF ur us treez) *n.* trees that produce cones to carry seeds

**Jackfruit, an Asian fruit, grows huge in the tropical wet climate of Hainan Island, China.**

# Climate and Vegetation

There are five broad types of climate: tropical, dry, temperate marine, temperate continental, and polar. Each climate has its own types of natural **vegetation,** or plants that grow in a region. This is because different plants require different amounts of water and sunlight and different temperatures to survive. The map titled The World: Natural Vegetation, on page 53, shows the location of Earth's vegetation regions. If you compare this map with the map on pages 44 and 45 titled The World: Climate Regions, you will see that climate regions and vegetation regions often cover similar areas.

**Tropical Climates** In the tropics, there are two main climates. Both are hot. A tropical wet climate has year-round rainfall. Its typical vegetation is tropical rain forest. A tropical wet and dry climate has two seasons: a rainy season and a dry season. This climate supports grasslands and scattered trees.

**Dry Climates** Arid and semiarid climates have very hot summers and generally mild winters. They get very little rain. The driest arid climate regions have little or no vegetation. Others have plants that need little water. Semiarid climates get a little more rain. They support shrubs and grasses.

**Temperate Marine Climates** Temperate marine climates are found in the middle latitudes, usually near coastlines. There are three types: Mediterranean, marine west coast, and humid subtropical. The marine west coast and humid subtropical climates get plenty of rain. In the humid subtropical climate, the rain falls mainly in summer. Mediterranean climates get less rain, and it falls mainly in winter. All of the climates have mild winters. Mediterranean and humid subtropical climates generally have hot summers. With their heavy rainfall, marine west coast and humid subtropical climates support a variety of forests. The drier Mediterranean climates have their own vegetation, known as Mediterranean vegetation.

**Temperate Continental Climates** In a humid continental climate, summer temperatures are moderate to hot, but winters can be very cold. This climate supports grasslands and forests. Regions with subarctic climates are drier, with cool summers and cold winters. Most subarctic climate regions are forested.

**Polar Climates** The polar climates are cold all year-round. The **tundra** is an area, near the Arctic Circle, of cold climate and low-lying vegetation. The word *tundra* refers both to the vegetation and the climate, which has short, cool summers and long, very cold winters. Ice cap climates are bitterly cold all year. These areas are covered with ice. No vegetation can grow there.

√ Reading Check **Why are climate and vegetation related?**

# Earth's Vegetation Regions

Geographers divide Earth into regions that share similar vegetation. A place's vegetation depends mainly on its climate, but also on other things, such as soil quality.

**Links to Science**

**Plant Fossils** In ancient rocks in Wyoming, scientists have found fossils of palm trees. Millions of years ago, sediments such as sand or ash buried the plants quickly. Over thousands of years, the sediment and plants within turned to rock. Scientists study fossils to learn about ancient climate and vegetation.

**Polar bears crossing the tundra in Churchill, Manitoba, Canada**

This tropical rain forest in Brazil supports dense vegetation.

**Use Context Clues** If you do not know what Mediterranean vegetation is, consider the examples and other information given by the context. What does the context tell you about this vegetation?

- **Tropical Rain Forest** Because there is so much sunlight, heat, and rain, thousands of kinds of plants grow in a rain forest. Some trees rise 130 feet (40 meters) into the air. The dense, leafy layer formed by the uppermost branches of the rainforest is called the **canopy.** Other plants grow to lower heights in the shade beneath the canopy.

- **Tropical Savanna** In tropical areas with winter dry seasons or more limited rainfall, there is a parklike landscape of grasslands with scattered trees known as **savanna.**

- **Desert** In the driest parts of deserts, there may be no vegetation at all. Elsewhere, plants grow far apart. Their roots absorb scarce water before it evaporates in the heat.

- **Desert Scrub** Semiarid areas and deserts with a little more rain support **desert scrub,** or low desert vegetation that needs little water. Some plants flower only when it rains, so that seeds have a better chance to survive.

- **Mediterranean Vegetation** Mediterranean vegetation includes grasses, shrubs, and low trees. These plants must hold water from the winter rains to survive warm, dry summers.

- **Temperate Grassland** Vast grasslands straddle regions with semiarid and humid continental climates. The wetter grasslands, in humid continental climates, have a mix of tall grasses and other plants that is sometimes called prairie.

- **Deciduous Forest** Marine west coast, humid subtropical, and humid continental climates all support forests of **deciduous trees,** or trees that lose their leaves in the fall.

- **Coniferous and Mixed Forest** These same climates also support areas of coniferous and mixed forest. **Coniferous trees** are trees that produce cones to carry seeds. They generally have needles, not leaves. These features protect trees in drier climates. Mixed forests combine both coniferous and deciduous trees.

- **Tundra** The tundra is an area of cold climate and low-lying vegetation. Tundra vegetation includes mosses, grasses, and low shrubs that bloom during the brief, cool summers.

- **Highland** In highland regions, vegetation depends on elevation, since temperatures drop as elevation rises. Tropical forests may grow at low elevations, with grasslands and coniferous forests farther up. Still higher, tundra vegetation may grow.

- **Ice Cap and Pack Ice** Around the poles, thick ice caps form on land. Masses of ice called pack ice cover the sea. No vegetation can grow there.

✔ Reading Check **What types of vegetation grow in deserts?**

# The World: Natural Vegetation

This map shows the natural vegetation regions of the world. The locations of these regions depend mainly on climate. Like the climates that support them, vegetation regions vary according to their distance from the Equator and the amount of precipitation they receive.

**The Sahara ▶**
The world's largest desert has vast sand dunes with little or no vegetation. This picture also shows an oasis, or a place in the desert where underground water allows trees or crops to grow.

**MAP MASTER™**
**Skills Activity**

**Location** In which parts of Earth do you find tropical rain forests? **Compare and Contrast** Find tropical wet climates on the map in the previous section titled The World: Climate Regions. How do those locations compare with the locations of tropical rain forests?

Go Online
PHSchool.com Use Web Code
lep-3214 for step-by-step map skills practice.

◀ **Lichen, Northern Russia**

◀ **Mixed Forest**
The mixed forests of California support trees such as pines, redwoods, and tan oaks.

0 miles 3,000
0 kilometers 3,000
Robinson

## KEY

| | | | |
|---|---|---|---|
| Tropical rain forest | | Desert scrub | |
| Deciduous forest | | Desert (no vegetation) | |
| Mixed forest | | Highland | |
| Coniferous forest | | Tundra | |
| Mediterranean forest | | Ice cap | |
| Tropical savanna | | Pack ice | |
| Temperate grassland | | National border | |
| | | Disputed border | |

# Vertical Climate Zones

The climate at the top of Mount Everest, in southern Asia, is like Antarctica's. But Mount Everest is near the Tropic of Cancer, far from the South Pole. It is so cold at the top of the mountain because the air becomes cooler as elevation increases. Mountains have vertical climate zones, where the climate and vegetation depend on elevation.

In a tropical region, vegetation that needs a tropical climate will grow only near the bottom of a mountain. Farther up is vegetation that can grow in a temperate climate. Near the top is vegetation that can grow in a polar climate.

Picture yourself on a hike up a mountain in a temperate climate. Grassland surrounds the base of the mountain, and temperatures are warm. You begin to climb and soon enter an area with more precipitation and lower temperatures than below. The grassland gives way to a coniferous forest.

As you continue to climb, you find only scattered, short trees. Finally, it is too cold even for them. There are only the low shrubs, short grasses, and mosses of a tundra. At the mountain's peak, you find permanent ice, where no vegetation grows.

**Forested valley at the foot of Machapuchare, a mountain in Nepal**

✓ **Reading Check** How does vegetation change with elevation?

---

## Section 4 Assessment

### Key Terms
Review the key terms at the beginning of this section. Use each term in a sentence that explains its meaning.

### Target Reading Skill
Find the phrase *tundra vegetation* on page 52. Use context to figure out its meaning. What do you think it means? What clues helped you find the meaning?

### Comprehension and Critical Thinking
**1. (a) List** What are the five main types of climate?
**(b) Evaluate** How do differences in climate affect plant life?

**(c) Analyze** Why do low-lying plants, such as scrub or tundra, grow in some climates, while rich forests grow in others?
**2. (a) Recall** How do desert plants survive in dry climates?
**(b) Transfer Information** What features of the plants in your region allow them to grow in your region's climate?
**3. (a) Define** What is a vertical climate zone?
**(b) Explain** How do vertical climate zones affect vegetation on a mountain?
**(c) Compare and Contrast** Why is vegetation at the top of a tall mountain different from vegetation at the bottom?

### Writing Activity
Look at the map titled The World: Natural Vegetation on page 53 in this section. Choose three places on the map that are in different natural vegetation regions. Then write a description of the types of plants you would expect to see if you visited each place you have chosen.

**Writing Tip** Since you are writing about three different types of natural vegetation, you may want to compare and contrast them. When you compare, you point out similarities. When you contrast, you focus on differences.

## ◆ Chapter Summary

### Section 1: Our Planet, Earth

- Earth's rotation on its axis changes day to night and night to day.
- The tilt of Earth's axis causes our seasons.

### Section 2: Forces Shaping Earth

- Earth's three main layers are the crust, the mantle, and the core.
- Forces inside Earth move plates of crust to form mountains and volcanoes.
- Wind, water, and ice wear down and reshape Earth's surface.

### Section 3: Climate and Weather

- Climate is the average weather in a region over a long period of time.
- Climate depends on latitude, landforms, and nearness to an ocean.
- Winds and ocean currents help spread Earth's warmth. They can also cause dangerous storms.

### Section 4: How Climate Affects Vegetation

- Vegetation depends mainly on climate.
- Earth can be divided into several natural vegetation regions.
- Climate and vegetation change with elevation.

**Delicate Arch, Utah**

## ◆ Key Terms

Each of the statements below contains a key term from the chapter. If the statement is true, write *true*. If it is false, rewrite the statement to make it true.

1. Earth's movement around the sun is called **rotation**.

2. The **mantle** is a thick, rocky layer around Earth's core.

3. Earth's **crust** is at the center of the planet.

4. **Magma** is hot, flowing rock beneath Earth's surface.

5. The Appalachian Mountains have been worn down over time by **erosion**.

6. If you want to know how hot it will be tomorrow, you can look at a **climate** report.

7. **Temperature** measures how hot or how cold something is.

8. **Vegetation** is a term for the plants that grow in a region.

9. **Deciduous forests** grow in polar climates.

## ◆ Comprehension and Critical Thinking

**10.** (a) **Recall** How many standard time zones is Earth divided into?
(b) **Analyze** How are time differences related to the rotation of Earth?

**11.** (a) **Identify** As Earth moves around the sun, what event happens about June 21?
(b) **Explain** How does Earth's movement make summers hot and winters cold?
(c) **Apply Information** Why is Antarctica cold even in summer?

**12.** (a) **Recall** How much of Earth's water is fresh?
(b) **Predict** If Earth's climate became colder, how might the fresh water supply be affected?

**13.** (a) **Recall** What causes winds?
(b) **Contrast** What are some negative and positive effects of wind and water in the tropics?

**14.** (a) **Describe** How do oceans shape climate?
(b) **Synthesize Information** Why do some coastal cities in the tropics stay cool?

**15.** (a) **Describe** How does climate affect vegetation?
(b) **Evaluate** A tropical climate has year-round rainfall. Can forests grow there? Explain why or why not.

## ◆ Skills Practice

**Using Special Geography Graphs** Review the steps you learned in the Skills For Life activity in this chapter. Then look at the climate graph for Helsinki, Finland, below. After you have analyzed the graph, write a paragraph that summarizes Helsinki's climate.

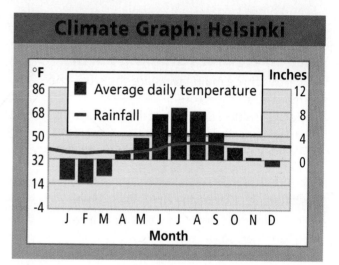

**Climate Graph: Helsinki**

## ◆ Writing Activity: Science

Reread the descriptions of dry climates and of desert vegetation regions. Then design a plant that could live in these regions. Describe how it would get light, water, and nutrients.

## MAP MASTER™
### Skills Activity

**Oceans and Seas**

**Place Location** For each place listed below, write the letter that marks its location on the map.

1. Atlantic Ocean
2. Arctic Ocean
3. Indian Ocean
4. Mediterranean Sea
5. Pacific Ocean
6. Southern Ocean

**Go Online**
PHSchool.com Use Web Code **lep-3215** for step-by-step **map skills practice.**

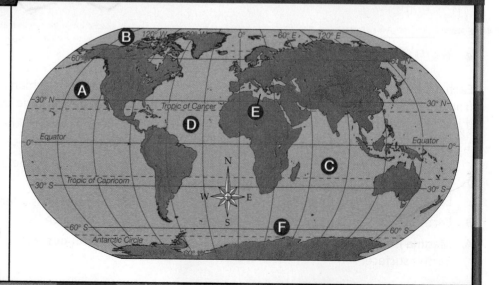

# Standardized Test Prep

## Test-Taking Tips

Some questions on standardized tests ask you to use map keys. Read the precipitation map key below. Then follow the tips to answer the sample question.

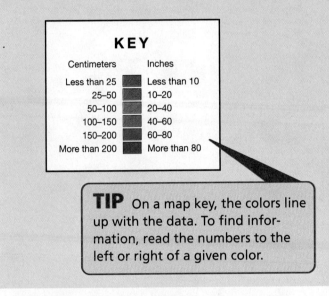

**TIP** On a map key, the colors line up with the data. To find information, read the numbers to the left or right of a given color.

Pick the letter that best answers the question.

On a precipitation map, the southern coastal states are colored dark green. According to the key at the left, how many inches of rain does this region get each year?

**A** 20–40

**B** 60–80

**C** 50–100

**D** 150–200

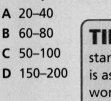

**TIP** To be sure you understand what the question is asking, restate it in your own words: *The color DARK GREEN on the map key stands for how many inches of rain each year?*

**Think It Through** The question asks about inches of rain, but the answers C and D show numbers from the centimeter column. The numbers 20–40 (answer A) are next to yellow, not dark green. The numbers 60–80 are next to dark green in the inches column. The answer is B.

## Practice Questions

Use the tips above and other tips in this book to help you answer the following questions:

1. When the Northern Hemisphere has days and nights of equal length, it is

   **A** summer solstice.

   **B** spring equinox.

   **C** New Year's Day.

   **D** winter solstice.

2. Which of the following is NOT an example of a landform?

   **A** a mountain

   **B** a plateau

   **C** a plain

   **D** an atmosphere

3. In which vegetation region would you find a plant with shallow roots, meant to absorb water before it evaporates?

   **A** desert

   **B** deciduous forest

   **C** coniferous forest

   **D** tropical savanna

Study the following map key and answer the question that follows.

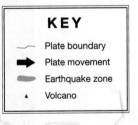

4. On a map with this key, you would find places where earthquakes happen by looking for

   **A** a brown area.

   **B** a red triangle.

   **C** a black arrow.

   **D** a black line.

**Go Online**
PHSchool.com

Use Web Code **lea-3201** for a **Chapter 2** self-test.

# Earth's Human Geography

## Chapter Preview

This chapter will introduce you to Earth's human geography, or the patterns of human activity on Earth.

### Target Reading Skill

**Comparison and Contrast** In this chapter you will focus on the text structure by learning how to compare and contrast. Comparing and contrasting can help you to sort out and analyze information.

▶ Woman harvesting rice on a terrace built by people in southern China

# Population

## Prepare to Read

### Objectives

In this section you will
1. Learn about population distribution.
2. Explore population density.
3. Investigate population growth.

### Taking Notes

Copy the concept web below. As you read this section, fill in the web with information about the causes and effects of population density and of population growth. Add more ovals as needed.

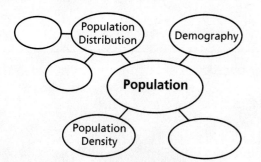

### Target Reading Skill

**Comparison and Contrast** Comparing and contrasting can help you sort out information. When you compare, you examine the similarities between things. When you contrast, you look at the differences. As you read this section, compare and contrast population distribution and population density. Look for the similarities and differences between these two concepts.

### Key Terms

• **population** (pahp yuh LAY shun) *n.* total number of people in an area

• **population distribution** (pahp yuh LAY shun dis trih BYOO shun) *n.* the way the population is spread out over an area
• **demography** (dih MAH gruh fee) *n.* the science that studies population distribution and change
• **population density** (pahp yuh LAY shun DEN suh tee) *n.* the average number of people per square mile or square kilometer
• **birthrate** (BURTH rayt) *n.* the number of live births each year per 1,000 people
• **death rate** (deth rayt) *n.* the number of deaths each year per 1,000 people

**A crowded village on the Nile River near Aswan, Egypt**

# Population Distribution

The world's **population,** or total number of people, lives in uneven clusters on Earth's surface. Some places have many people. Other places are almost empty. **Population distribution** is the way the population is spread out over an area.

**Demography** is the science that tries to explain how populations change and why population distribution is uneven. Demographers study rates of birth, marriage, and death. And they ask why people move from one place to another.

**Population and Places** People usually don't move without a good reason. People may move because they can live better in a new place. Other times, people are forced to move, or they move because they cannot feed their families. However, as long as people can make a living where they are, they usually stay in that area. So, regions with large populations tend to keep them.

**Population and History** In the past, most people lived on farms where they grew their own food. They lived where the climate provided enough water and warm weather to support crops. Regions with a long history of farming, good soil, and plenty of water became crowded. These regions still have large populations. Most places too cold or too dry for farming still have small populations.

**New Population Clusters** However, after about 1800, improved transportation and new ways of making a living changed things. Railroads and steamships made it easier for people to move long distances, even across oceans. New jobs in factories and offices meant that more people were living in cities, where they could make a living without farming the land. Crowded cities grew in regions that once had few people, such as the United States, Australia, and northern Europe.

**Villages in France have grown through centuries of farming.**

✓ **Reading Check** Why are some parts of the world more crowded than others?

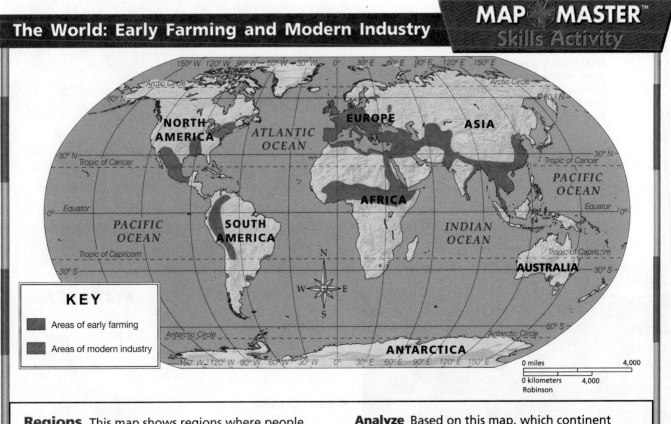

**MAP MASTER** Skills Activity

**The World: Early Farming and Modern Industry**

KEY

■ Areas of early farming

■ Areas of modern industry

Robinson

**Regions** This map shows regions where people were farming by 500 B.C. It also shows regions with modern industries. Population today is clustered in these two kinds of regions. **Identify** Which regions of the world have long histories of farming?

**Analyze** Based on this map, which continent probably has the most people?

Go Online Use Web Code lep-3321 for
PHSchool.com step-by-step **map skills practice.**

**Target Skill**

**Compare and Contrast**
How is population density different from population distribution?

# Population Density

How many people live in your neighborhood? How big is that neighborhood? If you take the population of an area and divide it by the size of that area in square miles or square kilometers, you can get a sense of how crowded or empty that area is. The average number of people per square mile or square kilometer is called **population density.**

Population distribution and population density both describe where people live. Population density differs from population distribution, however, because it gives an average number of people for an area. Population distribution gives actual numbers of people for an area.

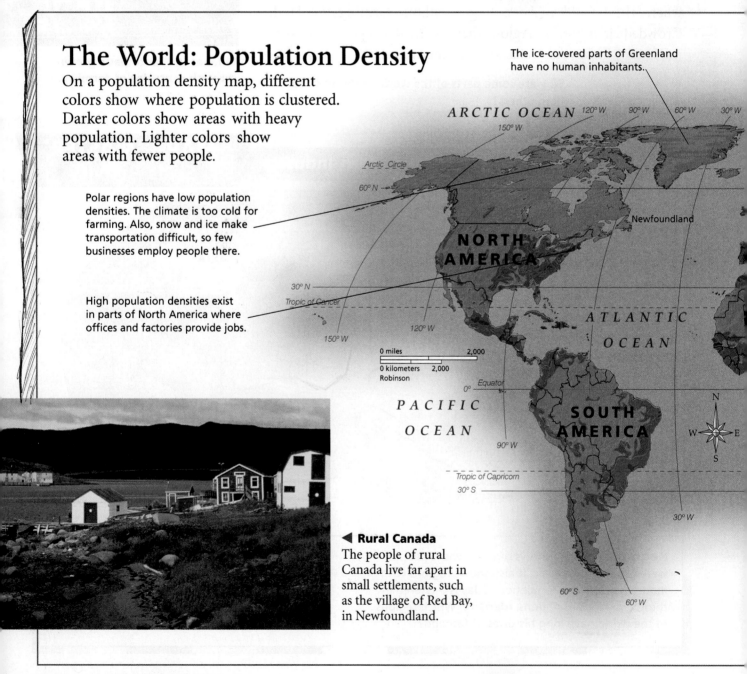

# The World: Population Density

On a population density map, different colors show where population is clustered. Darker colors show areas with heavy population. Lighter colors show areas with fewer people.

The ice-covered parts of Greenland have no human inhabitants.

Polar regions have low population densities. The climate is too cold for farming. Also, snow and ice make transportation difficult, so few businesses employ people there.

High population densities exist in parts of North America where offices and factories provide jobs.

ARCTIC OCEAN

Arctic Circle

NORTH AMERICA

Newfoundland

ATLANTIC OCEAN

PACIFIC OCEAN

SOUTH AMERICA

Tropic of Cancer

Equator

Tropic of Capricorn

0 miles 2,000
0 kilometers 2,000
Robinson

◄ **Rural Canada**
The people of rural Canada live far apart in small settlements, such as the village of Red Bay, in Newfoundland.

Population density varies from one area to another. In a country with a high density, such as Japan, people are crowded together. Almost half of Japan's 127 million people live on only 17 percent of the land, or an area the size of West Virginia. In Tokyo, there is a population density of more than 25,000 people per square mile (9,664 per square kilometer). In contrast, Canada has a low overall population density. It has about 9 people per square mile (3 per square kilometer). Canada is bigger than the United States, but has only about one ninth as many people.

**✓ Reading Check** **Which has a higher population density, a city or an area in the countryside?**

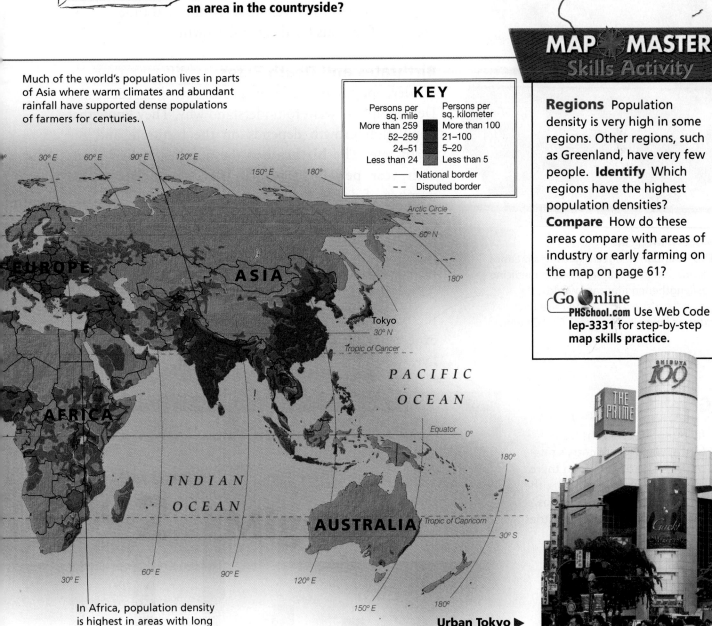

Much of the world's population lives in parts of Asia where warm climates and abundant rainfall have supported dense populations of farmers for centuries.

**KEY**

| Persons per sq. mile | Persons per sq. kilometer |
|---|---|
| More than 259 | More than 100 |
| 52–259 | 21–100 |
| 24–51 | 5–20 |
| Less than 24 | Less than 5 |

—— National border
– – Disputed border

EUROPE

ASIA

AFRICA

Tokyo

PACIFIC OCEAN

INDIAN OCEAN

AUSTRALIA

Arctic Circle

60° N

180°

30° N

Tropic of Cancer

Equator    0°

180°

Tropic of Capricorn

30° S

30° E    60° E    90° E    120° E    150° E    180°

30° E    60° E    90° E    120° E    150° E    180°

In Africa, population density is highest in areas with long histories of settled farming, such as the Nile Valley.

**Urban Tokyo ▶**
Tokyo, the world's largest urban area, is the capital of Japan, one of the world's most densely populated countries.

**MAP✦MASTER™**
**Skills Activity**

**Regions** Population density is very high in some regions. Other regions, such as Greenland, have very few people. **Identify** Which regions have the highest population densities? **Compare** How do these areas compare with areas of industry or early farming on the map on page 61?

**Go Online**
**PHSchool.com** Use Web Code **lep-3331** for step-by-step map skills practice.

# Population Growth

Suppose that all the years from A.D. 1 to A.D. 2000 took place in a single day. As the day began at midnight, there would be 300 million people in the world. Twelve hours later, at noon, there would be just 310 million people. By 8:24 P.M., the population would double to 600 million. It would double again by 10:05 P.M. to 1.2 billion. By 11:20, it would double again to 2.4 billion, and then double yet again by 11:48 to 4.8 billion, before reaching 6 billion as the day ended at midnight. As you can see, the world's population has grown very quickly in recent times. There are several reasons for this rapid growth.

**Birthrates and Death Rates** At different times in history, populations have grown at different rates. Demographers want to understand why. They know that population growth depends on the birthrate and the death rate. The **birthrate** is the number of live births each year per 1,000 people. The **death rate** is the number of deaths each year per 1,000 people.

For thousands of years, the world's population grew slowly. In those years, farmers worked without modern machinery. Food supplies often were scarce. People lived without clean water or waste removal. Many millions of people died of infectious diseases. As a result, although the birthrate was high, so was the death rate. The life expectancy, or the average number of years that people live, was short.

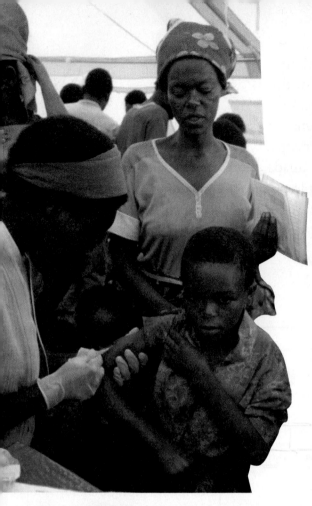

**Modern Medicine**
This Rwandan refugee is getting a measles vaccination in Tanzania. Modern medicine has lengthened lifespans worldwide.
**Analyze** *Does vaccination raise birth rates or lower death rates? Explain why.*

## Graph Skills

If you subtract deaths from births, you get a country's rate of natural growth. When there are more deaths than births, the native-born population drops. **Identify** Which of the countries shown here has the highest birthrate? **Compare** Where is the population growing, Russia or the United States?

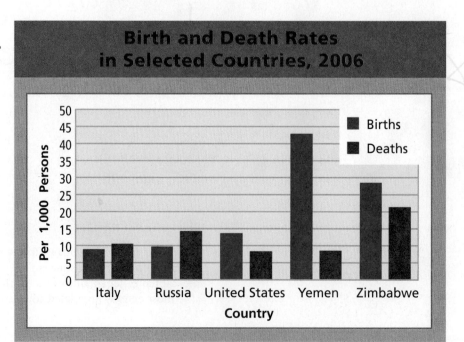

**Birth and Death Rates in Selected Countries, 2006**

Per 1,000 Persons

■ Births
■ Deaths

Country: Italy, Russia, United States, Yemen, Zimbabwe

**Reasons for Population Growth Today** This all changed after the 1700s. Death rates dropped sharply. In some countries, birthrates increased. As a result, populations have grown very fast. In some countries, the population has doubled in less than 20 years. Meanwhile, people live longer than ever. In the United States, people born in 1900 could expect to live for 47 years. Today, they can expect to live for 77 years.

Scientific progress explains much of this change. First, new farming methods have increased the world's food supply. Scientists have improved important food crops and found new ways to protect crops against insects. Scientists have also found ways to raise crops with less water. These recent scientific improvements in agriculture are called the Green Revolution.

The second set of scientific advances has come in health and medicine. Scientists have convinced local governments to provide clean drinking water and sanitary waste removal. These measures sharply reduce disease. Researchers have also developed vaccines to prevent disease and antibiotics to fight infections. As a result, people live many more years.

**Due to a high birthrate and a low death rate, Yemen's population is skyrocketing.**

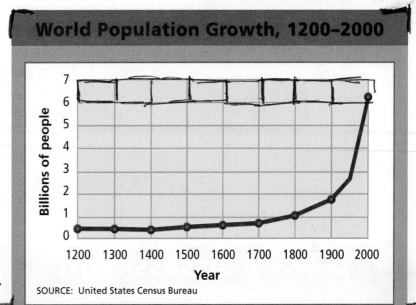

**World Population Growth, 1200–2000**

SOURCE: United States Census Bureau

**Overcrowding in Bangladesh**
These Bangladeshis are returning from a festival. Bangladesh's population has grown faster than its public services. This results in overcrowding, as seen on this train. **Infer** *What other aspects of life in Bangladesh might be affected by rapid population growth?*

**The Challenges of Population Growth** Today, food supplies have increased and people live longer. Even so, people in many countries still face serious problems. Some nations, such as those in Southwest Asia, do not have enough fresh water. In parts of Asia and Africa, the population is growing faster than the food supply. Often, these countries do not have enough money to buy food elsewhere.

Population growth puts pressure on all aspects of life. The populations of many countries are increasing so fast that not everyone can find jobs. There are not enough schools to educate the growing number of children. Decent housing is scarce. Public services such as transportation and sanitation are inadequate.

Rapid population growth also affects the environment. For instance, forests in many countries are disappearing. People in poorer countries cut down the trees for wood and fuel. Clearing forests causes other problems. In a forest, tree roots hold soil in place, and forest soils soak up rain. With the forest gone, heavy rainfall may wash away the soil and cause dangerous floods. Demand for wood and fuel in wealthier countries also uses up the world's scarce resources. All of Earth's people must work to meet this challenge.

✓ Reading Check **Why have populations risen rapidly in recent times?**

---

## Section 1 Assessment

**Key Terms**
Review the key terms at the beginning of this section. Use each term in a sentence that explains its meaning.

**Target Reading Skill**
How are population density and population distribution similar? How are they different?

**Comprehension and Critical Thinking**
1. (a) **Recall** In what parts of the world did most people live before modern times?
(b) **Explain** How does history help explain population distribution today?

(c) **Contrast** How is population distribution today different from the days before modern science was developed?
2. (a) **Define** What is population density?
(b) **Transfer Information** To figure out the population density of an area, what two pieces of information do you need?
3. (a) **Recall** How has population growth changed in 100 years?
(b) **Explain** What accounts for this change?
(c) **Identify Cause and Effect** What are the effects of this change in population growth?

**Writing Activity**
Suppose that you are a demographer studying the area where you live. How does population density vary across your area? Where is population growth taking place? Write a short description of your area's demography.

**Go Online**
**PHSchool.com**

**For:** An activity on population
**Visit:** PHSchool.com
**Web Code:** led-3301

# Migration

## Prepare to Read

### Objectives

In this section you will

1. Learn about migration, or people's movement from one region to another.
2. Investigate urbanization, or people's movement to cities.

### Taking Notes

Copy the chart below. As you read this section, fill in the chart with information about voluntary and involuntary migration and about urbanization.

```
                    Migration
    ┌──────────────┬──────────────┬──────────────┐
 Voluntary      Involuntary     Urbanization
 Migration       Migration
   •               •               •
   •               •               •
   •               •               •
   •               •
```

### Target Reading Skill

**Identify Contrasts**
When you contrast two situations, you examine how they differ. Although both voluntary and involuntary migration involve the movement of people, the reasons for that movement differ. As you read, list the differences between voluntary and involuntary migration.

### Key Terms

- **migration** (my GRAY shun) *n.* the movement of people from one place or region to another
- **immigrants** (IM uh grunts) *n.* people who move into one country from another
- **urbanization** (ur bun ih ZAY shun) *n.* the movement of people to cities, and the growth of cities
- **rural** (ROOR ul) *adj.* located in the countryside
- **urban** (UR bun) *adj.* located in cities and towns

# Why People Migrate

For thousands of years, people have moved to new places. People's movement from one place or region to another is called **migration**. **Immigrants** are people who move into one country from another.

In the years from 1850 to 1930, more than 30 million Europeans moved to live in the United States. Since 1971, more than 4.5 million people have migrated here from Mexico, and more than 2.5 million have migrated from the Caribbean islands. Since 1971, Central America, the Philippines, China, and Vietnam have all lost more than 1 million immigrants to the United States. More than 800,000 immigrants have come from both South Korea and India.

During the late 1800s and early 1900s, millions of immigrants to the United States stopped at Ellis Island in New York Harbor.

**Cubans in Little Havana**
These men ordering food at a cafe are part of a large community of Cuban immigrants in Miami, Florida.
**Analyze Images** *What aspects of their life in Cuba have these immigrants preserved in their new home?*

**Identify Contrasts** How is involuntary migration different from voluntary migration?

**Voluntary Migration in the Past** Voluntary migration is the movement of people by their own choice. Today, most people move by their own choice. The push-pull theory says that people migrate because difficulties "push" them to leave. At the same time, the hope for a better life "pulls" people to a new country.

The push-pull theory helps to explain the great Irish migration in the 1840s and 1850s. In those years, 1.5 million people left Ireland for the United States. What pushed so many Irish people to come to America? In the 1840s, disease destroyed Ireland's main crop—potatoes. Hunger pushed people to migrate. Job opportunities pulled Irish families to the United States.

**Voluntary Migration Today** The same theory explains most migration today. The main sources of migration are countries where many people are poor and jobs are few. In some countries, such as Vietnam and Central American countries, wars have made life dangerous and difficult.

In China, Vietnam, and Cuba, governments limit people's freedom. These problems push people to leave. Meanwhile, the possibility of good jobs and political freedom pulls people to the United States and other well-off, democratic countries.

**Involuntary Migration** Sometimes people are forced to move. Because these people do not choose to move, their movement is known as involuntary migration. During the early 1800s, the British sent prisoners to Australia to serve their sentences. When their sentences were done, many stayed. War also forces people to migrate to escape death or serious danger.

**The Transatlantic Slave Trade** Perhaps the biggest involuntary migration in history was the transatlantic slave trade. From the 1500s to the 1800s, millions of Africans were enslaved and taken against their will to European colonies in North and South America. These Africans traveled under inhumane conditions across the Atlantic Ocean, chained inside ships for more than a month.

At first, their descendants in the United States lived mainly on the east coast. As cotton farming spread west, many enslaved African Americans were forced to migrate again, this time to new plantations in the Mississippi Valley and Texas.

✓ **Reading Check** **Why do people migrate?**

# Migration in South Asia

At the end of British colonial rule in 1947, most of South Asia was divided along religious lines into two countries. India had a Hindu majority. Pakistan was mainly Muslim. Fearing religious discrimination or violence, Muslims from India and Hindus from Pakistan fled across the new borders. Many died when violence broke out during these massive migrations.

**Movement** This map shows migrations by South Asians. **Identify** Which countries did South Asia's largest migrations involve? **Contrast** How do the reasons for movement out of South Asia differ from the reasons for migration within the region?

Go Online
PHSchool.com Use Web Code **lep-3312** for step-by-step **map skills practice.**

Over a million people have left South Asian countries for Europe and North America, seeking better lives.

Present-day Bangladesh was part of Pakistan in 1947. Many Hindus from the region fled to India, while Muslims from India fled to what became Bangladesh.

70° E

*Indus R.*

80° E

30° N
30° N

**PAKISTAN**

**NEPAL**

**BHUTAN**

90° E

*Ganges R.*

Tropic of Cancer

*Arabian Sea*

**BANGLADESH (formerly part of Pakistan)**

When India and Pakistan were separated in 1947, 5.4 million Hindus and Sikhs fled from Pakistan to India, and 6.6 million Muslims fled to Pakistan.

20° N

**INDIA**

70° E

20° N

90° E

*Bay of Bengal*

Hundreds of thousands of South Asians have left the region for Southeast Asia, Australia, and the Pacific Islands.

N
W        E
S

10° N
10° N

*INDIAN OCEAN*

**SRI LANKA**

**MALDIVES**

80° E

▲ **Chaos in India and Pakistan**
The separation of India and Pakistan uprooted millions of people and drove them to flee across the new borders.

0 miles            500
0 kilometers       500
Lambert Azimuthal Equal Area

### KEY

➡ Involuntary migration of Hindus from Pakistan to India in 1947

➡ Involuntary migration of Muslims from India to Pakistan in 1947

➡ Voluntary migration of South Asians overseas after 1947

— National border

# Urbanization

Millions of people in many countries have migrated to cities from farms and small villages. In recent years, the population of some cities has grown tremendously. The movement of people to cities and the growth of cities is called **urbanization.**

**Cities and Suburbs** In Europe and North America, the growth of industry during the 1800s pulled people from the countryside to cities. They hoped for jobs in factories and offices. Since about 1950, urbanization has given way in Europe and North America to suburbanization, or the movement of people to growing suburbs. Suburbanization sometimes replaces valuable farmland with sprawling development. Because most people in suburbs rely on cars for transportation, suburban sprawl can increase pollution. However, people still move to suburbs to pursue the dream of home ownership.

## ■ Graph Skills

All over the world, city populations have soared. The photographs of Cape Town, South Africa, below, show how that city has expanded.
**Identify** What percent of the world's people lived in cities in 1800?
**Predict** Based on information from the graph, how do you think the world's rural and urban populations will compare in 2050?

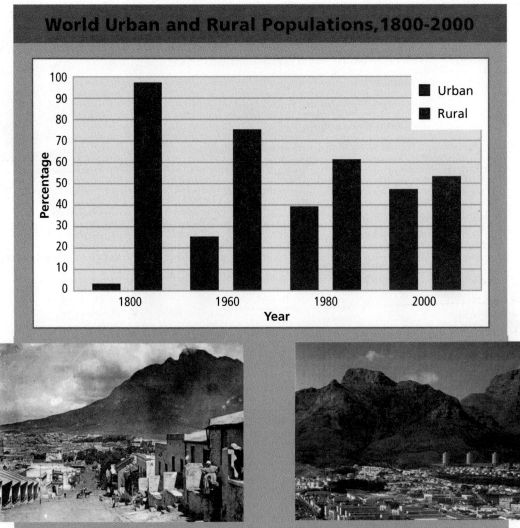

**World Urban and Rural Populations, 1800-2000**

Cape Town, 1938

Modern Cape Town

**Urbanization on Other Continents** In Asia, Africa, and Latin America, people are still streaming from the countryside to growing cities. Indonesia is an example. In the past, most Indonesians lived in **rural** areas, or areas in the countryside. Recently, more and more Indonesians have moved to **urban** areas, or areas in cities and nearby towns. For example, in 1970, about 3.9 million people lived in Greater Jakarta, Indonesia's capital. By 2000, its population was about 11 million. Jakarta is not unique. Greater São Paulo, Brazil, grew from 8 million residents in 1970 to nearly 18 million residents in 2000.

The problem in cities like Jakarta and São Paulo is that too many people are moving to the city too fast. Cities cannot keep up. They cannot provide the housing, jobs, schools, hospitals, and other services that people need. Traffic jams and crowds often make getting around a struggle.

With so many daily problems, why do people flock to São Paulo and other big cities? As hard as life is in the cities, it can be even harder in the countryside, where there are few jobs and a shortage of land to farm. Most migrants to the city are seeking a better life for their families. They are looking for jobs, modern houses, and good schools. Above all, most want better lives for their children.

**São Paulo, Brazil**
São Paulo is Brazil's largest city.
**Analyze Images** *Do you think that this city has a high or a low population density?*

✔ **Reading Check** **How is the population of urban areas changing in Africa, Asia, and Latin America?**

---

## Section 2 Assessment

### Key Terms
Review the key terms at the beginning of this section. Use each term in a sentence that explains its meaning.

### Target Reading Skill
Contrast involuntary migration and voluntary migration. How are these two forms of migration different? List at least two differences between the two kinds of migration.

### Comprehension and Critical Thinking
**1. (a) Identify** What are push factors and what are pull factors?
**(b) Explain** How do push factors and pull factors explain people's decision to migrate?
**(c) Compare and Contrast** Do push and pull factors account for involuntary migration? Explain why or why not.
**2. (a) Recall** What is urbanization?
**(b) Identify Cause and Effect** What are the causes and some of the effects of urbanization?

### Writing Activity
Suppose that you are moving to the United States from one of the countries listed in the second paragraph on page 67. Write a paragraph describing your reasons for leaving that country and what attracts you to the United States.

**Go Online** PHSchool.com

**For:** An activity on migration
**Visit:** PHSchool.com
**Web Code:** led-3302

# Analyzing and Interpreting Population Density Maps

**Crowds gather in Amsterdam on Queen's Day, a national holiday in the Netherlands.**

**H**ow dense is the population where you live? If you drew an imaginary five-mile square around your house and counted the number of people who lived within the square, would there be many residents, or few?

Population density is the average number of persons living within a certain area. You can find out how densely populated a place is by reading a population density map.

## Learn the Skill

To read and interpret a population density map, follow these steps.

**1** **Read the title and look at the map to get a general idea of what it shows.** The title and map key will show you that the topic of the map is population density.

**2** **Read the key to understand how the map uses symbols and colors.** Each color represents a different population density range, as explained in the map key.

**3** **Use the key to interpret the map.** Identify areas of various densities on the map. Some places average less than one person per square mile. In other places, thousands of people might be crammed into one square mile.

**4** **Draw conclusions about what the map shows.** The history, geography, and cultural traditions of a place affect its population density. Draw on this information, plus what you read on the map, to make conclusions about why particular areas have a higher or a lower population density.

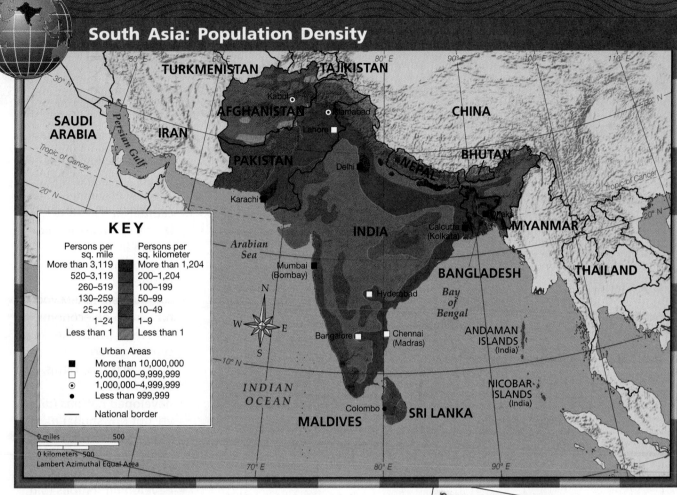

## South Asia: Population Density

**KEY**

| Persons per sq. mile | Persons per sq. kilometer |
|---|---|
| More than 3,119 | More than 1,204 |
| 520–3,119 | 200–1,204 |
| 260–519 | 100–199 |
| 130–259 | 50–99 |
| 25–129 | 10–49 |
| 1–24 | 1–9 |
| Less than 1 | Less than 1 |

**Urban Areas**

■ More than 10,000,000
□ 5,000,000–9,999,999
◉ 1,000,000–4,999,999
● Less than 999,999
— National border

0 miles 500
0 kilometers 500
Lambert Azimuthal Equal Area

## Practice the Skill

Use steps 1–4 to read and interpret the population density map above.

**1** What is the topic of this map? Notice that the map has relief—that is, markings that indicate hills and mountains. It also has labels for cities and nations of South Asia.

**2** Study the map key carefully. How many different colors are in the key? What color is used for the lowest population density? What color is used for the highest density?

**3** Using the key, identify the areas of highest and lowest population densities in South Asia. Write a sentence or two that describes where the most and the fewest people are located.

**4** Write a conclusion that makes a general statement about South Asia's population density and suggests possible reasons for the patterns shown on the map.

## Apply the Skill

Now take a closer look at the map titled The World: Population Density on pages 62 and 63. Find the areas of greatest density. From what you already know and what you see on the map, what features do you think influence where people choose to live? Think about rivers and mountains as well as nearness to a coast or to the Equator.

# Economic Systems

## Prepare to Read

### Key Questions

In this section you will
1. Examine different kinds of economies.
2. Investigate levels of economic development.
3. Study global trade patterns.

### Taking Notes

Copy the table below. As you read this section, fill in the table with information about economic terms, kinds of economies, levels of development, and world trade. Add columns and rows as needed.

| Economic Systems | |
| --- | --- |
| Kinds of Economies | • <br> • |
| Levels of Development | • <br> • |

### Target Reading Skill

**Make Comparisons**
Comparing economic systems enables you to see what they have in common. As you read this section, compare different kinds of economies and levels of economic development. Who makes decisions and how do people live?

### Key Terms

- **economy** (ih KAHN uh mee) *n.* a system in which people make, exchange, and use things that have value
- **producers** (pruh DOOS urz) *n.* owners and workers
- **consumers** (kun SOOM urz) *n.* people who buy and use products
- **capitalism** (KAP ut ul iz um) *n.* an economic system in which individuals own most businesses
- **communism** (KAHM yoo niz um) *n.* an economic system in which the central government owns factories, farms, and offices
- **developed nations** (dih VEL upt NAY shunz) *n.* nations with many industries and advanced technology
- **developing nations** (dih VEL up ing NAY shunz) *n.* nations with few industries and simple technology

**Consumers choose produce at a market in Honolulu, Hawaii.**

## Different Kinds of Economies

An **economy** is a system in which people make, exchange, and use things that have value and that meet their wants or needs. Economies differ from one country to another. In any economy, owners and workers are **producers.** The things they sell are called products **Consumers** are people who buy and use products.

There are three basic economic questions: What will be produced? How will it be produced? And, for whom will it be produced? The answers to these questions depend on the economy.

Modern economies differ in who owns workplaces. The owners generally decide how products are produced. In some countries, most workplaces are privately owned. In others, the government owns most workplaces.

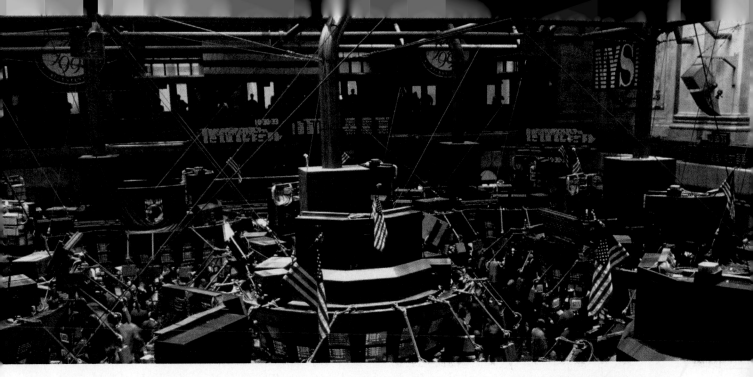

**Private Ownership Capitalism** is an economic system in which private individuals own most businesses. Capitalism is also called a free-market economy because producers compete freely for consumers' business.

In capitalism, people may save money in banks. Banks lend money to people and businesses in return for interest, or a percentage fee for the use of money. Banks also pay interest to savers. Under capitalism, people may directly invest in, or commit money to, a business. Owners of a business are also investors in that business.

**Government Ownership Communism** is an economic system in which the central government owns farms, factories, and offices. It controls the prices of goods and services, how much is produced, and how much workers are paid. The government decides where to invest resources. Today, only a few of the world's nations practice communism.

**Mixed Ownership** Hardly any nation has a "pure" economic system. For example, the United States has a capitalist economy. However, governments build and maintain roads and provide other services. In communist countries, you may find a few small private businesses.

In some countries, the government may own some industries, while others belong to private owners. This system of mixed ownership is sometimes called a mixed economy.

✔ Reading Check   **What are the differences between capitalism and communism?**

# Levels of Economic Development

Three hundred years ago, most people made their own clothes. Then came a great change. People invented machines to make goods. They found new sources of power to run the machines. Power-driven machines were a new technology, or way of putting knowledge to practical use. This change in the way people made goods was called the Industrial Revolution.

The Industrial Revolution created a new economic pattern. Nations with more industries and more advanced technology are considered **developed nations.** Because they are still developing economically, nations with fewer industries and simpler technology are considered **developing nations.** People live differently in developed and developing nations.

**Make Comparisons**
What do developed nations have in common with developing nations?

**Developed Nations**  Only about one fifth of the world's people live in developed nations. These nations include the United States, Canada, Japan, and most European nations. People in these nations use goods made in factories. Businesses use advanced technologies to produce goods and services.

In developed nations, most people live in towns and cities. They work in offices and factories. Machines do most of the work. Most people have enough food and water. Most citizens can get an education and healthcare.

In developed nations, most food is grown by commercial farmers. These are farmers who grow crops mainly for sale rather than for their own needs. Commercial farms use modern technologies, so they need fewer workers than traditional farms.

Developed nations can have some problems. Unemployment is a challenge. Not everyone can find a job. Industry and cars can cause air, land, and water pollution. Developed nations are working to solve these problems.

**Most of Thailand's subsistence farmers grow rice.**

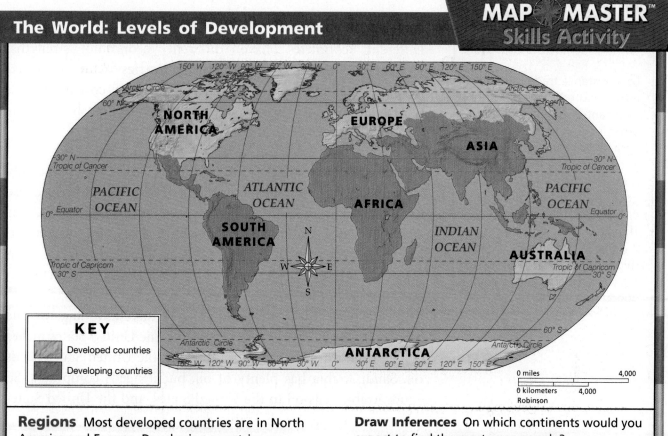

KEY

Developed countries

Developing countries

0 miles 4,000

0 kilometers 4,000

Robinson

**Regions** Most developed countries are in North America and Europe. Developing countries are mainly in South America, Africa, and Asia. **Identify** On which continents would you expect advanced industries, and farming that is mainly commercial?

**Draw Inferences** On which continents would you expect to find the most poor people?

Go Online Use Web Code **lep-3321** for
PHSchool.com step-by-step **map skills practice**.

**Developing Nations** Not every economy is like that of the United States. Most of the people in the world live in developing nations, which are mainly in Africa, Asia, and Latin America.

Developing nations do not have great wealth. Many people are subsistence farmers, or farmers who raise food and animals mainly to feed their own families. Their farms have little or no machinery. People and animals do most of the work.

Many developing nations face great challenges. These include disease, food shortages, unsafe water, poor education and healthcare, and political unrest.

People in developing nations are confronting these challenges. Some nations, such as Saudi Arabia and South Africa, have grown richer by selling natural resources. Others, such as Thailand and China, have built successful industries. The more industrial developing nations are gradually becoming developed countries themselves.

**Many people in developed nations work in offices.**

✓ Reading Check How do developed nations differ from developing nations?

**The Silk Road**
Long-distance trade is nothing new. Hundreds of years ago, merchants brought silks and other luxuries from China to ancient Rome along the Silk Road across Asia. However, those merchants had to load goods on the backs of animals or carry the goods themselves. They could take only light-weight, valuable goods. Today, ships, trains, and trucks can carry heavy and inexpensive goods long distances.

# World Trade Patterns

Different countries have different economic strengths. Developed nations have strong industries with advanced technology. Some developing nations have low-cost industries. Other developing nations may grow plantation cash crops, or they may produce oil or minerals.

**Different Specialties** Countries' economies differ not only because they are more or less developed. They also differ because each country has a different set of economic specialties. For example, Saudi Arabia has vast amounts of oil, and Switzerland has a long history of producing fine watches. Because each country has different specialties, each country has products that consumers in other countries want.

Countries trade with one another to take advantage of one another's special strengths. For example, the United States makes some of the world's best computers. But the United States needs oil. Saudi Arabia has plenty of oil, but it needs computers. So Saudi Arabia sells oil to the United States, and the United States sells computers to Saudi Arabia.

## How Does World Trade Work?

**Country A** produces more oil than it needs. It sells this oil so that it can buy computers and wheat.

**Country B** produces more wheat than it needs. It sells this wheat so that it can buy oil and computers.

**Country C** makes more computers than it needs. It sells computers so that it can buy wheat and oil.

**How Trade Works**
Countries sell what they have and what other countries want so that they can buy what they lack. **Predict** *Which country from the diagram would you expect to sell oil so that it can buy tea?*

**Interdependence** As world trade has grown, countries have grown interdependent, or dependent on one another. The United States depends on other countries for oil and inexpensive industrial goods. Meanwhile, other countries depend on the United States for computers and other products.

Developed nations tend to sell products made using advanced technologies. Developing nations tend to sell foods, natural resources such as oil, and simple industrial products. In return, they buy high-technology goods from developed countries.

Some countries have formed trade alliances to reduce the costs of trade. For example, the United States, Canada, and Mexico belong to the North American Free Trade Agreement, or NAFTA. Most European countries belong to the European Union. Businesses may face increased competition from foreign competitors within these alliances, and workers may lose their jobs. However, businesses may benefit from increased sales in other countries. Consumers benefit from these alliances because they pay less for products from other countries.

**Moving Goods**
Much of the world's trade travels on container ships, like this one in Dubai, United Arab Emirates. These ships can carry huge loads across oceans. **Draw Conclusions** *How does technology make world trade easier?*

✓ Reading Check **Why do countries trade with one another?**

## Section 3 Assessment

### Key Terms
Review the key terms at the beginning of this section. Use each term in a sentence that explains its meaning.

### Target Reading Skill
What are two ways developed and developing countries are similar?

### Comprehension and Critical Thinking
**1. (a) Identify** Who owns farms, factories, and offices in a communist economy?
**(b) Compare and Contrast** How is ownership different in a capitalist economy?

**2. (a) Identify** What is a country's level of development?
**(b) Describe** What are the main differences in level of development between countries?
**(c) Predict** What can we predict about a country's economy if we know its level of development?
**3. (a) List** What are two major trade alliances?
**(b) Explain** What is the main purpose of these alliances?
**(c) Analyze** What are some reasons why a country might want to join a trade alliance?

### Writing Activity
Suppose you run a company, and you want to expand to another nation. Would you choose a capitalist or communist nation? A developed or developing nation? Would you choose a nation that belongs to a trade alliance? Write a letter to investors explaining your choice.

**Go Online**
**PHSchool.com**

**For:** An activity on economic systems
**Visit:** PHSchool.com
**Web Code:** led-3303

# Political Systems

## Prepare to Read

### Objectives

In this section you will

1. Examine different types of states.
2. Investigate types of government.
3. Learn about alliances and international organizations.

### Taking Notes

Copy the table below. As you read, fill the table with information about types of states, types of governments, and international organizations.

| Political Systems | | |
| --- | --- | --- |
| Types of State | Types of Government | Alliances and International Organizations |
| • <br> • <br> • | • <br> • <br> • | • <br> • <br> • |

### Target Reading Skill

**Use Contrast Signal Words** Signal words point out relationships among ideas or events. Certain words, such as *like* or *unlike,* can signal a comparison or contrast. As you read this section, notice the comparisons and contrasts among different types of states and governments. What signal words indicate the comparisons and contrasts?

### Key Terms

- **government** (GUV urn munt) *n.* a body that makes and enforces laws
- **state** (stayt) *n.* a region that shares a government
- **dependency** (dee PEN dun see) *n.* a region that belongs to another state
- **nation-state** (NAY shun stayt) *n.* a state that is independent of other states
- **city-state** (SIH tee stayt) *n.* a small city-centered state
- **empire** (EM pyr) *n.* a state containing several countries
- **constitution** (kahn stuh TOO shun) *n.* a set of laws that define and often limit a government's power

In 1994, Eritreans celebrated the first anniversary of their country's independence.

## Types of States

Long ago, most people lived in small, traditional communities. All adults took part in group decisions. Some small communities still make decisions this way, but they are now part of larger units called nations. Nations are too large for everyone to take part in every decision. Still, nations have to protect people and resolve conflicts between individuals and social groups. In modern nations, these needs are met by **governments**, or organizations that set up and enforce laws.

You may remember that a region is an area united by a common feature. A **state** is a region that shares a government. You probably live in a state that is part of the United States. But the political units that we call "states" in the United States are just one kind of state. The entire United States can also be called a state. It is a region that shares a common government—the federal government.

**Dependencies and Nation-States** Some regions are **dependencies,** or regions that belong to another state. Others, like the United States, are **nation-states,** or states that are independent of other states. Each has a common body of laws. Nation-states are often simply called nations. Every place in the world where people live is part of a nation-state or dependency.

Most nation-states are large, but some are tiny. The smallest is Vatican City, which is surrounded by the city of Rome in Italy. Vatican City covers only about 109 acres (44 hectares)!

**How States Developed** The first real states formed in Southwest Asia more than 5,000 years ago when early cities set up governments. Small city-centered states are called **city-states.** Later, military leaders conquered large areas and ruled them as **empires,** or states containing several countries.

After about 1500, European rulers founded the first true nation-states. European nations established dependencies all over the world. When those dependencies became independent, they formed new nation-states.

✓ **Reading Check** **What is the difference between a government and a state?**

**Use Contrast Signal Words**

The first sentence in the paragraph at the left begins with the word *some*. The second sentence begins with *others*. These words signal that a contrast will be made. What contrast is being made?

**Vatican City**

St. Peter's Basilica, shown below, is the seat of the pope. He leads the Roman Catholic Church and rules Vatican City. **Infer** *What must be true about Vatican City for it to be a nation-state?*

**Kim Jong Il**
Kim Jong Il, the dictator of North Korea, making a rare public appearance.
**Analyze Images** *What group in North Korea might be a source of power for Kim Jong Il?*

# Types of Government

Each state has a government. There are many different kinds of government. Some governments are controlled by a single person or a small group of people. Others are controlled by all of the people.

**Direct Democracy** The earliest governments were simple. People lived in small groups. They practiced direct democracy, a form of government in which all adults take part in decisions. Many towns in New England today practice direct democracy. Decisions are made at town meetings where all adult residents can speak and vote.

**Tribal Rule** In time, communities banded together into larger tribal groups. Members of the tribe had a say in group decisions. But chiefs or elders usually made the final decision about what to do. Decisions were based upon the culture's customs and beliefs.

**Absolute Monarchy** Until about 200 years ago, one of the most common forms of government was absolute monarchy. In that system, a king or queen who inherits the throne by birth has complete control. Few absolute monarchies still exist today. Saudi Arabia is an example of a surviving absolute monarchy.

**Dictatorship** There are other countries today, however, where just one person rules. A leader who is not a king or queen but who has almost total power over an entire country is called a dictator. Dictatorship is rule by such a leader. Nations ruled by dictators include Cuba, Libya, and North Korea. Dictatorships differ from absolute monarchies because most dictators don't inherit power. Instead, they seize power. Dictators usually remain in power by using violence against their opponents. Dictators deny their people the right to make their own decisions.

**Oligarchy** Oligarchies are governments controlled by a small group of people. The group may be the leadership of a ruling political party. For example, China is an oligarchy controlled by the leadership of the Communist Party. There are other types of oligarchy. Myanmar, also called Burma, is run by a group of military officers. A group of religious leaders controls Iran. As in a dictatorship, ordinary people have little say in decisions.

**Constitutional Monarchy** Most monarchies today are constitutional monarchies, or governments in which the power of the king or queen is limited by law. The United Kingdom, the Netherlands, and Kuwait are examples. These nations have **constitutions,** or sets of laws that define and often limit the government's power. In a constitutional monarchy, the king or queen is often only a symbol of the country.

**Representative Democracy** Representative democracies are governments run by representatives that the people choose. Many constitutional monarchies are also representative democracies. In a representative democracy, the people indirectly hold power to govern and rule. They elect representatives who create laws. If the people do not like what a representative does, they can refuse to reelect that person. Citizens can also work to change laws they do not like. A constitution sets rules for elections, defines the rights of citizens, and limits the powers of the government. This system ensures that power is shared. The United States, Canada, and India are examples of representative democracies.

✓ Reading Check **What do absolute monarchies, dictatorships, and oligarchies have in common?**

**Queen Beatrix of the Netherlands heads a constitutional monarchy.**

**Representative Democracy**
Members of the United States House of Representatives, shown below, are elected by the people of their districts. **Contrast** *How does a representative democracy differ from a direct democracy?*

# International Organizations

Nations may make agreements to work together in an alliance. Members of an alliance are called allies. Alliances provide for nations to assist each other with defense. For example, members of the North Atlantic Treaty Organization (NATO) have agreed to defend any fellow member who is attacked.

Military bodies such as NATO are just one type of organization that is international, or involving more than one nation. Some international bodies are mainly economic in purpose. The European Union, for example, promotes economic unity among member nations in Europe.

The United Nations is an international organization meant to resolve disputes and promote peace. Almost all nations of the world belong to the United Nations. Every member has a vote in the General Assembly of the United Nations. But only the United Nations Security Council can make decisions over the use of force. The United States and four other permanent members have the power to prevent action in the Security Council.

The United Nations sponsors other international organizations with special purposes. For example, the Food and Agriculture Organization combats hunger worldwide. The United Nations Children's Fund (UNICEF) promotes the rights and well-being of children.

**The United Nations headquarters in New York, New York**

✓ Reading Check **What is the purpose of the United Nations?**

# Section 4 Assessment

## Key Terms
Review the key terms at the beginning of this section. Use each term in a sentence that explains its meaning.

## Target Reading Skill
Reread the first paragraph on page 82. Which two main types of government are contrasted? Look for contrast signal words.

## Comprehension and Critical Thinking
**1. (a) Identify** What were the earliest types of states?

**(b) Compare and Contrast** How did those early states differ from modern nation-states?

**2. (a) List** What are the main types of government?

**(b) Categorize** In which types of government do ordinary citizens take part in decisions?

**3. (a) Define** What is an alliance?

**(b) Compare and Contrast** What are the differences and similarities between alliances and other international organizations?

## Writing Activity
Which type of government described in this section appeals most to you? Write a paragraph explaining your preference, and why it appeals to you.

**Writing Tip** When you write a paragraph, state the main idea in a topic sentence. In this case, the topic sentence will tell the type of government that you prefer. Other sentences should support the main idea with arguments.

# Review and Assessment

## ◆ Chapter Summary

### Section 1: Population
- Where people live depends on factors such as climate, soil, and history.
- Population density measures the average number of people living in an area.
- Scientific progress has spurred population growth, which is straining Earth's resources.

### Section 2: Migration
- People migrate to seek a better life, or, in some cases, because they have no other choice.
- Cities are growing rapidly in some regions.

### Section 3: Economic Systems
- Economic systems may have private ownership of businesses, government ownership, or a mixture of both.
- Developed countries have more industry and technology than developing countries.
- Trade connects countries as buyers and sellers.

### Section 4: Political Systems
- The world is divided into nation-states.
- States have governments that differ in the amount of power that citizens have.
- Nation-states may join together in alliances and international organizations.

**Harvesting rice in China**

## ◆ Key Terms

Each of the statements below contains a key term from the chapter. If the statement is true, write *true*. If it is false, rewrite the statement to make it true.

1. A country's **population** is the number of people who live there.

2. **Population density** measures the size of cities.

3. The movement of people from one region to another is **migration.**

4. **Urbanization** is the movement of people to cities.

5. An **economy** is a system of government.

6. **Consumers** are people who sell products.

7. **Developing nations** have few industries and simple technologies.

8. A **government** is a body that makes and enforces laws and resolves conflicts among its people.

9. A **state** is a system of government.

## ◆ Comprehension and Critical Thinking

**10. (a) Define** What is population distribution?
**(b) Explain** What factors affect population distribution in a region?
**(c) Compare and Contrast** How are those factors different today than they were when most people were farmers?

**11. (a) Identify** How has the size of world populations changed in recent years?
**(b) Identify Cause and Effect** What difficulties have resulted from the change in the size of world populations?

**12. (a) Define** What is voluntary migration?
**(b) Make Generalizations** Why do people choose to migrate?

**13. (a) Define** What is capitalism?
**(b) Contrast** How does capitalism differ from communism?

**14. (a) List** What are some challenges faced by developing countries?
**(b) Infer** Why do developing countries face these challenges?

**15. (a) Identify** What are two types of democracy?
**(b) Contrast** How do democracies differ from other forms of government?

## ◆ Skills Practice

**Using Population Density Maps** In the Skills for Life activity in this chapter, you learned how to read a population density map using the map key.

Review the steps you followed to learn this skill. Then review the map on pages 62 and 63, titled The World: Population Density. Using the map key, describe what each color on the map represents and then list the most sparsely populated areas shown. Finally, draw conclusions about why these areas have such small populations.

## ◆ Writing Activity: Math

Suppose you are a demographer projecting population growth for three countries. Use the following information to create a population bar graph for each country:

|  | Birthrate | Death Rate |
|---|---|---|
| **Country A** | 14.2 | 8.7 |
| **Country B** | 9.8 | 9.7 |
| **Country C** | 9.4 | 13.9 |

Then, write a brief paragraph explaining your graph. For each country, is the population increasing, decreasing, or stable? Explain why.

## MAP MASTER™
### Skills Activity

**Place Location** For each place listed below, write the letter from the map that shows its location.

1. Asia
2. Antarctica
3. Africa
4. South America
5. North America
6. Europe
7. Australia

**Go Online**
**PHSchool.com** Use Web Code **lep-3215** for an **interactive map.**

**Continents**

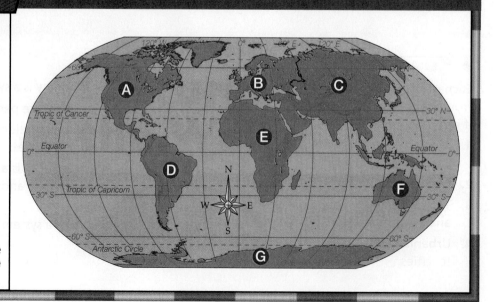

# Standardized Test Prep

## Test-Taking Tips

Some questions on standardized tests ask you to analyze a reading selection for a main idea. Read the passage in the box below. Then follow the tips to answer the sample question.

> This region has one of the highest population densities in the world. As many as 5,000 people per square mile live in parts of the region. There are good reasons for this heavy population density. The land is fertile. Though the desert is not far away, the river contains plenty of water for the people who live there.

**TIP** As you read each sentence, think about what main idea it supports.

**Pick the letter that best answers the question.**

Which sentence states this passage's main idea?

- A ~~Demographers study human populations.~~
- B Egypt's Nile River valley supports a large population.
- C ~~People find ways to adapt to their environment.~~
- D Many people live near the Mississippi River.

**TIP** Cross out answer choices that don't make sense. Then pick from the remaining choices the one that BEST answers the question.

**Think It Through** The passage does not mention demographers. So you can cross out answer A. You can also rule out C, because the passage does not discuss people adapting to their environment. Answers B and D both mention specific regions. Which region does the paragraph describe? The paragraph mentions a desert. There is no desert near the Mississippi River. So the answer is B.

## Practice Questions

Use the tips above and other tips in this book to help you answer the following questions.

1. The number of people per square mile is a region's
   - A population distribution.
   - B population.
   - C elevation.
   - D population density.

2. People moving to a different region to seek better farming opportunities is an example of
   - A trade.
   - B voluntary migration.
   - C involuntary migration.
   - D urbanization.

3. In which of the following does the government own most workplaces?
   - A capitalism
   - B developing country
   - C communism
   - D developed country

**Read the following passage, and answer the question that follows.**

A constitutional monarch has little power. Under some constitutions, elected representatives have the law-making power instead of the monarch. In such cases, the government works much like other representative democracies.

4. What is the main idea of this passage?
   - A An absolute monarch has great power.
   - B Constitutions are always democratic.
   - C A constitutional monarchy may also be a representative democracy.
   - D A constitutional monarch cannot interfere with representative democracy.

Go Online PHSchool.com
Use Web Code **lea-3301** for a **Chapter 3 self-test.**

# My Side of the Mountain
## By Jean Craighead George

## Prepare to Read

### Background Information

Have you ever camped out overnight? Have you ever built a fire in order to keep warm? Suppose you had no electricity or your home had no heating system. How would you cope with the natural world without modern technology? Do you think that living closer to the natural world would change you in any significant way?

Sam Gribley is the fictional hero of the novel *My Side of the Mountain*. When he decided to live close to nature, he built a tree house in the Catskill Mountains of New York and then moved in with his only companion, Frightful, a falcon. This excerpt describes their first winter in the mountains.

### Objectives

As you read this selection, you will

• Identify the skills Sam needed to survive alone in the wilderness.

• Discover how Sam came to understand the natural world.

I lived close to the weather. It is surprising how you watch it when you live in it. Not a cloud passed unnoticed, not a wind blew untested. I knew the moods of the storms, where they came from, their shapes and colors. When the sun shone, I took Frightful to the meadow and we slid down the mountain on my snapping-turtle-shell sled. She really didn't care much for this.

When the winds changed and the air smelled like snow, I would stay in my tree, because I had gotten lost in a blizzard one afternoon and had to hole up in a rock ledge until I could see where I was going. That day the winds were so strong I could not push against them, so I crawled under the ledge; for hours I wondered if I would be able to dig out when the storm blew on. Fortunately I only had to push through a foot of snow. However, that taught me to stay home when the air said "snow." Not that I

**Fog-shrouded woodland in the Catskill Mountains, New York**

was afraid of being caught far from home in a storm, for I could find food and shelter and make a fire anywhere, but I had become as attached to my <u>hemlock</u> house as a brooding bird to her nest. Caught out in the storms and weather, I had an urgent desire to return to my tree, even as The Baron Weasel returned to his den, and the deer to their <u>copse</u>. We all had our little "patch" in the wilderness. We all fought to return there.

I usually came home at night with the nuthatch that roosted in a nearby sapling. I knew I was late if I tapped the tree and he came out. Sometimes when the weather was icy and miserable, I would hear him high in the trees near the edge of the meadow, <u>yanking</u> and yanking and flicking his tail, and then I would see him wing to bed early. I considered him a pretty good <u>barometer</u>, and if he went to his tree early, I went to mine early too. When you don't have a newspaper or radio to give you weather bulletins, watch the birds and animals. They can tell when a storm is coming. I called the nuthatch "Barometer," and when he holed up, I holed up, lit my light, and sat by my fire <u>whittling</u> or learning new tunes on my reed whistle. I was now really into the <u>teeth of winter</u>, and quite fascinated by its activity. There is no such thing as a "still winter night." Not only are many animals running around in the breaking cold, but the trees cry out and limbs snap and fall, and the wind gets caught in a ravine and screams until it dies.

✔ **Reading Check** **What did Sam name the nuthatch? Explain why.**

**hemlock** (HEM lahk) *n.* an evergreen tree with drooping branches and short needles
**copse** (kahps) *n.* a thicket of small trees or shrubs
**yank** (yangk) *v.* to give the call made by a nuthatch
**barometer** (buh RAHM uh tur) *n.* an instrument for forecasting changes in the weather; anything that indicates a change
**whittle** (WHIT ul) *v.* to cut or pare thin shavings from wood with a knife
**teeth of winter** (teeth uv WIN tur) *n.* the coldest, harshest time of winter

## About the Selection

*My Side of the Mountain,* by Jean Craighead George (New York: E. P. Dutton, 1959), includes sketches of Sam Gribley's adventures.

# Review and Assessment

## Comprehension and Critical Thinking

**1. (a) Identify** When the weather is bad, what is Sam's "urgent desire"?
**(b) Compare** To what does Sam compare this desire?
**(c) Interpret** What does Sam tell us about himself when he makes a comparison?
**2. (a) Recall** What are some of the clues Sam has about what the weather will be like?
**(b) Describe** What parts of the natural world does Sam seem to notice most?
**(c) Evaluate** Sometimes Sam talks about the wind and trees as if they were alive. Think about your relationship with nature. How is it like Sam's? How is it different?

## Writing Activity

Make a list of sounds you hear only in winter. What are the tastes and smells that make you think of winter? List them. What are the sights of winter? Add them to your list. Then write an essay describing the place you most like to be in winter and explain why.

## About the Author

**Jean Craighead George** (b. 1919) often went camping, climbed trees, and studied living things as she grew up. Ms. George has been writing about nature and its lessons since she was eight years old, and has written more than 80 books for young readers.

*Literature* **89**

# Cultures of the World

## Chapter Preview

This chapter will introduce you to the concept of culture, the things that make up culture, and the ways in which cultures change.

**Section 1**
Understanding Culture

**Section 2**
Culture and Society

**Section 3**
Cultural Change

### Target Reading Skill

**Sequence** In this chapter, you will focus on the text structure by identifying the order, or sequence, of events. Noting the sequence of events can help you understand and remember the events.

▶ Young women in traditional dress at a festival in Pushkar, India

# Understanding Culture

## Prepare to Read

### Objectives

In this section you will
1. Learn about culture.
2. Explore how culture has developed.

### Taking Notes

Copy the concept web below. As you read this section, fill in the web with information about culture, its relation to the environment, and how it has developed. Add ovals as needed for concepts in the section.

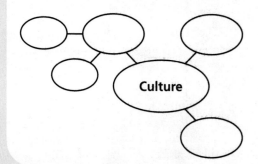

### Target Reading Skill

**Understand Sequence**
A sequence is the order in which a series of events occurs. Noting the sequence of important events can help you understand and remember the events. You can show the order of events by making a sequence chart. Write the first event, or thing that sets the other events in motion, in the first box. Then write each additional event in a box. Use arrows to show how one event leads to the next.

### Key Terms

- **culture** (KUL chur) *n.* the way of life of a people, including their beliefs and practices
- **cultural landscape** (KUL chur ul LAND skayp) *n.* the parts of a people's environment that they have shaped and the technology they have used to shape it
- **civilization** (sih vuh luh ZAY shun) *n.* an advanced culture with cities and a system of writing
- **institution** (in stuh TOO shun) *n.* a custom or organization with social, educational, or religious purposes

**A grandfather in Japan teaching his grandson to use chopsticks**

## What Is Culture?

**Culture** is the way of life of a people, including their beliefs, customs, and practices. The language people speak and the way they dress are both parts of their culture. So are the work people do, what they do after work or school, and the ideas that influence them.

**Elements of Culture** Parents pass culture on to their children, generation after generation. Ideas and ways of doing things are called cultural traits. Over time, cultural traits may change.

Some elements of a culture are easy to see. They include material things, such as houses, television sets, food, and clothing. Sports and literature are visible elements of culture as well. Things you cannot see or touch are also part of culture. They include spiritual beliefs, government, and ideas about right and wrong. Finally, language is a very important part of culture.

**People and Their Land** Geographers study themes of culture, especially human activities related to the environment. The theme of human-environment interaction deals with these activities. Geographers want to know how the environment affects culture. For example, Japan is a nation of mountainous islands, with limited farmland. So the Japanese have turned to the sea. Fish and seaweed are popular foods in Japan.

However, environment does not dictate culture. Like Japan, Greece is a nation of mountainous islands and peninsulas surrounded by the sea. The Greeks eat some fish, but they have cleared mountainsides as well for use as pasture. Goats and sheep graze on the mountainsides and provide food for the Greeks.

Geographers are also interested in the effect people have on their environment. Often the effect is tied to a culture's technology, even if that technology is simple. For example, the Greeks have cleared their rugged land for pasture. The Japanese harvest seaweed.

A **cultural landscape** is the parts of a people's environment that they have shaped and the technology they have used to shape it. This varies from place to place. On hilly Bali (BAH lee), in Indonesia, farmers have carved terraces into hillsides. On the plains of northern India, farmers have laid out broad, flat fields.

✓ **Reading Check** **How are culture and environment related?**

Learn more about culture.

**Balinese Terraces**
A farmer on the island of Bali, in Indonesia, crosses terraced rice fields.
**Analyze** *How has Bali's environment affected its culture? How has Bali's culture affected its environment?*

# The Development of Culture

Scientists think that early cultures had four major advances in technology. First was the invention of tools millions of years ago. Second and third were the control of fire and the beginnings of agriculture. Fourth was the development of **civilizations,** or advanced cultures with cities and the use of writing.

**Technology and Civilization** For most of human existence, people were hunters and gatherers. While traveling from place to place, they collected wild plants, hunted game, and fished.

Later, people discovered how to grow crops. They tamed wild animals to help them with work or to raise for food. Over time, more and more people relied on farming for most of their food. Historians call this great change the Agricultural Revolution.

Agriculture provided a steady food supply. Agriculture let farmers grow more food than they needed. In parts of Asia and Africa, some people worked full time on crafts such as metalworking. They traded their products for food. People began to develop laws and government. To store information, they developed writing. These advances in culture produced the first true civilizations about 5,000 years ago.

Early civilizations developed new technologies, such as irrigation, that let people grow more crops. Over time, farming and civilization spread throughout the world.

## The Development of Agricultural Technology

**Sickle**
The first farmers used hand-held sickles to harvest grain. The first sickles had stone blades. Later sickles, like the one shown here, had metal blades.

**Horse-drawn reaper**
By the late 1800s, farmers were using animal-powered machinery, such as this sail reaper, to harvest grain.

**Tools for Harvesting** When the Agricultural Revolution began, people used simple hand-powered tools. The Industrial Revolution later brought industrial tools to the fields. **Draw Conclusions** *How do you think the development of tools for harvesting affected the amount that each farmer could harvest?*

**Combine harvester**
Today, farmers harvest grain with large-scale, motorized machinery, such as this combine.

Then, about 200 years ago, people began to invent new technologies that used power-driven machinery. This change marked the beginning of the Industrial Revolution. It led to the growth of cities, science, and even more advanced technologies, such as computers and space flight.

**Understand Sequence** What important events led to the Industrial Revolution?

**Development of Institutions** Before the Agricultural Revolution, people had simple **institutions,** customs and organizations with social, educational, or religious purposes. These included extended families and simple political institutions, such as councils of elders.

As people gathered in larger groups and formed cities, they needed more complex institutions. People developed organized religions, with priests, ceremonies, and temples. Armies and governments appeared with states. Teachers started schools.

In the modern world, we have many different kinds of institutions, including museums, sports clubs, corporations, political parties, and universities. These institutions are important parts of our culture.

Oxford University, in Oxford, England, is more than 800 years old.

✓ **Reading Check** What allowed civilizations to develop?

---

## Section 1 Assessment

### Key Terms
Review the key terms at the beginning of this section. Use each term in a sentence that explains its meaning.

### Target Reading Skill
Place the following events in the order in which they occurred: the development of civilization; the invention of tools; the development of industry; and the beginnings of agriculture.

### Comprehension and Critical Thinking
1. (a) **Define** What is a cultural landscape?
(b) **Explain** What are the most important cultural traits that shape a people's cultural landscape?
(c) **Identify Cause and Effect** If two cultures occupy similar environments, why might their cultural landscapes still differ?
2. (a) **Identify** What was the Agricultural Revolution?
(b) **Sequence** What cultural advances followed the Agricultural Revolution?

### Writing Activity
Think of all the ways that the culture of your region has shaped its landscape. Write a short paragraph describing your cultural landscape and the cultural traits that shaped it.

**Go Online** PHSchool.com

**For:** An activity on culture
**Visit:** PHSchool.com
**Web Code:** led-3401

# Culture and Society

## Prepare to Read

### Objectives

In this section you will
1. Learn how people are organized into groups.
2. Investigate language.
3. Explore the role of religion.

### Taking Notes

Copy the outline below. As you read this section, fill in the outline with information about how society is organized, about language, and about religion. Add letters and numbers as needed.

```
I. How society is organized
   A. Social classes
   B.
      1.
      2.
II. Language
    A.
```

### Target Reading Skill

**Understand Sequence**
Noting the sequence of important changes can help you understand and remember the changes. You can show a sequence of changes by simply listing the changes in the order in which they occurred. As you read this section, list the sequence of the changes in people's ability to improve their status.

### Key Terms

- **society** (suh SY uh tee) *n.* a group of people sharing a culture
- **social structure** (SOH shul STRUK chur) *n.* a pattern of organized relationships among groups of people within a society
- **social class** (SOH shul klas) *n.* a grouping of people based on rank or status
- **nuclear family** (NOO klee ur FAM uh lee) *n.* a mother, a father, and their children
- **extended family** (ek STEN did FAM uh lee) *n.* a family that includes several generations

**A nuclear family in the United Kingdom**

## How Society Is Organized

Think about the people you see every day. Do you spend each day meeting random strangers? Or do you see the same family members, classmates, and teachers every day? Chances are, there is a pattern to your interactions.

A group of people sharing a culture is known as a **society.** Every society has a **social structure,** or a pattern of organized relationships among groups of people within the society. A society may be as small as a single community or as large as a nation or even a group of similar nations. Smaller groups within a society work together on particular tasks. Some groups work together to get food. Others protect the community. Still others educate children. Social structure helps people work together to meet one another's basic needs.

The family is the basic, most important social unit of any society. Families teach the customs and traditions of the culture to their children. Through their families, children learn how to dress, to be polite, to eat, and to play.

**Social Classes** Cultures also have another kind of social organization—**social classes,** or groupings of people based on rank or status. A person's status or position may come from his or her wealth, land, ancestors, or education. In some cultures in the past, it was often hard—or impossible—for people to move from one social class to another. Today, people in many societies can improve their status. They can obtain a good education, make more money, or marry someone of a higher class.

**Kinds of Families** Not all cultures define family in the same way. In some cultures, the basic unit is a **nuclear family,** or a mother, a father, and their children. This pattern is common in developed nations such as the United States, Australia, and Germany. The nuclear family gets its name from the word *nucleus*, which means "center."

Other cultures have **extended families,** or families that include several generations. In addition to a central nuclear family of parents and their sons or daughters, there are the wives or husbands of those sons or daughters. The family also includes grandchildren, or the children of those sons or daughters. In extended families, older people often help care for the children. They are respected for their knowledge and experience. Older family members pass on traditions. Extended families are less common than they used to be. As rural people move to cities, nuclear families are becoming more common.

✓ Reading Check  **What is the basic social unit of societies?**

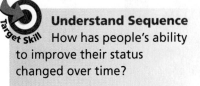

**Understand Sequence** How has people's ability to improve their status changed over time?

**A Salvadoran-American Family**
This family includes grandparents and more than one set of parents. **Infer** *Is this a nuclear family or an extended family?*

**A teacher using sign language with hearing-impaired students**

# Language

All cultures have language. In fact, language provides a basis for culture. People learn their cultures mainly through language. Most communication with others depends on language. Think how hard it would be if you had no way to say, "Meet me by the gate after school." How could you learn if you could not ask questions?

A culture's language reflects the things that are important in that culture. For example, English has words for Christian and Jewish concepts, such as *baptism* and *sabbath.* Some languages lack words for these concepts because their speakers are not Jewish or Christian. But those languages have words for concepts in their people's religions that have no English translation.

## The World: Major Language Groups

This map shows the locations of the world's major language groups. Languages in each of these groups share a common ancestor, a language spoken long ago that gradually changed to become several related languages. For example, English and German are both Indo-European languages that share a common ancestor. Can you recognize the German words *Land, Mann,* and *Wagen?*

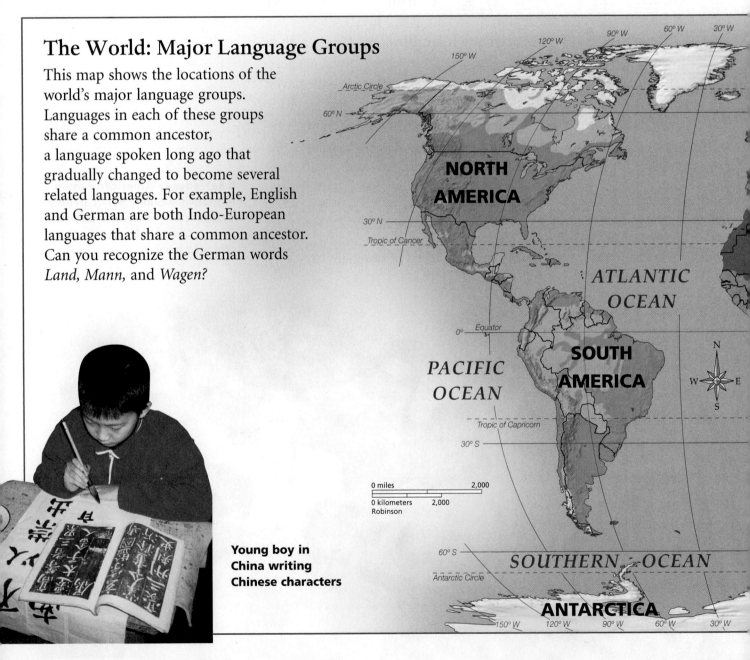

**Young boy in China writing Chinese characters**

In some countries, people speak more than one language. For example, Canada has two official languages, French and English. In the United States, you may usually hear English, but you can also hear Spanish, Chinese, Haitian Creole, and many other languages. India has 16 official languages, but people there speak more than 800 languages!

People who speak each language are culturally different in some ways from other people in their country who speak other languages. They may celebrate different festivals or have different customs for such things as dating or education. That is because each language preserves shared ideas and traditions.

✔ **Reading Check** **What is the relation between language and culture?**

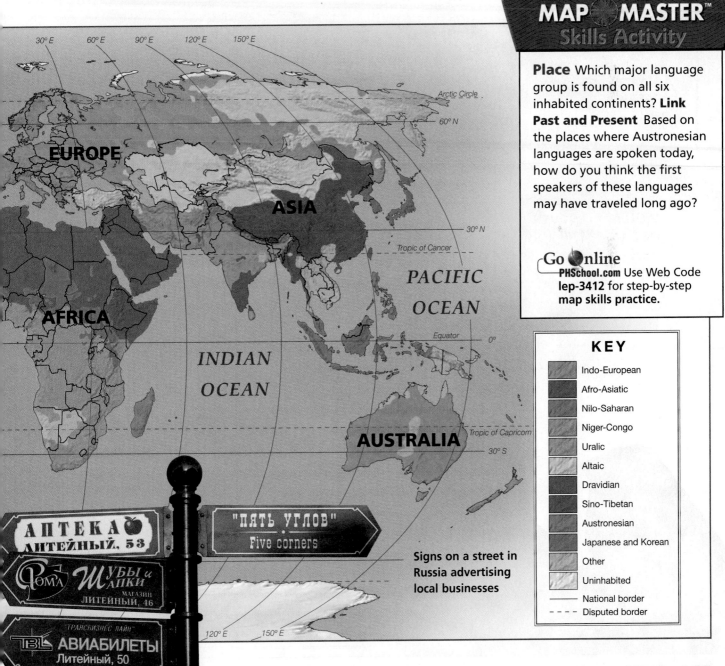

## MAP MASTER™
### Skills Activity

**Place** Which major language group is found on all six inhabited continents? **Link Past and Present** Based on the places where Austronesian languages are spoken today, how do you think the first speakers of these languages may have traveled long ago?

Go Online
PHSchool.com Use Web Code lep-3412 for step-by-step map skills practice.

**Signs on a street in Russia advertising local businesses**

### KEY

- Indo-European
- Afro-Asiatic
- Nilo-Saharan
- Niger-Congo
- Uralic
- Altaic
- Dravidian
- Sino-Tibetan
- Austronesian
- Japanese and Korean
- Other
- Uninhabited
- National border
- - - - Disputed border

# The World: Major Religions

The major religions of the world all began in Asia. India was the birthplace of Sikhism, Hinduism, and Buddhism, all of which later spread to other countries. The other great world religions had their start in Southwest Asia: first Judaism, then Christianity, and finally Islam. These religions also later spread to other parts of the world.

**Young Buddhist monks in Thailand**

## MAP MASTER™
### Skills Activity

**Place** Which of the continents has the greatest variety of religions?
**Draw Inferences** Why do you think this is so?

**Go Online**
**PHSchool.com** Use Web Code **lep-3422** for step-by-step map skills practice.

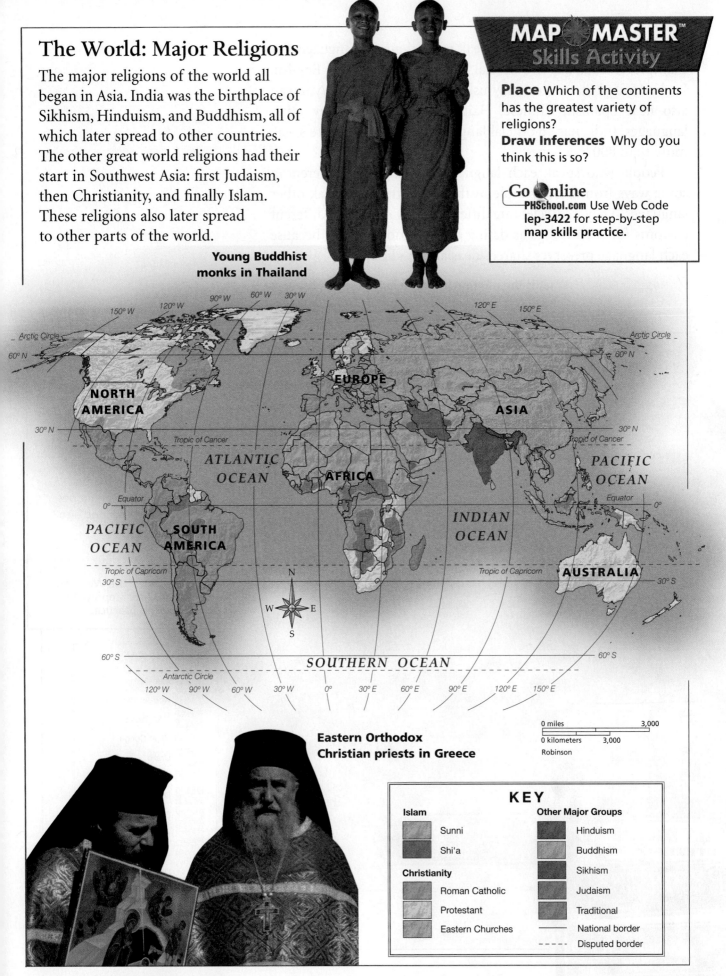

**Eastern Orthodox Christian priests in Greece**

0 miles 3,000
0 kilometers 3,000
Robinson

### KEY

**Islam**
- Sunni
- Shi'a

**Christianity**
- Roman Catholic
- Protestant
- Eastern Churches

**Other Major Groups**
- Hinduism
- Buddhism
- Sikhism
- Judaism
- Traditional
- —— National border
- – – – Disputed border

**100** Foundations of Geography

# Religion

Religion is an important part of every culture. For example, most of the people of Saudi Arabia are Muslim. In some countries, such as the United States, people follow more than one religion. Beliefs and practices may differ among religions. However, religion remains important to many people.

Religion can help people make sense of the world. Religion can provide comfort and hope for people facing difficult times. And religion can help answer questions about the meaning and purpose of life. Religion also guides people in ethics, or standards of accepted behavior.

Religious beliefs vary. Members of some religions, such as Islam, Judaism, and Christianity, believe in one God. Members of other religions, such as Hinduism and traditional religions, believe in more than one god. But all religions have prayers and rituals. Every religion celebrates important places and times. And all religions expect people to treat one another well and to behave properly.

✓ **Reading Check** **Why is religion important to people?**

This temple, in Amritsar, India, is a holy place of Sikhism.

---

## Section 2 Assessment

### Key Terms
Review the key terms at the beginning of this section. Use each term in a sentence that explains its meaning.

### Target Reading Skill
Place the following events in young people's lives in the correct sequence: learning their culture's language and learning their culture's beliefs.

### Comprehension and Critical Thinking
**1. (a) Identify** What is the role of social structure in society?
**(b) Explain** What is the place of families in a social structure?
**(c) Predict** Would you expect the members of one family to fall within one social class or more than one?
**2. (a) Recall** How is language related to culture?
**(b) Identify Cause and Effect** Why do you think people who speak different languages tend to have different cultures?
**3. (a) Identify** What values do all religions share?
**(b) Draw Conclusions** How might those values help people of different religions overcome conflicts?

### Writing Activity
In a journal entry, explore the ways in which family and language connect you to other people in your society.

> **Writing Tip** When you write a journal entry, write about experiences from your own life. You may also express your own opinions and perspectives. For this exercise, think about which of your activities and interests involve family or the use of language.

# Making Valid Generalizations

**A** generalization is a broad conclusion. Some generalizations are valid—that is, they have value or worth—because they can be drawn reasonably from specific facts. Other generalizations are not valid, because they draw unreasonably broad conclusions and are not based on fact.

Many statements have clues that tell you they should be evaluated for validity. For example, statements with words such as *everybody* or *everyone* are very broad. They should always be evaluated. Is the statement "Everybody needs salt" a valid generalization? It is, because it is based on the scientifically proven fact that humans cannot survive without salt in our diet. However, generalizations such as "Everybody loves chocolate" are not valid. They draw unreasonably broad conclusions and cannot be proved.

You need to know how to evaluate a generalization to see if it is valid. You also have to know how to make a valid generalization yourself.

## Testing for Validity

To find whether a generalization is valid, ask

• Are there enough facts—at least three in a short passage—to support the generalization?

• Do I know any other facts that support the generalization?

• Does the statement overgeneralize or stereotype a group of people? Words such as *all*, *always*, or *every* signal overgeneralization. Words such as *some*, *many*, *most*, and *often* help prevent a statement from being overgeneralized.

## Learn the Skill

To make a valid generalization, follow these steps:

**1** **Identify specific facts contained within a source of information.** Make sure you understand the topic that the facts support.

**2** **State what the facts have in common, and look for patterns.** Do any of the facts fit together in a way that makes a point about a broad subject? Do data in a table or graph point toward a general statement?

**3** **Make a generalization, or broad conclusion, about the facts.** Write your generalization as a complete sentence or a paragraph.

**4** **Test the generalization and revise it if necessary.** You can test the validity of a generalization by using the guidelines in the box at the left.

## Practice the Skill

Read the passage at the right describing three cultures, and then make a generalization about these cultures.

 What is the topic of the text? List at least three specific facts that relate to that topic.

 What do the facts you listed have in common? Do they suggest a general idea about the topic?

 Make a generalization about the topic. Write it in a complete sentence. List three facts that support it.

④ Test your generalization to see if it is valid. If it is not valid, try rewriting it so that it is more limited. Be careful of exaggerated wording.

## Apply the Skill

Turn to page 97 and read the paragraph under the heading Kinds of Families. Make as many generalizations as you can, and test them for their validity. Explain why each generalization is or is not valid.

The Maya thrived in present-day Mexico and Central America from about A.D. 300 to 900. Corn was their principal crop. They developed a sophisticated civilization, but they had abandoned their great cities by about A.D. 900. At about that time, the Hohokam people were growing corn and beans in what is now Arizona. The Hohokam left their settlements during the 1400s, possibly because of drought. Meanwhile, between about A.D. 900 and 1300, the Anasazi people lived to the northeast. They also grew corn. The Anasazi built multistory dwellings up against high cliff walls. Many families lived in these homes. During a drought in the late 1200s, the Anasazi abandoned some of their villages.

**An extended Islamic family, spanning three generations, from the rural east coast of Malaysia**

# Cultural Change

## Prepare to Read

### Objectives
In this section you will
1. Explore how cultures change.
2. Learn how ideas spread from one culture to another.

### Taking Notes
Copy the concept web below. As you read this section, fill in the web with information about cultural change. Add ovals as needed for the concepts in the section.

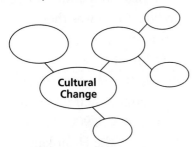

Cultural Change

### Target Reading Skill
**Recognize Words That Signal Sequence**
Signal words point out relationships among ideas or events. To help keep the order of events clear, look for words such as *first, later,* or *at that time* that signal the order in which the events took place.

### Key Terms
- **cultural diffusion** (KUL chur ul dih FYOO zhun) *n.* the movement of customs and ideas
- **acculturation** (uh kul chur AY shun) *n.* the process of accepting new ideas and fitting them into a culture

**Blue jeans and denim shirts have changed with the times.**

## How Cultures Change

All cultures change over time. The history of blue jeans is an example of cultural change. Some people think that blue jeans are typical American clothes. But many cultures contributed to them. Blue jeans were invented in the United States in the 1800s. They were marketed by Levi Strauss. Strauss was a German-born merchant who moved to California. He made the jeans with a cloth called denim. This may be a shortened form of *serge de Nîmes,* the name of a similar cloth from France.

At first, only Americans wore blue jeans, but they later became popular in other countries. In the 1980s, the Japanese and the French developed stonewashing. It made brand-new denim jeans look worn. Since then, designers from Asia, Europe, and America have promoted new styles, such as ripped and "dirty" denim. Today, jeans are popular all over the world. And the word *jeans* comes from an old French name for Genoa, an Italian city where a cloth similar to denim was first made. What could be more American than jeans?

**Why Cultures Change** Just as jeans have changed over time, so, too, has American culture. Cultures change all the time. Because culture is an entire way of life, a change in one part changes other parts. Changes in the natural environment, technology, and ideas all affect culture.

**New Technologies** New technologies also change a culture. During the 1800s and early 1900s, the growth of industry and the spread of factories drew large numbers of Americans from the countryside to the nation's cities. Factories offered jobs to thousands of men, women, and children. Limited transportation meant that people had to live close to the factories. Cities grew larger as a result.

This all changed after the invention of the car in the late 1800s. Within a few years, advances in technology made cars more affordable. By 1920, many Americans had cars. People could live farther from their jobs and drive to work. Soon after, the idea of owning a house with a yard became more popular. The result has been the growth of sprawling suburbs since the mid-1900s and a new culture based on car travel.

**A teenager using a cell phone**

**A "bullet train" in Japan**
Japanese engineers have developed new technologies that allow these trains to travel at speeds of more than 180 miles (300 kilometers) per hour. **Infer** *How might such high speeds affect how far away people can live from their work?*

**How One Change Can Lead to Others** Think of other ways technology has changed the culture of the United States. Radio and television brought entertainment and news into homes. Today instant information is part of our culture. Computers change how and where people work. Computers even help people live longer since doctors use computers to diagnose and treat patients. Radio, television, and computers add new words to our language, such as *broadcast, channel surfing,* and *hacker.* What other new words can you think of?

**Cultural Change Over Time** Cultural change has been going on for a long time. Controlling fire helped early people survive in colder climates. When people started raising animals and growing crops, ways of life also changed. People began to work in the same fields year after year. Before that, they had roamed over a wider area looking for wild plant and animal foods.

**Target Skill** **Recognize Words That Signal Sequence** What do the words *before that,* in the paragraph at the right, tell you about the sequence of events? Which happened first — the events after those words or the events in the preceding sentence?

✓ **Reading Check** **How did the invention of cars change culture?**

# How Ideas Spread

Advances in transportation technology, such as the airplane, make it easier for people to move all over the world. When they move, people bring new kinds of clothing and tools with them. They also bring ideas about such things as ways to prepare food, teach children, practice their religion, or govern themselves.

Ideas can travel to new places in other ways. People may obtain goods from another culture by trade and then learn to make those goods themselves. People may also learn from other cultures through written material. The movement of customs and ideas is called **cultural diffusion.**

**How Cultures Adopt New Ideas** One example of cultural diffusion is the game of baseball. Baseball began as an American sport, but today it is played in countries all around the world. That is an example of cultural diffusion. The Japanese love baseball. However, they have changed the game to fit their culture. These changes are an example of **acculturation,** or the process of accepting new ideas and fitting them into a culture. Americans value competition. They focus on winning. A game of baseball does not end until one team wins. But in Japan, a game can end in a tie. The Japanese do not mind a tie game. In Japan, how well you play is more important than winning.

**A woman practicing yoga, a form of meditation that spread from Asia to Europe and North America**

## Communication Technology and the Speed of Change

What's the fastest way to get from your house to Japan? Would you use a jet plane? A phone call? The Internet? A fax? All these answers can be correct. The answer depends on whether you want to transport your body, your voice, a picture, or just words on a sheet of paper.

For thousands of years, cultures changed slowly. People and goods moved by foot or wagon or sailing ship, so ideas and technology also moved slowly. Recently, communication technology has increased the speed of change. Faxes and computers transport information almost instantly. Magazines and television shows can bring ideas and information from all over the world to any home. This rapid exchange of ideas speeds up cultural change.

Technology has brought many benefits. Computers let scientists share information about how to cure diseases. Telephones let us instantly talk to relatives thousands of miles away. In the Australian Outback, students your age use closed-circuit television and two-way radios to take part in class from their own homes.

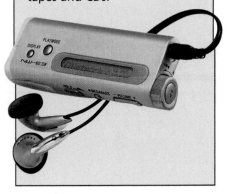

**World Internet Users, 1996–2005**

(Graph: y-axis "Internet Users (millions)" ranging 0 to 1100; x-axis "Year" 1996 to 2005. The line rises from about 25 million in 1996 to about 1030 million in 2005.)

### Graph Skills

Internet use grew rapidly after 1996. **Identify** What was the number of Internet users in 2005?

**Predict** Based on the trend shown in the graph, how do you think the number of Internet users has changed since 2005?

**Defending Their Heritage**
In 1988 Aborigines, descendants of Australia's original inhabitants, protested the 200th anniversary of the arrival of Europeans.
**Analyze Images** *What evidence do you see that the Aborigines' culture has changed over the past 200 years?*

**Defending Traditions** Change can help, but it can also hurt. If things change too fast, people may feel that their culture is threatened. Valuable traditions can disappear. Once traditional knowledge has been lost, it can never be regained. In many parts of the world, people are working to preserve, or save, their own cultures before it is too late. They do not want to lose what is valuable in their culture. They want to save the artistic traditions, the religious beliefs, and the wisdom that enriched the lives of past generations for the sake of future generations.

✓ **Reading Check** How has technology affected the speed of cultural change?

# Section 3 Assessment

## Key Terms
Review the key terms at the beginning of this section. Use each term in a sentence that explains its meaning.

## Target Reading Skill
Review the second paragraph on page 107. Find the words that signal a sequence of events related to communication technologies.

## Comprehension and Critical Thinking
**1. (a) Describe** What cultural changes in America followed the invention of cars?

**(b) Explain** How did cars change where people lived and worked?
**(c) Predict** Suppose that gasoline became more expensive and computers allowed more people to work at home. How might American culture change?
**2. (a) List** What are two main ways in which ideas travel from one culture to another?
**(b) Describe** Give an example of an idea that has passed from one culture to another.
**(c) Compare and Contrast** How has the spread of ideas changed with modern communication technologies?

## Writing Activity
What parts of your own culture come from other countries? Make a list detailing the foods, fashions, music, or customs that are part of your life and that come from other countries.

**For:** An activity on cultural change
**Visit:** PHSchool.com
**Web Code:** led-3403

# Review and Assessment

## ◆ Chapter Summary

### Section 1: Understanding Culture

- Culture is an entire way of life that is shaped by people's environment and that also shapes people's environment.
- Culture developed over time from simple technologies and institutions to more advanced technologies and institutions.

### Section 2: Culture and Society

- A society is a group of people sharing a culture and held together by a social structure.
- Language expresses the basic concepts of a culture and transmits those concepts to young people.
- Religions help people make sense of the world. They are an important source of values for cultures and teach people to treat one another fairly.

### Section 3: Cultural Change

- Changes in the environment or in technology lead to changes in culture.
- Ideas move among cultures through the movement of people, through trade, and through communication technologies.

**Traditional dress in India**

## ◆ Key Terms

Each of the statements below contains a key term from the chapter. If the statement is true, write *true*. If it is false, rewrite the statement to make it true.

1. The **culture** of a people is their way of life, including their beliefs and customs.

2. A **civilization** is an organization with social, educational, or religious purposes.

3. An **institution** is an advanced culture with cities and the use of writing.

4. A **society** is a group of people sharing a culture.

5. A pattern of organized relationships among groups of people is a **social structure**.

6. An **extended family** consists of two parents and their children.

7. A **nuclear family** includes two grandparents, their children, and their grandchildren.

8. **Cultural diffusion** is the movement of customs or ideas from one culture to another.

9. **Acculturation** is an accumulation of several cultures in a single place.

## ◆ Comprehension and Critical Thinking

**10. (a) Describe** What elements make up a culture?
**(b) Apply Information** Which of these elements might influence a people's environment, and how?

**11. (a) Describe** What was the Agricultural Revolution?
**(b) Explain** How did it affect population?
**(c) Draw Conclusions** How did it allow the growth of cities?

**12. (a) Describe** How does social class affect a person's status in society?
**(b) Link Past and Present** How has people's ability to improve their status changed?

**13. (a) Recall** Which major religions started in Asia?
**(b) Infer** What might explain their spread?

**14. (a) Describe** How did the development of industry and factories change culture?
**(b) Compare and Contrast** How do those changes compare with the ways technology has changed culture in your lifetime?

**15. (a) List** What technologies contribute to cultural change today?
**(b) Draw Conclusions** How have new technologies affected the rate of cultural change?

## ◆ Skills Practice

**Making Valid Generalizations** In the Skills for Life activity in this chapter, you learned to make generalizations. You also learned how to make sure that generalizations are valid, or justified, based on facts. You learned not to overgeneralize, or make claims that go beyond the facts.

Review the steps that you followed to learn this skill. Then reread the paragraphs on pages 94 and 95 under the heading Development of Culture. List several facts about the changes described there. Finally, use these facts to make a valid generalization about those changes.

## ◆ Writing Activity: Math

Look at the graph titled World Internet Users 1996–2005 on page 107. Find the number of Internet users in 1996 and the number of Internet users nine years later in 2005. How many more users were there in 2005 than in 1996? Based on this information, predict how many Internet users there will be in 2014, nine years after the latest date shown on this graph. Write a short paragraph describing your results and your prediction.

## MAP MASTER Skills Activity

**Place Location** For each religion listed below, write the letter that marks its location on the map.
1. Buddhism
2. Eastern Christianity
3. Hinduism
4. Islam
5. Protestant Christianity
6. Roman Catholic Christianity
7. Traditional religions

**Go Online** PHSchool.com Use Web Code lep-3414 for an interactive map.

### World Religions

# Standardized Test Prep

## Test-Taking Tips

Some questions on standardized tests ask you to supply information using prior knowledge. Analyze the web diagram below. Then follow the tips to answer the sample question.

**TIP** The title in the center circle describes all of the languages. Think about the word *Indo-European* and how it describes languages.

**Pick the letter that best answers the question.**

Another language that belongs on this web is

  A ~~Mandarin Chinese.~~

  B Swahili.

  C ~~Japanese.~~

  D Greek.

**TIP** Use your prior knowledge—what you know about history, geography, or government—to help you rule out choices.

**Think It Through** The word *Indo-European* describes languages of India and Europe. Therefore, you can rule out answers A and C because these languages do not come from India or Europe. That leaves Swahili and Greek. You may not be sure about where Swahili is spoken, but you probably know from prior reading that Greece (where people speak Greek) is in Europe. The correct answer is D.

## Practice Questions

**Use the tips above and other tips in this book to help you answer the following questions:**

1. The Agricultural Revolution led

  A to a rebellion by farmers against taxes.

  B to widespread hunger.

  C to an increase in population.

  D people to begin using tools.

2. How does family structure change when countries become more developed?

  A People lose interest in their families.

  B Nuclear families become more common.

  C People move in with their grandparents, aunts, and uncles.

  D Extended families become more common.

3. Which of the following does NOT contribute to cultural change?

  A technological change

  B migration

  C tradition

  D television

**Read the following passage, and answer the question that follows.**

This country is the birthplace of three major religions. It is located on Earth's largest continent. Its neighbors include Bangladesh and Sri Lanka. The country has more than a billion inhabitants. Its people speak hundreds of different languages. Many people from this country have migrated overseas.

4. What country does the passage describe?

  A Israel

  B Mexico

  C India

  D China

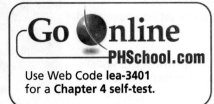

Use Web Code **lea-3401** for a **Chapter 4 self-test.**

## Chapter Preview

This chapter will introduce you to the ways in which people interact with their natural surroundings.

### Target Reading Skill

**Main Idea** In this chapter you will construct meaning by identifying the main idea in a paragraph and the details that support it. Identifying a paragraph's main idea can help you remember what you have read.

▶ Windmills capturing the wind's energy in Tehachapi Pass, California

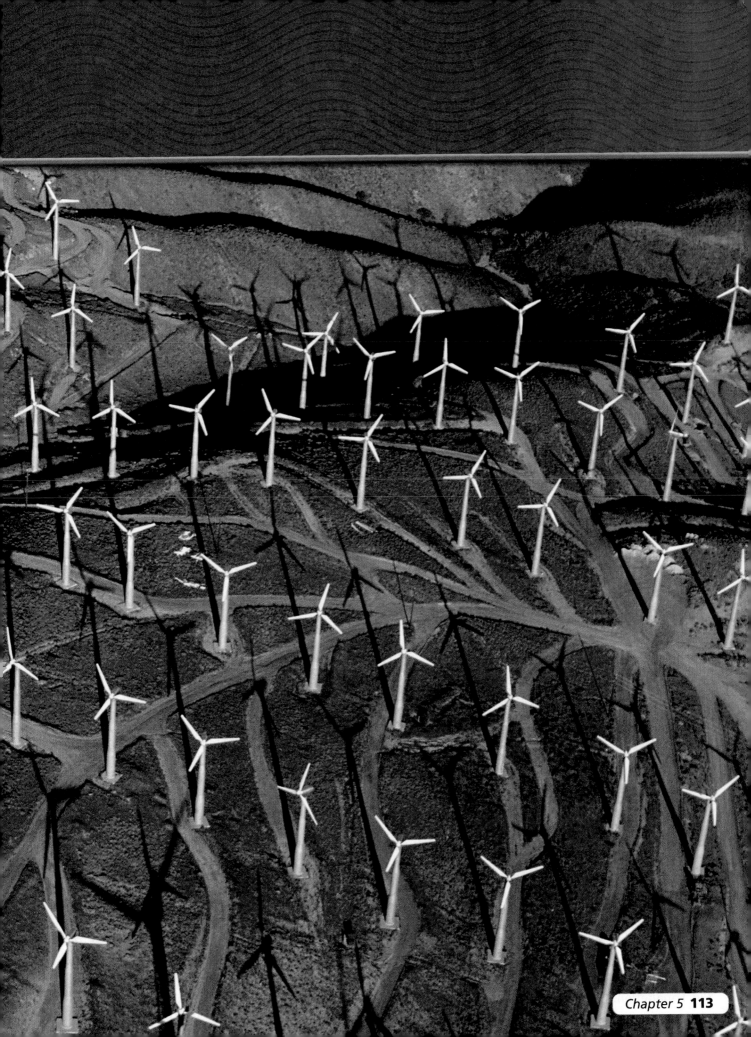

# Natural Resources

## Prepare to Read

### Objectives

In this section you will
1. Learn about natural resources.
2. Investigate energy.

### Taking Notes

Copy the outline below. Add letters, numbers, and headings as needed. As you read this section, fill in the outline with information about natural resources and energy.

I. Natural resources
  A. Renewable resources
  B.
    1.
    2.
II. Energy
  A.

### Target Reading Skill

**Identify Main Ideas**
Good readers identify the main idea in every written paragraph. The main idea is the most important point—the one that includes all of the other points. Sometimes this idea is stated directly. For example, in the first paragraph below, the first sentence states the paragraph's main idea. As you read, note the main idea of each paragraph.

### Key Terms

- **natural resources** (NACH ur ul REE sawr siz) *n.* useful materials found in the environment
- **raw materials** (raw muh TIHR ee ulz) *n.* natural resources that must be worked to be useful
- **renewable resources** (rih NOO uh bul REE sawr siz) *n.* natural resources that can be replaced
- **nonrenewable resources** (nahn rih NOO uh bul REE sawr siz) *n.* natural resources that cannot be replaced

**Men constructing a wooden hut in Kenya**

## What Are Natural Resources?

Everything that people use or consume is made with **natural resources,** or useful materials found in the environment. When people talk about natural resources, they usually mean such things as water, minerals, and vegetation.

All people need water, food, clothing, and shelter to survive. People drink water. People eat food that the soil produces. So do the animals that provide eggs, cheese, meat, and wool. Homes are made from wood, clay, and steel.

People can use some resources just as they are found in nature. Fresh water is one of these. But most resources must be changed before people can use them. Natural resources that must be worked to be useful are called **raw materials.** For example, people cannot just go out and cut down a tree if they want paper. Trees are the raw materials for paper and wood. To make paper, the wood must be soaked and broken up to create pulp. (Pulp is a kind of soup of wood fibers.) Machines collect the wet fibers on screens to form sheets of paper.

**Renewable Resources** The environment is filled with natural resources, but not all resources are alike. Geographers divide them into two main groups.

The first group is **renewable resources,** or resources that can be replaced. Some resources are replaced naturally because of the way Earth works. In the water cycle, water evaporates into the air and falls as rain, snow, hail, or sleet. This happens over and over again. Therefore, Earth has an unchanging amount of water. Other materials that go through natural cycles include nitrogen and carbon.

Some types of energy are also renewable resources. Using wind to make electricity will not use the wind up. Wind results from differences in the way the sun heats Earth. As long as the sun shines, there will always be more wind. Solar energy, or energy from the sun, is a renewable resource. No matter how much people use, there will always be more. Geothermal energy uses differences in heat between Earth's surface and its interior. This heat difference will not disappear in the foreseeable future.

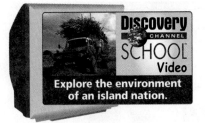
**Discovery CHANNEL SCHOOL Video**
**Explore the environment of an island nation.**

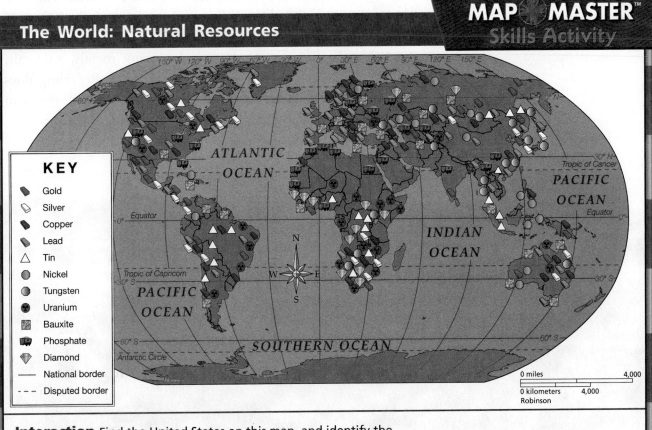

**Identify Main Ideas** Which sentence states the main idea of the paragraph at the left?

**MAP MASTER™**
*Skills Activity*

**The World: Natural Resources**

**KEY**

- Gold
- Silver
- Copper
- Lead
- △ Tin
- Nickel
- Tungsten
- Uranium
- Bauxite
- Phosphate
- Diamond
- —— National border
- - - - Disputed border

ATLANTIC OCEAN

PACIFIC OCEAN

INDIAN OCEAN

PACIFIC OCEAN

SOUTHERN OCEAN

Tropic of Cancer
Equator
Tropic of Capricorn
Antarctic Circle

0 miles 4,000

0 kilometers 4,000
Robinson

**Interaction** Find the United States on this map, and identify the natural resources shown on the map that the United States lacks.
**Infer** How do you think the lack of these resources in the United States affects its trade with other countries?

**Go Online**
**PHSchool.com** Use Web Code lep-3213 for step-by-step **map skills practice.**

**Solar cells on the roof of a house in Felsberg, Germany**

**Living Resources** Living things that provide natural resources, such as plants and animals, are also renewable resources. Like other resources, they must be properly managed so that people do not overuse them.

For example, a timber company may cut down all the trees in an area for use as wood. But the company may then plant new trees to replace the ones they cut. Even if they do not, seeds left in the ground will probably produce new trees. Every day, the people of the world eat many chickens and ears of corn. But farmers always make sure to grow more corn and chickens to replace what people eat. If people are careful, they can have a steady supply of these renewable living resources.

**Nonrenewable Resources** The second major group of resources is called **nonrenewable resources**, or resources that cannot be replaced. Most nonliving things, such as metal ores, most minerals, natural gas, and petroleum—or crude oil—are nonrenewable resources. If people keep mining minerals and burning fuels such as coal and oil, they will eventually run out. Therefore, people need to use these resources carefully. If they do run out, people will need to find substitutes for them.

Although they are nonrenewable, many metals, minerals, and materials such as plastics can be recycled. Recycling does not return these materials to their natural state. Still, they can be recovered and processed for reuse. Recycling these materials helps to conserve nonrenewable resources.

**Fossil Fuels** Most scientists think that coal, natural gas, and petroleum are fossil fuels, or fuels created over millions of years from the remains of prehistoric living things. If people continue using coal at today's rate, known supplies may run out in several hundred years. At current rates of use, known supplies of oil and natural gas may run out in less than 100 years.

If oil and natural gas are fossil fuels, they are renewable, since living things today will become fossil fuels in millions of years. But if these fuels take so long to develop, they are nonrenewable for our purposes.

✓ **Reading Check** **What is the difference between renewable and nonrenewable resources?**

## A Special Resource: Energy

Many natural resources are sources of energy. People use energy not only from fossil fuels, but also from the wind and the sun. Dams produce hydroelectric power by harnessing the power of falling water.

Energy is itself a resource that is needed to make use of other natural resources. Consider cotton. It takes energy to harvest cotton from a field, to spin the cotton into thread, and to weave it into fabric. Workers use energy to travel to a garment factory. It takes energy to sew a shirt with a sewing machine. It also takes energy to transport the shirt by ship and truck to a retail store. Finally, the consumer uses energy to bring the shirt home.

**Located on the border between Oregon and Washington, the Bonneville Dam produces hydroelectric power.**

**Strip Mining Coal**
The machine below extracts coal from this exposed deposit in Banwen Pyrddin, Wales, United Kingdom.
**Apply Information** *Do you think that coal is a recyclable, renewable, or nonrenewable resource?*

**Pipes running across an oil field in Meyal, Pakistan**

**Energy "Have's" and "Have Not's"** People in every country need energy. But energy resources are not evenly spread around the world. Certain areas are rich in energy resources. Others have very few.

Countries with many rivers, such as Canada and Norway, can use water energy to create electricity. Countries like Saudi Arabia and Mexico have huge amounts of oil that they sell to other countries. Countries like Japan and the United States do not produce as much energy as they use. These countries have to buy energy from other countries.

**Meeting Energy Needs in the Future** Over time, energy use worldwide has grown rapidly. Yet our supplies of fossil fuels may be limited. It seems likely that the world's people will need to find other sources of energy. Many possibilities exist.

Already, some countries, such as Denmark and Germany, are developing renewable energy sources such as wind and solar energy. Other sources of energy that will not run out are tidal energy, from the rise and fall of Earth's oceans, and geothermal energy, or energy from the heat of Earth's interior. Biomass, or plant material, is a renewable source of energy. These energy sources can reduce a country's need for imported oil.

Atomic energy uses radioactive materials, which are non-renewable but plentiful. Some people oppose atomic energy because radioactive materials can be dangerous. Others support it as a plentiful energy source that does not pollute the air.

## ■ Graph Skills

Some countries produce more oil than they use. These countries can sell their extra oil to other countries. Others consume more oil than they produce and have to buy it from other countries. **Identify** Which of the countries on this graph have to buy almost all of their oil? **Compare and Contrast** Which country buys the most oil?

### The World's Top Petroleum Producers and Consumers

Percentage of World Total

- Consumption
- Production

Country: Canada, China, Germany, India, Iran, Japan, Mexico, Russia, Saudi Arabia, USA

SOURCE: *Energy Information Administration*

Fossil fuels will last longer if people use less energy. New technologies, such as hybrid cars, can reduce a country's need for imported oil by burning less gas per mile. Other technologies offer energy savings in heating and lighting buildings and in making new products. If people manage to use less energy, they will not need to buy as much from foreign countries. They will also have an easier time meeting their energy needs in the future.

**Geothermal power**
In addition to producing energy, the geothermal power plant at Svartsengi, Iceland, heats the mineral-rich water of the Blue Lagoon. **Infer** *Are fossil fuels used to heat this pool?*

✔ Reading Check **Why do some countries have to import energy?**

## Section 1 Assessment

### Key Terms
Review the key terms at the beginning of this section. Use each term in a sentence that explains its meaning.

### Target Reading Skill
State the main idea of the paragraph on this page.

### Comprehension and Critical Thinking
**1. (a) Identify** Why is wood considered a renewable resource?

**(b) Apply Information** What needs to happen after trees are cut in order for wood to remain a renewable resource?
**2. (a) List** Name some sources of energy other than fossil fuels.
**(b) Categorize** What do these energy sources have in common, and how do they differ from fossil fuels?
**(c) Draw Conclusions** Why might we need to use more of these energy sources in the future?

### Writing Activity
Think about what you did this morning before you came to school. Write a journal entry describing the natural resources that you used and all of the ways that you used energy at home and on your way to school.

**Go Online**
PHSchool.com

**For:** An activity on natural resources
**Visit:** PHSchool.com
**Web Code:** led-3501

# Land Use

## Prepare to Read

### Objectives

In this section you will
1. Study the relation between land use and culture.
2. Investigate the relation between land use and economic activity.
3. Explore changes in land use.

### Taking Notes

Copy the concept web below. As you read the section, fill in the ovals with information about land use. Add ovals as needed.

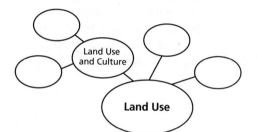

### Target Reading Skill

**Identify Supporting Details** Sentences in a paragraph may provide details that support the main idea. These details may give examples or explanations. In the second paragraph on this page, this sentence states the main idea: "Even in similar environments, people may use land differently because they have different cultural traits." Note three details in the paragraph that explain this main idea.

### Key Terms

- **environment** (en VY run munt) *n.* natural surroundings
- **manufacturing** (man yoo FAK chur ing) *n.* the large-scale production of goods by hand or by machine
- **colonization** (kahl uh nih ZAY shun) *n.* the movement of settlers and their culture to a new country
- **industrialization** (in dus tree ul ih ZAY shun) *n.* the growth of machine-powered production in an economy

**A peanut farmer in Georgia inspecting his crop**

# Land Use and Culture

How people use the land depends on their culture. People may use their land differently because their cultures have developed in different **environments**, or natural surroundings. For example, the Inuit live in a cold, arctic climate. It is too cold to grow crops, so the Inuit use their land mainly for hunting wild animals, and they rely heavily on fishing. The Japanese live in a warmer, moister climate. Although much of Japan is too steep to farm, the Japanese use much of the remaining land for crops. Their main crop is rice, which grows well in the warm, moist climate of Japan.

Even in similar environments, however, people may use land differently because they have different cultural traits. For example, Georgia has a warm, moist climate like that of southern Japan. But Georgia does not produce much rice. Instead, Georgians raise chickens and grow crops such as peanuts. While the Japanese eat rice at nearly every meal, Americans eat more meat and peanut butter.

**Cultures and Landscapes** The examples of the Inuit and the Japanese show how people's environments help to shape their cultures. People's cultures, in turn, help shape the landscapes where they live. For example, in some parts of the Philippines, a culture of rice farming and a shortage of level land has led people to carve terraces into hillsides. Thousands of years ago, Western Europe was covered with forests. As farming cultures spread across that region, people cleared forests to use the land for farming. Today, most of Western Europe is open fields and pastures. Few forests remain.

**Land Use and Cultural Differences** As the examples of Japan and Georgia show, however, similar environments do not necessarily produce similar cultures. People may respond differently to those environments, depending on their culture. For example, much of the western United States has a dry climate. Many crops need irrigation, or an artificial water supply. The Middle East also has climates too dry for most crops to grow without irrigation. However, the two regions have different cultures and different responses to this challenge. In the western United States, farmers use modern irrigation systems. For example, drip irrigation provides water to each plant through little pipes or tubes. Some Middle Eastern farmers use qanats, or brick irrigation channels, to bring water to their crops. Both cultures face similar environments, but they interact with those environments differently.

✓ **Reading Check** How is land use related to culture?

**Drip irrigation of grape vines in eastern Washington State**

**Irrigation in Yemen**
This man is walking along a qanat, or brick irrigation channel, in Jiblah, Yemen.
**Analyze Images** *What clues do you see in this landscape that suggest a need for irrigation?*

## Land Use and Economic Activity

In some places, people use the land and its resources to make a living by farming, fishing, or mining. In other places, people work in factories, where they turn natural resources into finished products. In still other places, people sell or distribute products and make a living by providing services. These three ways of making a living correspond to three stages of economic activity. Geographers use stages of economic activity as a way to understand land use.

**Target Skill**
**Identify Supporting Details**
Which details in the paragraph at the right give examples of first-level activities?

**First-Level Activities** In the first stage, people use land and resources directly to make products. They may hunt, cut wood, mine, or fish. They also may herd animals or raise crops. This is the first stage of activities. At this stage, people interact directly with the land or the sea. Most of the world's land is used for first-level activities. However, in developed countries such as the United States, only a small percentage of the people make a living at first-level activities.

## Stages of Economic Activity

A series of economic activities connect a flock of sheep in a pasture to a wool sweater in a store. Sheep-raising, a first-level activity, makes it possible to manufacture woolen goods such as sweaters, a second-level activity. Manufacturing makes it possible to deliver sweaters to stores. Stores can then sell the sweaters. Delivery and sales are both third-level activities.

**A flock of sheep being driven to a pasture in New Zealand**

▲ **Farming, a first-level activity**
This farmer is shearing a sheep, or trimming away its wool. Raising and shearing sheep are first-level activities, or direct uses of natural resources.

**Second-Level Activities** At the second stage, people process the products of first-level activities. Most second-level activity is **manufacturing**, or the large-scale production of goods by hand or by machine. Manufacturing may turn a farmer's corn crop into cornflakes for your breakfast. Manufacturing, especially in urban areas, is an important land use in developed countries.

**Third-Level Activities** At the third stage, a person delivers boxes of cornflakes to your local grocery store. Third-level activities are also known as services. These activities do not produce goods. They may help sell goods. They often involve working directly for customers or for businesses. Many businesses offering services—doctors' offices, banks, automobile repair shops, shopping malls, and fast-food restaurants—are part of everyday living. Services are also clustered in urban areas, especially in developed countries.

✓ **Reading Check** How is most of the world's land used?

### GEOGRAPHY SKILLS PRACTICE

**Human-Environment Interaction** Each activity shown here occurs in a different part of New Zealand.
**Apply Information** Which activities occur in rural areas, and which activities are likely to occur in urban areas?

▲ **Manufacturing, a second-level activity**
Second-level activities process natural resources to make goods, such as the wool this worker is processing at a New Zealand mill.

**Retail sales, a third-level activity** ▶
Selling manufactured goods, such as this sweater, in a store is a third-level activity. This woolen-goods store is in New Zealand.

# Boston: A Changing Landscape

English colonists founded Boston, Massachusetts, on a narrow peninsula surrounded by water, marshes, and forest. The colonists cleared most of the forest for farmland. The colonists also built dams, piers, and retaining walls along the waterfront. By the 1800s, Boston's growing industries and growing population of workers faced a land shortage. Boston's solution was to drain marshes and to create new land by filling in areas of water. At first, Boston's people filled in around existing piers. Then, they filled in tidal ponds behind dams. Finally, they filled in whole bodies of open water.

## MAP MASTER™
### Skills Activity

**Human-Environment Interaction** Colonization and industrialization transformed Boston's landscape. **Identify** How much of the forest around Boston remained after colonization? **Compare and Contrast** How did Boston's land area change between colonial times and today?

**Go Online**
**PHSchool.com** Use Web Code **lep-3312** for step-by-step map skills practice.

Charlestown

Cambridge

Boston

*Charles River*

*Shawmut Peninsula*

*Boston Harbor*

*Back Bay*

*South Cove*

*Governor's Island*

*South Bay*

Castle Island

South Boston

**KEY**

- Forested area before colonization
- Forested area after colonization
- Land area before colonization
- Land area after colonization
- Additional land area, after industrialization

N
W E
S

0 miles 1
0 kilometers 1

**This replica of a colonial ship is docked in view of modern skyscrapers in Boston, Massachusetts.**

# Changes in Land Use

When a region undergoes **colonization,** or a movement of new settlers and their culture to a country, the newcomers may change that region's landscape to fit their cultural practices. For example, if farmers move to a region without farms, they will create farms. Similarly, as people find new ways of making a living, they start using the land in new ways, too.

**Colonization** Before European colonists came to Australia, there was no farming and no livestock raising. In North and South America before colonization, European crops such as wheat and grapes were unknown. So were livestock such as cows and chickens. When Europeans settled these continents, they cleared large areas for use as farmland and livestock pasture.

**Industrialization and Sprawl** Since the 1800s, the growth of machine-powered production, or **industrialization,** has changed landscapes in many countries. Cities have grown around industrial facilities worldwide. Since 1900, suburbs have spread out from cities in the United States and other developed countries to cover more and more land. The spread of cities and suburbs is known as sprawl.

✔ **Reading Check** How did European colonization change landscapes in North and South America?

**Vineyards in Australia**
Grapes did not grow in Australia before European colonists arrived. Now grapes thrive in Australia's Hunter Valley. **Infer** *What would have been different about this landscape before European colonization?*

---

## Section 2 Assessment

### Key Terms
Review the key terms at the beginning of this section. Use each term in a sentence that explains its meaning.

### 🎯 Target Reading Skill
State three details that explain the main idea of the second paragraph on page 120.

### Comprehension and Critical Thinking
**1. (a) Describe** How have rice farmers in the Philippines transformed the landscape?

**(b) Infer** Why is the Philippines' farm landscape different from Western Europe's?

**2. (a) Recall** What are second-level activities?

**(b) Categorize** Name some examples of second-level activities.

**(c) Compare and Contrast** How do second-level activities differ from third-level activities?

**3. (a) Recall** What is industrialization?

**(b) Identify Causes** How is industrialization related to sprawl?

### Writing Activity
Write a short encyclopedia article on land use around your hometown. Describe how culture has affected land use. Mention the different levels of economic activity around your town. Finally, give an example of a change in land use in or near your hometown.

**Writing Tip** Encyclopedia articles contain descriptions and statements of facts. Be careful not to express personal thoughts or opinions.

**Many American presidents, who work and live in the White House, shown above, have had to carefully try to predict the consequences of their decisions.**

**W**hen you watch an adventure movie, half the fun is in predicting what happens next. Decision makers, such as American presidents, make predictions, too, and their predictions guide their decisions. Good decision makers take actions that they predict will have good results. When you predict, you make an educated guess about the effects of a certain cause. The key word here is *educated*. Without knowledge, you can't predict—you just guess.

## Learn the Skill

Follow these steps to make a good prediction.

**1** **Identify a situation that has not been resolved.** As you read information, ask yourself questions, such as, "What will happen next? What effects will this situation produce?"

**2** **Make a list of probable outcomes, or effects.** If possible, analyze examples of similar causes that have known effects.

**3** **Make an educated guess about which outcome is most likely.** In order to make an *educated* guess, use information that you know or that you research.

**4** **State your prediction.** In your prediction, explain why you think the cause will produce a particular effect, or outcome.

## Practice the Skill

Read the text in the box at the right. Then predict the consequences of global struggles for water.

 From what you have read about water supplies in Southwest Asia, identify a major issue that has not been resolved. State the problem as a question.

**2** This chapter discusses problems in global oil supply. How are oil and water issues similar? What effects have resulted from world oil shortages? Study the graphic organizer below. It shows results that might occur when one country controls other countries' water.

**3** Of the possible outcomes in the graphic organizer, which seems the most likely? Make an educated guess, using what you know about the oil issue.

**4** Here's how your prediction might begin: "As the world's need for water grows, water-rich countries will probably _____."

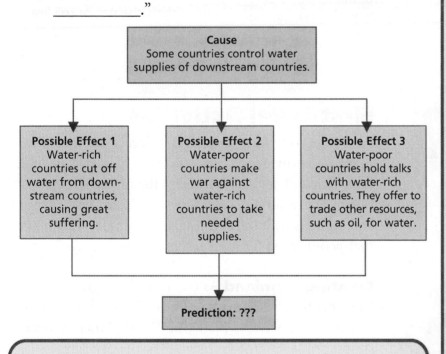

**Cause**
Some countries control water supplies of downstream countries.

**Possible Effect 1**
Water-rich countries cut off water from downstream countries, causing great suffering.

**Possible Effect 2**
Water-poor countries make war against water-rich countries to take needed supplies.

**Possible Effect 3**
Water-poor countries hold talks with water-rich countries. They offer to trade other resources, such as oil, for water.

**Prediction: ???**

During the 1900s, oil-rich nations became wealthy and powerful by controlling world oil supplies. In the present century, water supplies may determine who is rich or poor. Much of the world's usable fresh water comes from rivers that flow through many countries. Nearly half the people in the world live in international river basins. Yet many of the countries that share rivers have no water treaties. Countries along these rivers build dams to store water for themselves. Nations downstream worry that they might run out of water. In Southwest Asia, Turkey controls sources of water flowing south into Syria and Iraq. A proposed system of 22 dams could allow Turkey to withhold water from its neighbors. Syria and Iraq have plentiful oil but not enough water.

## Apply the Skill

Study the graph on page 118. Note how much oil the United States consumes and produces. What do you learn from these facts? Make a prediction about what America might do when world oil supplies run low. Create a graphic organizer like the one on this page to help you make a prediction.

# People's Effect on the Environment

## Prepare to Read

### Objectives

In this section you will
1. Investigate how first-level activities affect the environment.
2. Explore how second- and third-level activities affect the environment.

### Taking Notes

Copy the table below. As you read this section, fill in the table with information about people's effect on the environment. Add rows to the table as needed.

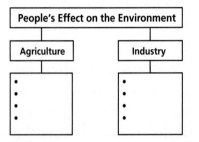

People's Effect on the Environment

| Agriculture | Industry |
|---|---|
| • | • |
| • | • |
| • | • |
| • | • |

### Target Reading Skill

**Identify Implied Main Ideas** Identifying main ideas can help you remember what you read. The details in a paragraph can add up to the main idea, even if it is not stated directly. For example, the details in the first paragraph below add up to this main idea: "While first-level activities are necessary for human survival, they also reshape the environment."

### Key Terms

- **deforestation** (dee fawr uh STAY shun) *n.* a loss of forest cover in a region
- **biodiversity** (by oh duh VUR suh tee) *n.* a richness of different kinds of living things in a region
- **civil engineering** (SIV ul en juh NIHR ing) *n.* technology for building structures that alter the landscape, such as dams, roads, and bridges
- **pollution** (puh LOO shun) *n.* waste, usually man-made, that makes the air, water, or soil less clean

## First-Level Activities

First-level activities, or direct interaction with raw materials, provide the food and resources that people need to live. They also transform the physical environment. For example, agriculture replaces wild plants and animals with the domesticated plants and animals that people need for food and other products.

**Creating Farmland** As countries have grown, they have met the challenge of feeding their people in different ways. The Great Plains of North America once supported wild grasses and buffalo. Today, farmers in that region grow corn and wheat and raise cattle. In the Netherlands, the people have drained lakes, bays, and marshes to create dry farmland. While creating new farmland destroyed wild grasslands and wetlands, the new land has fed millions.

**A rancher driving cattle in Manitoba, Canada**

**Environmental Challenges** Agriculture, forestry, and fishing provide food and resources that people need to live. At the same time, they sometimes have harmful effects on the environment. For example, wood is needed to build houses. But cutting down too many trees can result in **deforestation,** or the loss of forest cover in a region. Cutting forests may result in the loss of more than trees and other plants. Animals that depend on the forest for survival may also suffer. Deforestation can lead to a loss of **biodiversity,** which is a richness of different kinds of living things. So timber companies face the challenge of harvesting needed wood while limiting damage to the environment.

Farmers often use fertilizers and other chemicals to grow more crops. This makes it possible to feed more people. But when rain washes these chemicals into streams, they sometimes harm fish and other water-dwelling creatures. Fish are a tasty and healthy food source. But if fishers catch too many, they may threaten the fishes' survival. Farmers and fishers face the challenge of feeding the world's people without harming important resources.

**Finding a Balance** The key is to find a balance. Around the world, governments, scientists, and business people are working to find ways of meeting our need for food and resources without harming the environment. One solution is planting tree farms for timber. When the trees are mature, they can be cut and new trees can be replanted without harming ancient forests. Farmers can grow crops using natural methods or use chemicals that will not damage waterways. Fishers can limit their catch of endangered fish and harvest fish that are more plentiful.

✓ Reading Check  **How do people benefit when new farmland is created?**

**Deforestation**
Timber companies and farmers have cut down rain forests in Indonesia.
**Apply Information** *What are some of the advantages and disadvantages of cutting down forests?*

**Links to**
# Math

**Acres and Timber Yields**
Tree farms, like the one below, in Newbury, England, are one way to fight deforestation. If these oak trees grow to yield 80,000 board feet of timber per acre (466 cubic meters per hectare), and the farm covers 300 acres (121 hectares), how much timber will the farm produce?

# The Hybrid Car

Cars with gasoline engines are fast and can go long distances, but they pollute. Electric cars don't emit dangerous chemicals, but they can be driven only for a short distance before their batteries need to be recharged. The hybrid car combines the best features of gasoline and electric cars. It is fast and can go long distances, but it uses less gasoline and pollutes less. The hybrid car gets about 46 miles per gallon, while the conventional car of the same size gets about 33.

**Traffic Jam**
Today, traffic jams are common as drivers commute daily in and out of cities. Waiting in traffic jams wastes a lot of fuel and adds to air pollution.

Hybrid cars are made of lightweight materials. It takes less fuel to move a lighter car.

The electric motor draws energy from the battery to accelerate the car. When the car's brakes are applied, the motor recharges, or sends energy back to, the battery.

The small gasoline engine has the same power as a motorcycle, but it uses less fuel. It pollutes less than an ordinary car engine.

Fuel tank

The battery drives an electric motor, which assists the engine during acceleration.

The tires are inflated to a higher pressure than in an ordinary car. The higher pressure reduces energy loss.

**ANALYZING IMAGES**
How do hybrid cars save fuel?

# Second- and Third-Level Activities

Over the years, industry, or second-level activities, and services, or third-level activities, have transformed deserts, prairies, woodlands, and marshes. They have created our familiar urban landscapes of housing developments, offices, factories, railroads, and highways.

**Providing Jobs, Reshaping the Environment** Industrial and service activities provide most of the jobs in developed countries such as the United States. Those activities are the basis for the developed countries' prosperity. They are also the main land use in urban areas.

The main purpose of some of these activities is to change the environment. **Civil engineering** is technology for building structures that alter the landscape, such as dams, canals, roads, and bridges. Dams create reservoirs that cover large areas with water. They also provide water for farms and cities and protect areas downstream from flooding.

Other industrial and service activities have side effects on the environment. For example, shopping malls require large areas to be paved for parking. Industries use large amounts of resources and release industrial wastes into the environment. Service activities require the construction of roads, telephone lines, and power lines.

**Identify Implied Main Ideas**
In one sentence, state what all the details in the paragraph at the left are about.

**A Landscape Shaped by Industry** The waterfront in Rotterdam, Netherlands, has been shaped to meet the needs of industry. **Analyze Images** How might this landscape have been different before it was shaped by industry?

**Recycling**
These seventh-grade students in Syracuse, New York, are sorting materials for recycling. **Apply Information** *What environmental problems does recycling help to solve?*

**Environmental Challenges** Industry is not the only source of **pollution**, waste that makes the air, soil, or water less clean. The trash that we throw away may pollute the soil, water, or air. Exhaust from cars and trucks is another source of air pollution. Many scientists believe that air pollution may cause higher temperatures or other changes in our climate.

**Finding Solutions** Working together, scientists, governments, businesses, and ordinary people can find solutions to these problems. One solution is to use more fuel-efficient vehicles, such as hybrid cars. Vehicles that burn less fuel create less air pollution. Renewable energy sources, such as solar power and wind power, can also reduce the need to burn fuels that pollute the air. In addition, reducing pollution may reduce the risk of harmful climate changes.

Many cities and counties in the United States have introduced waste recycling. Recycling reduces the amount of waste that local governments must burn or dump. It also saves natural resources. For example, when paper is recycled, fewer trees must be cut down to make new paper.

Finding solutions to environmental problems is one of the greatest challenges of our time. If we all work together, we can meet this challenge.

✓ **Reading Check** **How do industrial activities affect the environment?**

---

## Section 3 Assessment

**Key Terms**
Review the key terms at the beginning of this section. Use each term in a sentence that explains its meaning.

**Target Reading Skill**
State the main idea of each paragraph on this page.

**Comprehension and Critical Thinking**
**1. (a) Recall** What are the causes of deforestation?

**(b) Identify Cause and Effect** How does deforestation threaten the environment?
**2. (a) List** List ways in which industrial and service activities transform landscapes.
**(b) Categorize** Which of these ways are common to both industrial and service activities?
**(c) Analyze** How are industrial activities different from service activities in their impact on the environment?

**Writing Activity**
Write a journal entry in which you discuss how your own activities today may have affected the environment.

**Go Online**
**PHSchool.com**

**For:** An activity on the environment
**Visit:** PHSchool.com
**Web Code:** led-3503

# Review and Assessment

## ◆ Chapter Summary

### Section 1: Natural Resources
- Almost everything that people use or consume is made with natural resources, which are either renewable or nonrenewable.
- Energy is a special resource needed for most economic activities, but some sources of energy are in limited supply, and some nations need to buy energy resources from others.

### Section 2: Land Use
- How people use the land depends on their culture.
- Three levels of economic activity account for most land use.
- Land use changes when newcomers settle a region and as cultures change over time.

### Section 3: People's Effect on the Environment
- First-level activities provide needed food and resources, but they reduce the land available for wild plants and animals.
- Second- and third-level activities provide jobs, but they can also pollute the environment.

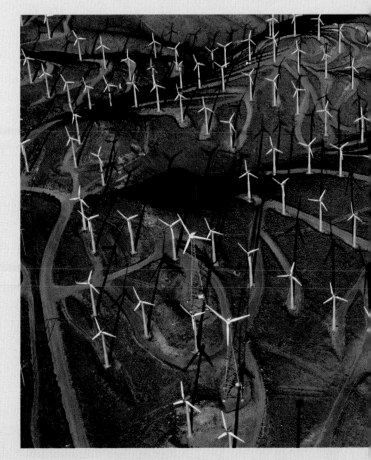

**Windmills in California**

## ◆ Key Terms

Each of the statements below contains a key term from the chapter. If the statement is true, write *true*. If it is false, rewrite the statement to make it true.

1. **Raw materials** are natural resources that can be used without reworking.

2. **Renewable resources** are natural resources that can be replaced.

3. Natural resources that cannot be replaced are called **nonrenewable resources.**

4. Our **environment** is our natural surroundings.

5. **Manufacturing** does not produce goods but involves working directly for customers.

6. **Industrialization** is the growth of manufacturing in an economy.

7. **Deforestation** is the planting of trees to replace forests cut down for timber.

8. **Biodiversity** is the loss of plant and animal life due to deforestation.

9. **Pollution** is waste, usually made by people, that makes air, soil, or water less clean.

## ◆ Comprehension and Critical Thinking

**10. (a) List** List at least three renewable resources.
**(b) Explain** Why is each of these resources renewable?
**(c) Compare and Contrast** How do renewable resources differ from nonrenewable resources?

**11. (a) Recall** Do all countries have adequate energy supplies?
**(b) Analyze** What energy sources are available to all countries?

**12. (a) Recall** Does culture affect land use?
**(b) Predict** What might happen to land use in a region if people with a different culture colonized it?

**13. (a) List** List three first-level activities.
**(b) Compare and Contrast** How do those activities differ from second- and third-level activities?

**14. (a) Describe** How can people obtain wood without cutting down wild forests?
**(b) Predict** How would leaving forests in place affect biodiversity?

**15. (a) Describe** What causes pollution?
**(b) Infer** How might companies and individuals reduce pollution?

## ◆ Skills Practice

**Making Predictions** In the Skills for Life activity on pages 126 and 127, you learned to make predictions. You also learned how to make sure that a prediction is an educated guess. That is, predictions should be based on information about the situation or about similar situations.

Review the steps that you followed to learn this skill. Then reread the paragraphs on pages 118 and 119 under the heading Meeting Energy Needs in the Future. List several facts about the issues described there. Finally, use these facts to make a prediction about how those issues might be resolved in the future.

## ◆ Writing Activity: Language Arts

Identify an environmental problem that interests you. Write a story about people solving the environmental problem. For your story, create characters with different roles in creating or solving the environmental problem. You should also create a plot for your story that describes how people come up with a solution to the problem and carry out that solution.

---

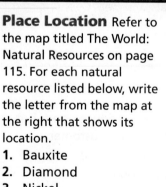

**MAP MASTER™**
**Skills Activity**

**Natural Resources**

**Place Location** Refer to the map titled The World: Natural Resources on page 115. For each natural resource listed below, write the letter from the map at the right that shows its location.

1. Bauxite
2. Diamond
3. Nickel
4. Phosphates
5. Tungsten

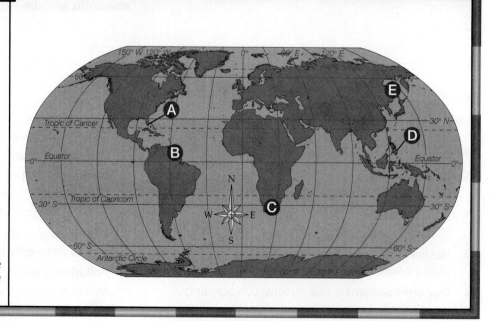

**Go Online**
**PHSchool.com** Use Web Code **lep-3514** for an **interactive map.**

# Standardized Test Prep

## Test-Taking Tips

Some questions on standardized tests ask you to find a main idea by analyzing a reading selection. Read the passage below. Then follow the tips to answer the sample question.

> Saudi Arabia, Mexico, Iraq, Venezuela, and Russia have large oil reserves. The United States and China are rich in coal and natural gas. Many Northern European countries have rivers with water energy to create electricity. By contrast, Japan has few energy sources.

**TIP** As you read the paragraph, try to identify its main idea, or most important point. Every sentence in a paragraph supports this main idea.

**Pick the letter that best answers the question.**

This paragraph describes which kind of resources?

**A** capital resources

**B** human resources

**C** natural resources

**D** entrepreneurial resources

**TIP** Look for key words in the question and in the answer choices that connect to the paragraph. In this case, the key word is *resources*.

**Think It Through** Start with the main idea of the paragraph: Different countries have different energy sources. What kind of resources are these energy sources: oil, coal, gas, and water? Energy is not a human resource. You may not know the words *entrepreneurial* or *capital*. But you probably recognize *natural resources* as useful materials found in the environment—such as oil, coal, gas, and water. The correct answer is C.

## Practice Questions

Use the tips above and other tips in this book to help you answer the following questions:

1. Wind energy is a

   **A** fossil fuel.

   **B** raw material.

   **C** renewable resource.

   **D** nonrenewable resource.

2. When colonists settle in a new environment,

   **A** they will use land just as they did in their old environment.

   **B** the environment will not change.

   **C** they will adjust their previous land uses to the new environment.

   **D** they will give up all familiar land uses.

3. Which of the following environmental problems does paper recycling help solve?

   **A** deforestation

   **B** pollution

   **C** deforestation and pollution

   **D** neither deforestation nor pollution

Read the following passage and answer the question that follows.

Sierra Leone's economy produces raw materials and cash crops. The country's people mine diamonds, iron ore, and aluminum ore. People on the coast catch fish. Its farmers produce coffee, cocoa, rice, and palm oil. They also raise poultry and other livestock.

4. The passage's main idea refers to which type of activities?

   **A** first-level activities

   **B** second-level activities

   **C** third-level activities

   **D** financial activities

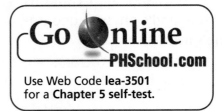

Go Online
PHSchool.com

Use Web Code **lea-3501** for a **Chapter 5 self-test.**

# Projects

Create your own projects to learn more about geography. At the beginning of this book, you were introduced to the **Guiding Questions** for studying the chapters and the special features. But you can also find answers to these questions by doing projects on your own or with a group. Use the questions to find topics you want to explore further. Then try the projects described on this page or create your own.

**1** **Geography** What are Earth's major physical features?

**2** **History** How have people's ways of life changed over time?

**3** **Culture** What is a culture?

**4** **Government** What types of government exist in the world today?

**5** **Economics** How do people use the world's natural resources?

## Project

### CREATE A PHYSICAL MAP

**Focus on Part of the Whole**
The world and its population are extremely varied. Choose a particular region or country. If you are working with a group, have each person choose a different country on a continent. Learn everything you can about the country's physical geography, the population, and the lifestyles of the people there. Use encyclopedias, almanacs, or other books.

Set up a display based on your research. Prepare a large map that includes important physical features of the land. Add captions that explain how the land's physical geography affects people's lives.

## Project

### RESEARCH A COUNTRY'S CULTURE

**Desktop Countries**
What countries did your ancestors come from? Select one country and do some research on it. Interview someone, perhaps a relative from that country, or read about it. Find a recipe you can prepare to share with the class. Then make a desktop display about the country you have chosen. Write the name of the country on a card and put it on your desk. Add a drawing of the country's flag or map, or display a souvenir. On place cards, write several sentences about each object. Take turns visiting everyone's "desktop countries."

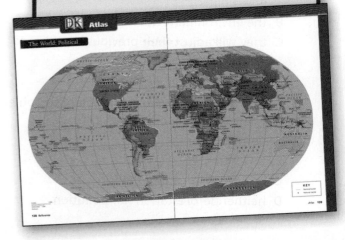

# Contents

# The World: Political

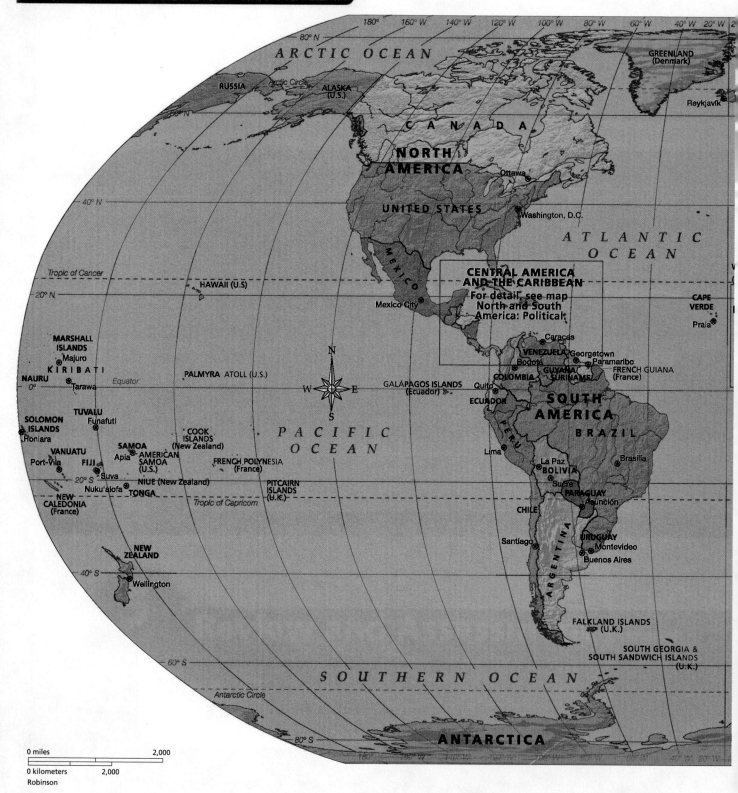

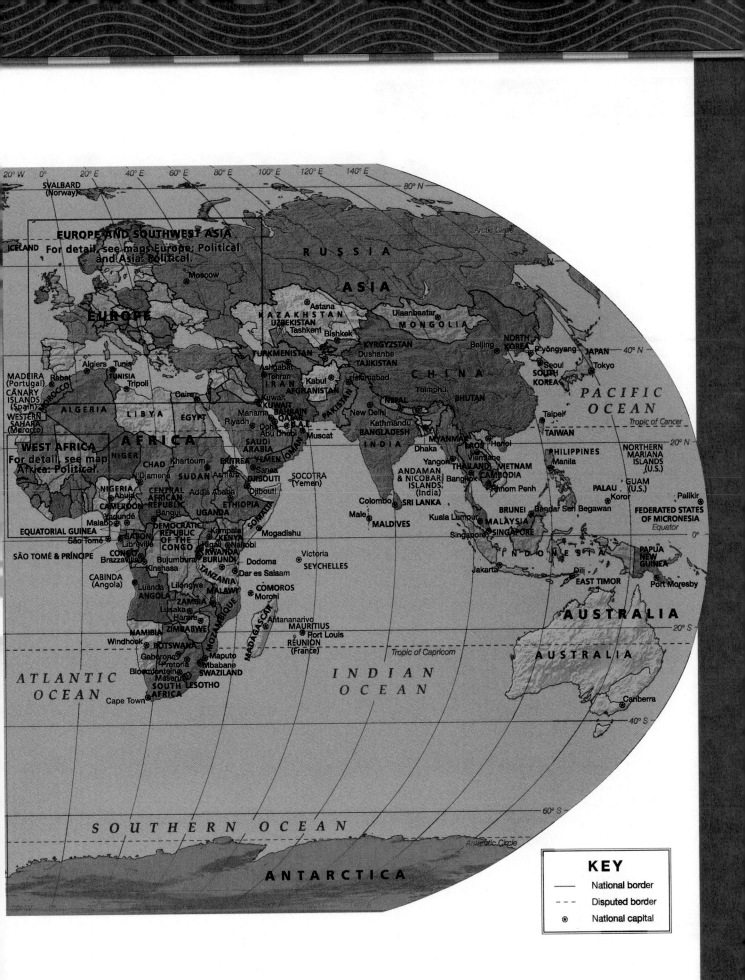

# The World: Physical

0 miles 2,000
0 kilometers 2,000
Robinson

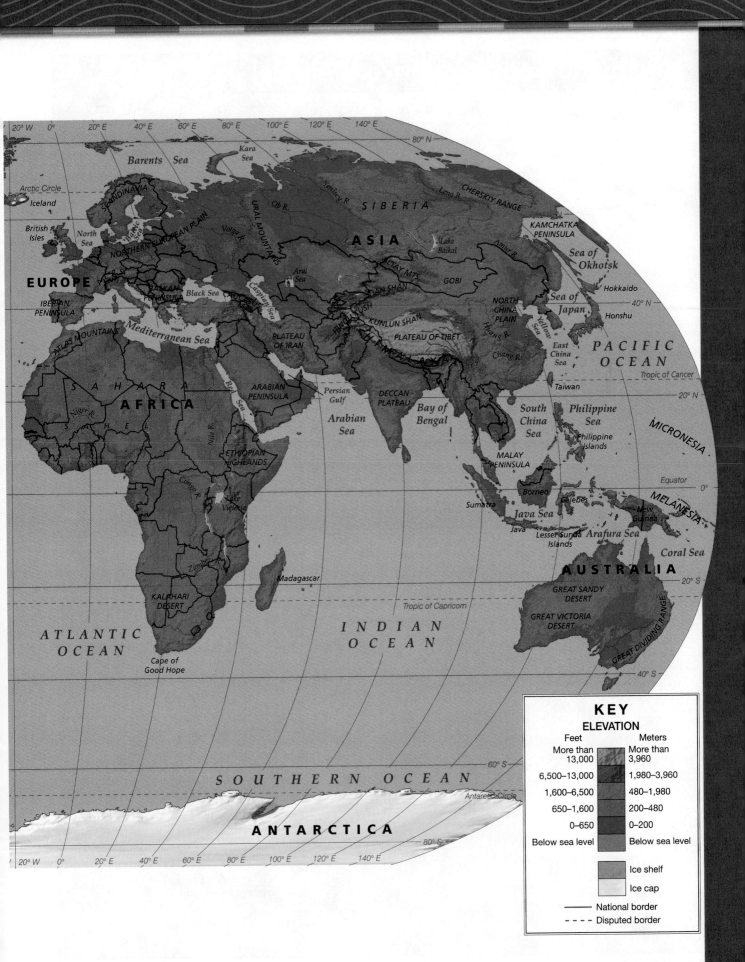

KEY
**ELEVATION**

| Feet | | Meters |
|------|------|------|
| More than 13,000 | | More than 3,960 |
| 6,500–13,000 | | 1,980–3,960 |
| 1,600–6,500 | | 480–1,980 |
| 650–1,600 | | 200–480 |
| 0–650 | | 0–200 |
| Below sea level | | Below sea level |

Ice shelf

Ice cap

National border

Disputed border

# North and South America: Political

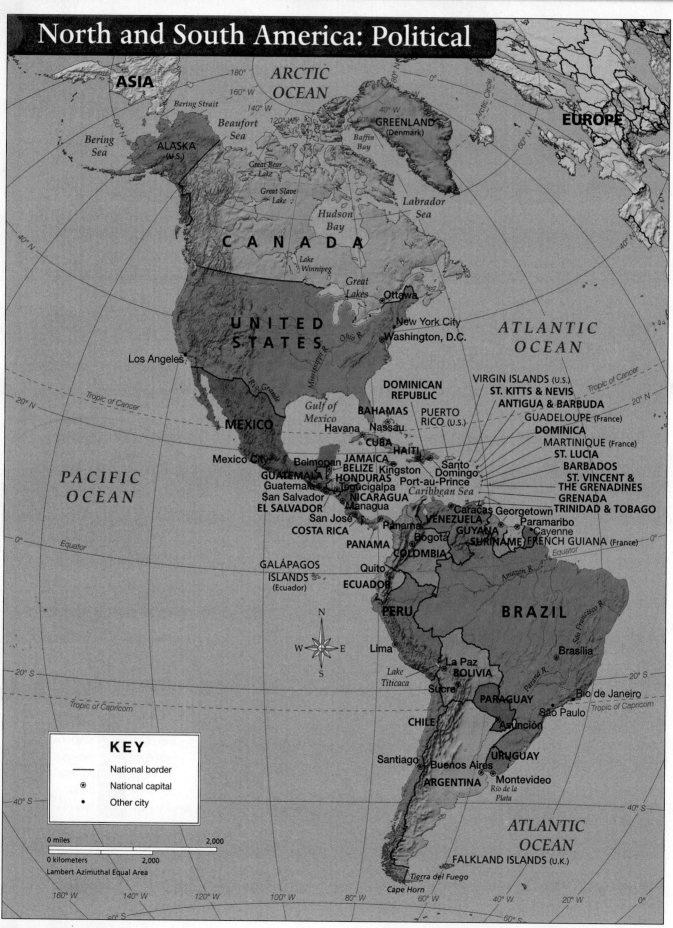

ASIA

ARCTIC OCEAN

180°
160° W
140° W
120° W

Bering Strait

Beaufort Sea

Bering Sea

ALASKA (U.S.)

Great Bear Lake

Great Slave Lake

40° N

Arctic Circle

GREENLAND (Denmark)

40° W
60° W

Baffin Bay

Labrador Sea

EUROPE

60° N

CANADA

Hudson Bay

Lake Winnipeg

Great Lakes

Ottawa

UNITED STATES

Ohio R.

New York City
Washington, D.C.

ATLANTIC OCEAN

Mississippi R.

Los Angeles

Rio Grande

Tropic of Cancer

20° N

Gulf of Mexico

MEXICO

Havana  Nassau

Mexico City

Belmopan

GUATEMALA
Guatemala
San Salvador
EL SALVADOR

BELIZE  Kingston
HONDURAS
Tegucigalpa
NICARAGUA
Managua
San José
COSTA RICA

PACIFIC OCEAN

DOMINICAN
REPUBLIC

BAHAMAS

CUBA

HAITI

JAMAICA

Santo
Domingo
Port-au-Prince

PUERTO
RICO (U.S.)

VIRGIN ISLANDS (U.S.)
ST. KITTS & NEVIS
ANTIGUA & BARBUDA
GUADELOUPE (France)
DOMINICA
MARTINIQUE (France)
ST. LUCIA
BARBADOS
ST. VINCENT &
THE GRENADINES
GRENADA
TRINIDAD & TOBAGO

Tropic of Cancer

20° N

Caribbean Sea

Panama

PANAMA

Caracas  Georgetown
VENEZUELA
GUYANA
SURINAME

Paramaribo
Cayenne
FRENCH GUIANA (France)

Bogotá

COLOMBIA

0°  Equator

GALÁPAGOS
ISLANDS
(Ecuador)

Quito

ECUADOR

Equator  0°

Amazon R.

PERU

BRAZIL

São Francisco R.

N

W        E

S

Lima

La Paz
BOLIVIA

Brasília

Rio de Janeiro

20° S

Lake
Titicaca

Sucre

Parana R.

PARAGUAY

São Paulo

Tropic of Capricorn  20° S

Tropic of Capricorn

CHILE

Asunción

KEY

—— National border
⊛ National capital
• Other city

Santiago

Buenos Aires

ARGENTINA

URUGUAY

Montevideo
Río de la
Plata

0 miles                    2,000

0 kilometers            2,000

Lambert Azimuthal Equal Area

ATLANTIC OCEAN

FALKLAND ISLANDS (U.K.)

Tierra del Fuego
Cape Horn

160° W    140° W    120° W    100° W    80° W    60° W    40° W    20° W    0°

60° S

# North and South America: Physical

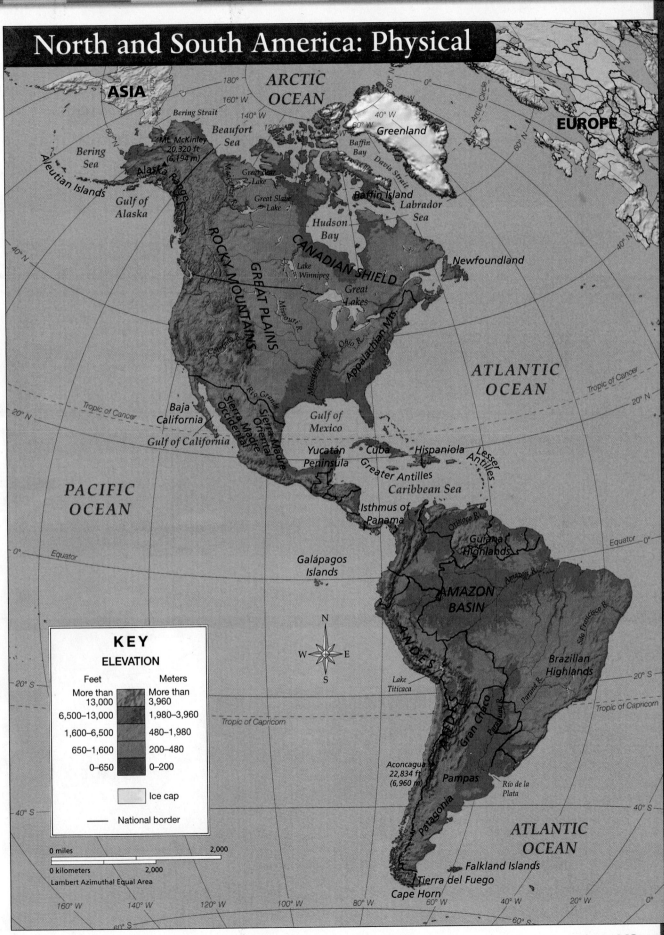

ASIA

ARCTIC OCEAN

EUROPE

Bering Strait

Beaufort Sea

Mt. McKinley 20,320 ft (6,194 m)

Bering Sea

Aleutian Islands

Alaska Range

Gulf of Alaska

Greenland

40° W

60° W

Baffin Bay

Davis Strait

Baffin Island

Labrador Sea

Great Bear Lake

Mackenzie R.

Great Slave Lake

Hudson Bay

CANADIAN SHIELD

Newfoundland

ROCKY MOUNTAINS

GREAT PLAINS

Lake Winnipeg

Great Lakes

Missouri R.

Mississippi R.

Ohio R.

Appalachian Mts.

Columbia R.

ATLANTIC OCEAN

Tropic of Cancer

Baja California

Sierra Madre Occidental

Sierra Madre Oriental

Rio Grande

Gulf of Mexico

Gulf of California

Yucatán Peninsula

Cuba

Hispaniola

Greater Antilles

Lesser Antilles

Caribbean Sea

Isthmus of Panama

PACIFIC OCEAN

Galápagos Islands

Equator

Guiana Highlands

Orinoco R.

Amazon R.

AMAZON BASIN

ANDES

São Francisco R.

Brazilian Highlands

Lake Titicaca

Gran Chaco

Pilcomayo R.

Paraguay R.

Paraná R.

Tropic of Capricorn

## KEY

### ELEVATION

| Feet | Meters |
|---|---|
| More than 13,000 | More than 3,960 |
| 6,500–13,000 | 1,980–3,960 |
| 1,600–6,500 | 480–1,980 |
| 650–1,600 | 200–480 |
| 0–650 | 0–200 |

Ice cap

National border

0 miles 2,000

0 kilometers 2,000

Lambert Azimuthal Equal Area

N W E S

Aconcagua 22,834 ft (6,960 m)

Pampas

Río de la Plata

Patagonia

ATLANTIC OCEAN

Falkland Islands

Tierra del Fuego

Cape Horn

# United States: Political

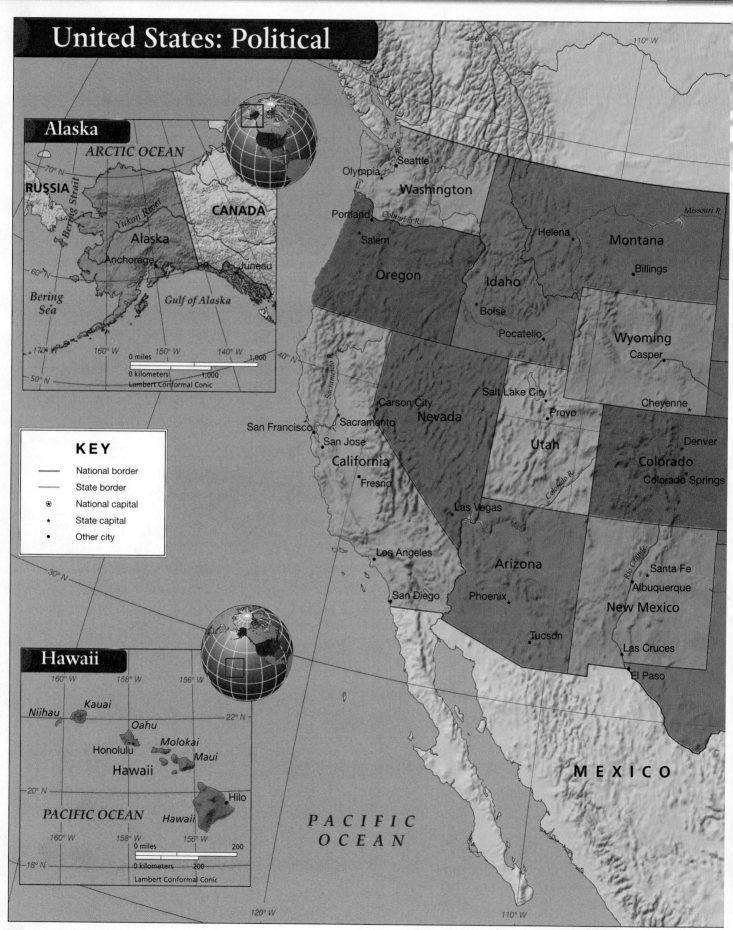

**Alaska**

ARCTIC OCEAN

RUSSIA

70° N

Bering Strait

Yukon River

CANADA

Alaska

60° N

Anchorage

Juneau

Bering
Sea

Gulf of Alaska

170° W   160° W   150° W   140° W

0 miles                    1,000
0 kilometers               1,000

Lambert Conformal Conic

Arctic Circle

50° N

40° N

## KEY

— National border

— State border

⊛ National capital

★ State capital

• Other city

30° N

**Hawaii**

160° W    158° W    156° W

Niihau    Kauai

Oahu

Honolulu    Molokai

Maui

Hawaii

Hilo

PACIFIC OCEAN    Hawaii

160° W    158° W    156° W

0 miles                200
0 kilometers           200

Lambert Conformal Conic

22° N

20° N

18° N

Seattle

Olympia    ★

Washington

Portland    Columbia R.

Salem    ★

Oregon

Helena    ★

Montana

Billings

Idaho

Boise

Pocatello

Missouri R.

Wyoming

Casper

110° W

Sacramento R.

San Francisco

Sacramento

Carson City

San Jose

California

Fresno

Nevada

Salt Lake City

Provo

Utah

Colorado R.

Cheyenne    ★

Denver    ★

Colorado

Colorado Springs

Los Angeles

San Diego

Las Vegas

Arizona

Phoenix    ★

Tucson

Rio Grande

Santa Fe    ★

Albuquerque

New Mexico

Las Cruces

El Paso

PACIFIC
OCEAN

MEXICO

120° W                110° W

CANADA

North Dakota
Bismarck★
Fargo•

Minnesota

South Dakota
Pierre★
Sioux Falls•

Minneapolis•
St. Paul★

*Lake Superior*

Wisconsin
*Mississippi R.*
Milwaukee•
Madison★

Michigan

*Lake Michigan*
*Lake Huron*
Grand Rapids•
Lansing★

Maine
Augusta★

Vermont
Montpelier★
Portland•

New Hampshire
Concord★

Boston•
Massachusetts

*Lake Ontario*
Albany★
New York
Buffalo•

Providence•
Hartford★
Rhode Island
Connecticut
New York City•

Nebraska
Omaha•
Lincoln•

Iowa
Des Moines★

*Missouri R.*

Chicago•
Cedar Rapids•

Fort Wayne•

Illinois
Springfield★

Indiana
Indianapolis★

Detroit•
*Lake Erie*

Cleveland•
Pittsburgh•

Columbus★
Ohio

Pennsylvania
Harrisburg★

New Jersey
Trenton★
Philadelphia•

Delaware

Baltimore•
Washington, D.C.
*Ohio R.*
Cincinnati•

West
Virginia
Charleston★

Dover★
Annapolis★
Maryland

District of Columbia

Kansas
Topeka★
Wichita•

Kansas City•
Jefferson City★
St. Louis•

Louisville•
Frankfort★
Kentucky

Richmond★
Virginia

Norfolk•

*Arkansas R.*

Missouri

Nashville•
Knoxville•

Raleigh★
North Carolina
Charlotte•

Oklahoma
Tulsa•
Oklahoma City★

Arkansas
Fort Smith•
Little Rock★

Memphis•
*Mississippi R.*

Tennessee

*Tennessee R.*

South Carolina
Columbia★
Charleston•

*Red R.*

Dallas•
Fort Worth•

Shreveport•
Louisiana

Mississippi
Jackson★

Birmingham•
Alabama
Montgomery★

Atlanta★

Georgia
Columbus•

Savannah•

ATLANTIC
OCEAN

Texas

Austin★
San Antonio•

Houston•

Baton Rouge★
Gulfport•
New Orleans•

Mobile•

Tallahassee★

Jacksonville•

Florida

Orlando•
Tampa•

*Gulf of Mexico*

N
W   E
S

Miami•

0 miles        250
0 kilometers   250
Lambert Azimuthal Equal Area

100° W
90° W
80° W
70° W
50° N
40° N
30° N

# Europe: Political

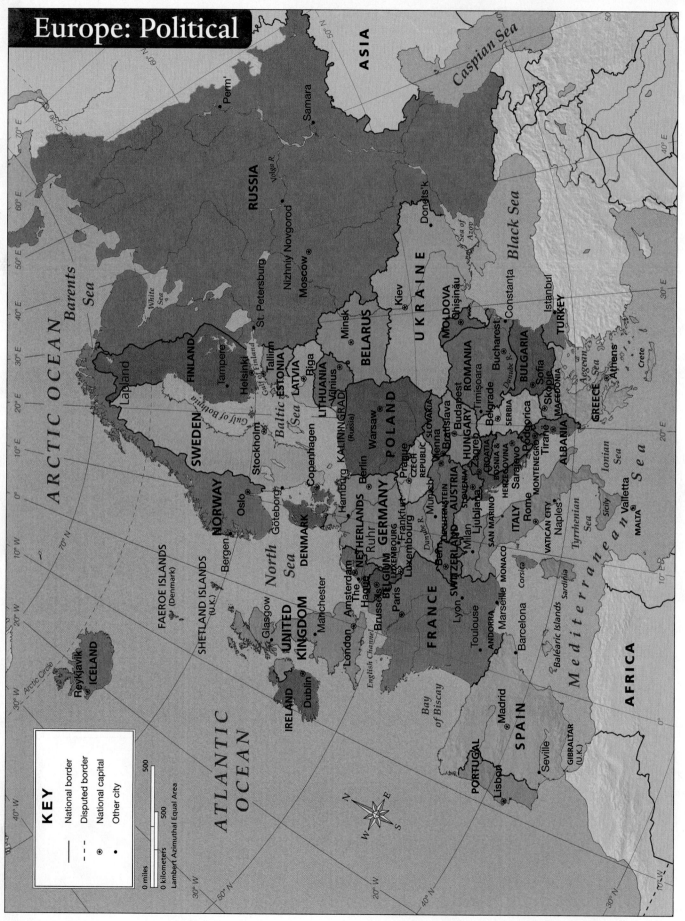

ASIA

*Caspian Sea*

Perm'

Samara

RUSSIA

*Volga R.*

Nizhniy Novgorod

Moscow

Donets'k

Sea of Azov

*Black Sea*

Kiev

UKRAINE

MOLDOVA

Chişinău

Constanța

Istanbul

TURKEY

St. Petersburg

Minsk

BELARUS

BULGARIA

Sofia

ROMANIA

Bucharest

Belgrade

SERBIA

Podgorica

Skopje

MACEDONIA

ALBANIA

Tirane

GREECE

Athens

Crete

*Aegean Sea*

White Sea

*Barents Sea*

ARCTIC OCEAN

FINLAND

Tampere

Helsinki

Tallinn

ESTONIA

Riga

LATVIA

LITHUANIA

Vilnius

Lapland

Gulf of Finland

Gulf of Bothnia

SWEDEN

Stockholm

*Baltic Sea*

KALININGRAD (Russia)

Warsaw

POLAND

SLOVAKIA

Bratislava

Budapest

HUNGARY

ROMANIA

Timişoara

CROATIA

Zagreb

BOSNIA & HERZEGOVINA

Sarajevo

MONTENEGRO

*Danube R.*

NORWAY

Oslo

Bergen

North Sea

DENMARK

Copenhagen

Hamburg

Berlin

GERMANY

Prague

CZECH REPUBLIC

Vienna

AUSTRIA

LIECHTENSTEIN

SLOVENIA

Ljubljana

Milan

SAN MARINO

ITALY

Rome

VATICAN CITY

Naples

*Tyrrhenian Sea*

Sicily

Valletta

MALTA

FAEROE ISLANDS (Denmark)

SHETLAND ISLANDS (U.K.)

Glasgow

UNITED KINGDOM

Manchester

London

Amsterdam

NETHERLANDS

The Hague

Brussels

BELGIUM

LUXEMBOURG

Luxembourg

Paris

FRANCE

Lyon

SWITZERLAND

Bern

MONACO

Marseille

Toulouse

ANDORRA

Corsica

Sardinia

*Balearic Islands*

Barcelona

*Ionian Sea*

*Mediterranean Sea*

Ruhr

Frankfurt

Munich

Göteborg

English Channel

ICELAND

Reykjavík

IRELAND

Dublin

Arctic Circle

*Bay of Biscay*

ATLANTIC OCEAN

SPAIN

Madrid

Seville

GIBRALTAR (U.K.)

PORTUGAL

Lisbon

AFRICA

## KEY

— National border

- - - Disputed border

⊛ National capital

• Other city

0 miles 500

0 kilometers 500

Lambert Azimuthal Equal Area

N E S W

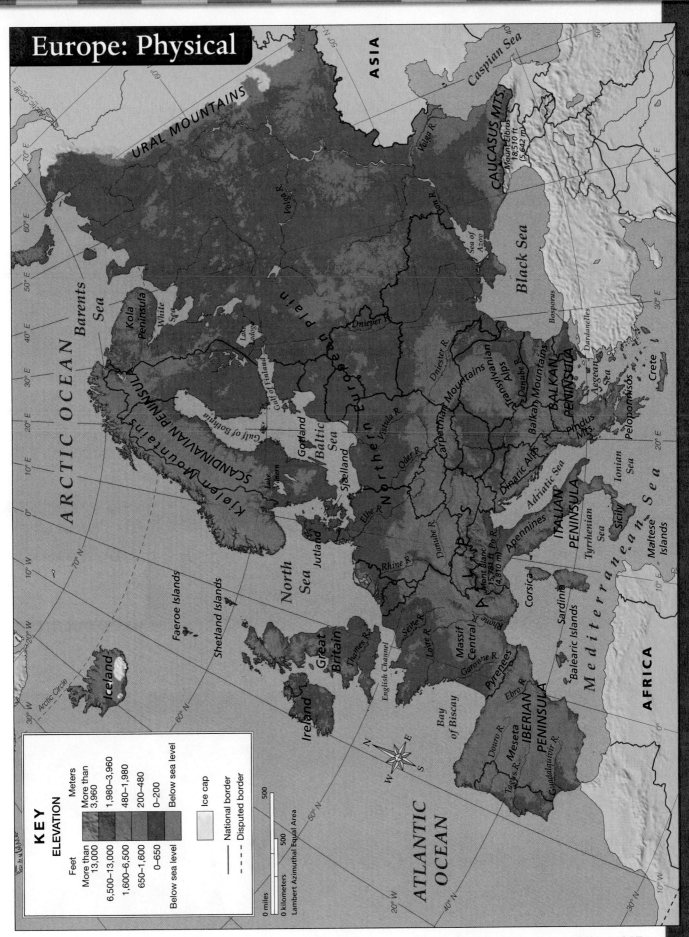

# Europe: Physical

ASIA

URAL MOUNTAINS

Caspian Sea

CAUCASUS MTS.
Mount Elbrus
18,510 ft
(5,642 m)

Volga R.

Don R.

Sea of Azov

Black Sea

Northern European Plain

Dnieper

Dniester R.

Bosporus

Barents Sea

White Sea

Kola Peninsula

Lake Ladoga

Carpathian Mountains

Transylvanian Alps

Danube

Balkan Mountains

BALKAN PENINSULA

Dardanelles

ARCTIC OCEAN

SCANDINAVIAN PENINSULA

Kjølen Mountains

Gulf of Bothnia

Gulf of Finland

Gotland

Baltic Sea

Vistula R.

Oder R.

Dinaric Alps

Adriatic Sea

Pindus Mts.

Aegean Sea

Peloponnisos

Crete

Lake Vänern

Sjælland

Elbe R.

Danube R.

Apennines

ITALIAN PENINSULA

Tyrrhenian Sea

Sicily

Ionian Sea

Maltese Islands

North Sea

Jutland

Rhine R.

Mont Blanc
15,781 ft
(4,810 m)

Corsica

Sardinia

Mediterranean Sea

Great Britain

Thames R.

English Channel

Seine R.

Loire R.

Massif Central

Rhône R.

Garonne R.

Pyrenees

Balearic Islands

Ireland

Bay of Biscay

Ebro R.

IBERIAN PENINSULA

Douro R.

Meseta

Tagus R.

Guadalquivir R.

Faeroe Islands

Shetland Islands

Iceland

Arctic Circle

ATLANTIC OCEAN

AFRICA

## KEY

### ELEVATION

| Feet | Meters |
|---|---|
| More than 13,000 | More than 3,960 |
| 6,500–13,000 | 1,980–3,960 |
| 1,600–6,500 | 480–1,980 |
| 650–1,600 | 200–480 |
| 0–650 | 0–200 |
| Below sea level | Below sea level |

Ice cap

National border

Disputed border

0 miles 500
0 kilometers 500
Lambert Azimuthal Equal Area

N E S W

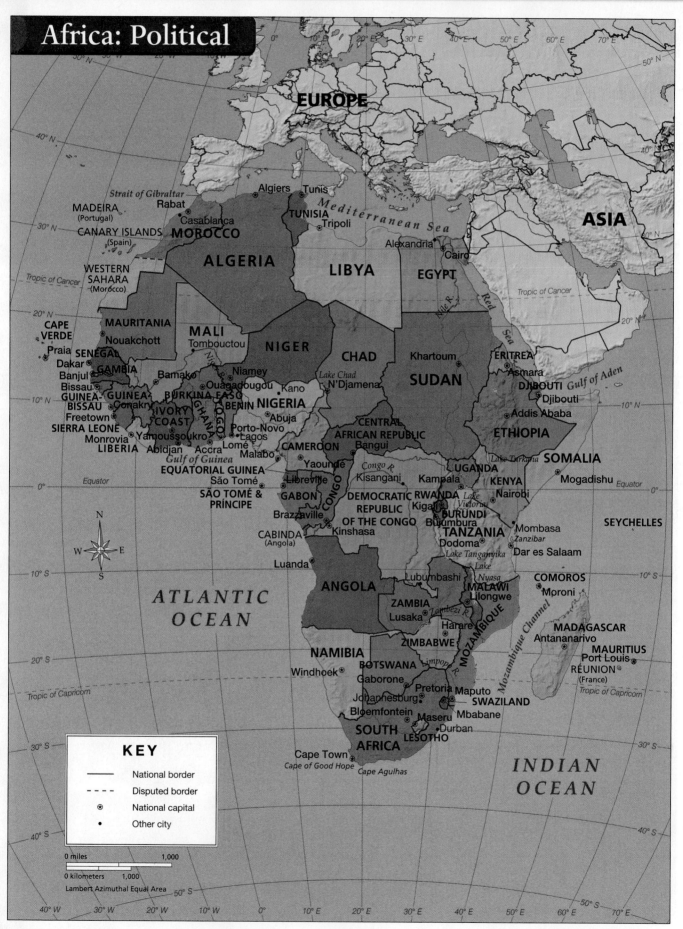

# Africa: Political

EUROPE

ASIA

*Mediterranean Sea*

Strait of Gibraltar
MADEIRA
(Portugal)
Rabat
CANARY ISLANDS
(Spain)
MOROCCO
Casablanca
Algiers · Tunis
TUNISIA
Tripoli
Alexandria
Cairo

WESTERN
SAHARA
(Morocco)
ALGERIA
LIBYA
EGYPT

*Tropic of Cancer*

CAPE
VERDE
Praia
MAURITANIA
Nouakchott
MALI
Tombouctou
NIGER
Niamey
CHAD
Khartoum
SUDAN
ERITREA
Asmara
DJIBOUTI  *Gulf of Aden*
Djibouti

SENEGAL
Dakar
GAMBIA
Banjul
Bissau
GUINEA-
BISSAU
Bamako
Ouagadougou
Kano
N'Djamena
Lake Chad
*Red Sea*

Conakry
GUINEA
Freetown
SIERRA LEONE
Monrovia
LIBERIA
BURKINA FASO
IVORY
COAST
Yamoussoukro
Abidjan
GHANA
TOGO
BENIN
Accra
Lomé
Porto-Novo
Lagos
NIGERIA
Abuja
CENTRAL
AFRICAN REPUBLIC
Bangui
Addis Ababa
ETHIOPIA
SOMALIA

*Gulf of Guinea*
Malabo
CAMEROON
Yaoundé
*Congo R.*
Kisangani
UGANDA
Kampala
Lake Turkana
Mogadishu
*Equator*

EQUATORIAL GUINEA
São Tomé
SÃO TOMÉ &
PRÍNCIPE
Libreville
GABON
Brazzaville
CONGO
DEMOCRATIC
REPUBLIC
OF THE CONGO
Kinshasa
RWANDA
Kigali
BURUNDI
Bujumbura
Lake
Victoria
KENYA
Nairobi
SEYCHELLES

CABINDA
(Angola)
TANZANIA
Dodoma
Mombasa
Zanzibar
Dar es Salaam

Luanda
Lubumbashi
*Lake Tanganyika*
*Lake Nyasa*
COMOROS
Moroni

ANGOLA
ZAMBIA
Lusaka
MALAWI
Lilongwe
MADAGASCAR
Antananarivo
MAURITIUS
Port Louis
RÉUNION
(France)

Harare
ZIMBABWE
*Zambezi R.*
MOZAMBIQUE
*Mozambique Channel*

NAMIBIA
Windhoek
BOTSWANA
Gaborone
*Limpopo R.*

*ATLANTIC
OCEAN*

Pretoria
Johannesburg
Bloemfontein
Maputo
SWAZILAND
Mbabane
Maseru
Durban
LESOTHO
SOUTH
AFRICA
Cape Town
Cape of Good Hope
Cape Agulhas

*INDIAN
OCEAN*

## KEY

| | |
|---|---|
| —— | National border |
| - - - | Disputed border |
| ⊛ | National capital |
| • | Other city |

0 miles 1,000
0 kilometers 1,000
Lambert Azimuthal Equal Area

# Africa: Physical

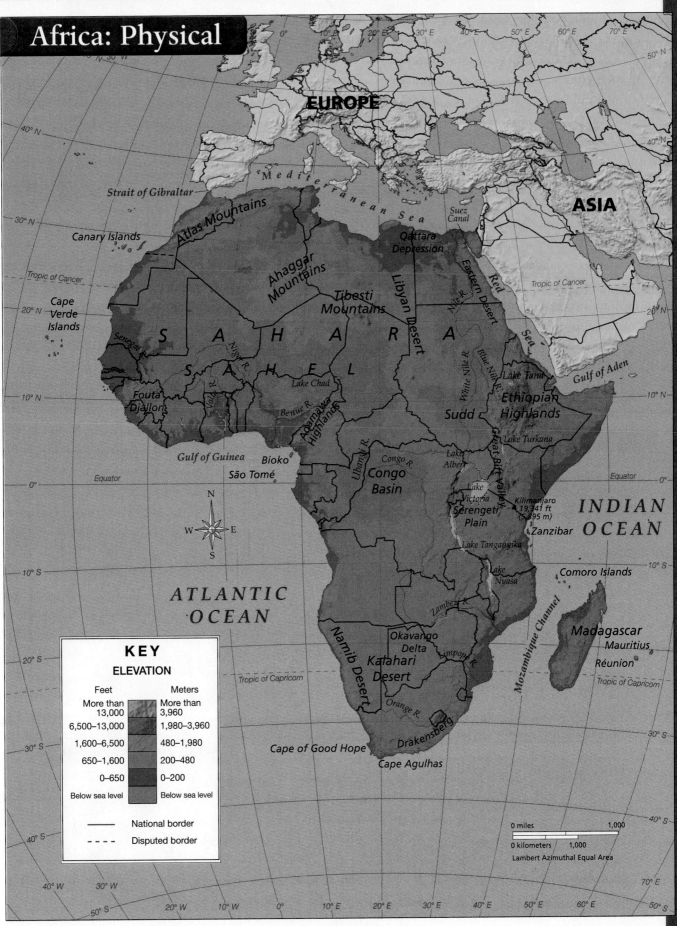

EUROPE

ASIA

Strait of Gibraltar

Mediterranean Sea

Suez Canal

Canary Islands

Atlas Mountains

Qattara Depression

Tropic of Cancer

Cape Verde Islands

Ahaggar Mountains

Tibesti Mountains

Libyan Desert

Red Sea

Eastern Desert

Nile R.

Tropic of Cancer

S A H A R A

Senegal

Niger R.

Lake Chad

White Nile R.

Blue Nile R.

Lake Tana

Gulf of Aden

S A H E L

Fouta Djallon

Volta R.

Benue R.

Adamawa Highlands

Sudd

Ethiopian Highlands

Gulf of Guinea

Bioko

São Tomé

Ubangi R.

Congo R.

Congo Basin

Lake Albert

Lake Victoria

Lake Turkana

Great Rift Valley

Equator

Serengeti Plain

Kilimanjaro 19,341 ft (5,895 m)

Zanzibar

INDIAN OCEAN

Equator

Lake Tanganyika

Lake Nyasa

Comoro Islands

ATLANTIC OCEAN

Zambezi R.

Madagascar

Mauritius

Réunion

Okavango Delta

Limpopo R.

Namib Desert

Kalahari Desert

Mozambique Channel

Tropic of Capricorn

Orange R.

Drakensberg

Tropic of Capricorn

Cape of Good Hope

Cape Agulhas

## KEY
### ELEVATION

| Feet | Meters |
|---|---|
| More than 13,000 | More than 3,960 |
| 6,500–13,000 | 1,980–3,960 |
| 1,600–6,500 | 480–1,980 |
| 650–1,600 | 200–480 |
| 0–650 | 0–200 |
| Below sea level | Below sea level |

—— National border

- - - Disputed border

0 miles 1,000

0 kilometers 1,000

Lambert Azimuthal Equal Area

# Asia: Political

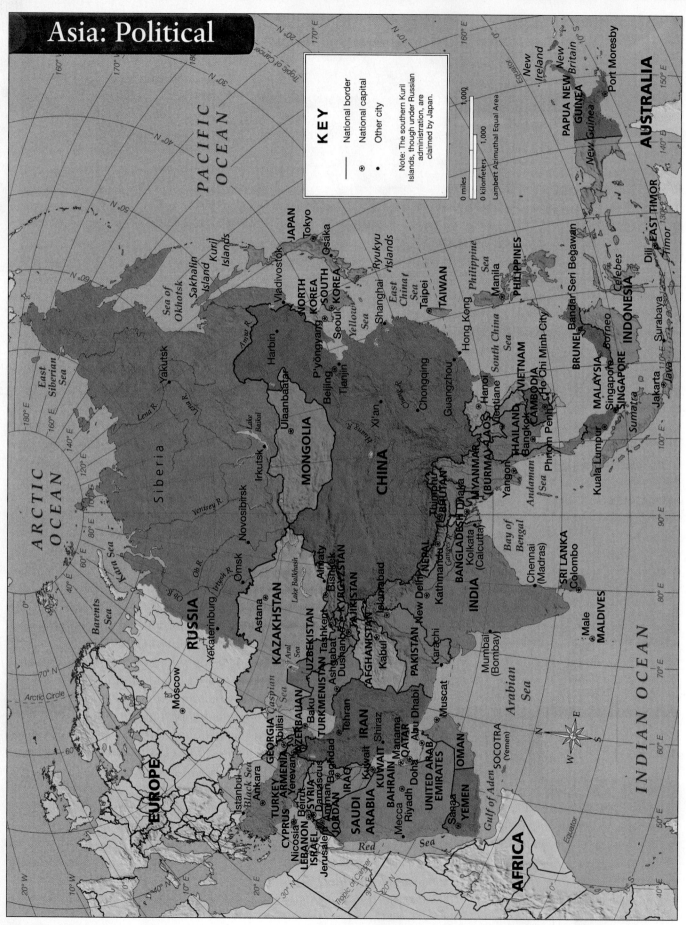

KEY

— National border
⊛ National capital
• Other city

Note: The southern Kuril Islands, though under Russian administration, are claimed by Japan.

1,000

0 miles 1,000
0 kilometers
Lambert Azimuthal Equal Area

ARCTIC OCEAN

PACIFIC OCEAN

Arctic Circle

EUROPE

Barents Sea

Kara Sea

East Siberian Sea

Sea of Okhotsk

Sakhalin Island

Kuril Islands

JAPAN
Tokyo
Osaka

Vladivostok

NORTH KOREA
P'yŏngyang
SOUTH KOREA
Seoul

Ryukyu Islands

East China Sea

Yellow Sea

Shanghai

TAIWAN
Taipei

Philippine Sea

PHILIPPINES
Manila

New Ireland
New Britain
Port Moresby
PAPUA NEW GUINEA
New Guinea

AUSTRALIA

Moscow

RUSSIA

Siberia

Lena R.

Lena R.

Yenisey R.

Novosibirsk

Omsk

Yekaterinburg

Ob R.

Irtysh R.

Astana

Lake Balkhash

KAZAKHSTAN

Aral Sea

Caspian Sea

Black Sea

Istanbul
Ankara
TURKEY
CYPRUS
Nicosia
LEBANON Beirut
ISRAEL Damascus
Jerusalem Amman
JORDAN
SYRIA
Baghdad
IRAQ
SAUDI ARABIA
Mecca
Riyadh
BAHRAIN
QATAR
Doha
UNITED ARAB EMIRATES
Abu Dhabi
Sanaa
YEMEN
OMAN
Muscat
SOCOTRA (Yemen)
Gulf of Aden
Red Sea

GEORGIA
Tbilisi
ARMENIA
Yerevan
AZERBAIJAN
Baku
Tehran
IRAN
Shiraz
KUWAIT
Kuwait
Mariana

TURKMENISTAN
Ashgabat
UZBEKISTAN
Tashkent
Dushanbe
TAJIKISTAN
KYRGYZSTAN
Bishkek
Almaty

AFGHANISTAN
Kabul

PAKISTAN
Islamabad
Karachi

Irkutsk

Lake Baikal

Ulaanbaatar

MONGOLIA

Harbin

Amur R.

Beijing
Tianjin

CHINA

Xi'an

Chang R.

Huang R.

Chongqing

Guangzhou

Hong Kong

South China Sea

VIETNAM
Hanoi
LAOS
Vientiane
THAILAND
Bangkok
CAMBODIA
Phnom Penh
Ho Chi Minh City

MYANMAR (BURMA)
Yangon

Andaman Sea

BRUNEI
Bandar Seri Begawan

MALAYSIA
Kuala Lumpur
SINGAPORE
Singapore

Borneo

Celebes

INDONESIA

Sumatra

Java
Jakarta
Surabaya

Dili
EAST TIMOR
Timor

NEPAL
Kathmandu

BHUTAN
Thimphu

BANGLADESH
Dhaka

Kolkata (Calcutta)

INDIA

New Delhi

Ganges R.

Mumbai (Bombay)

Chennai (Madras)

Bay of Bengal

SRI LANKA
Colombo

Male
MALDIVES

Arabian Sea

INDIAN OCEAN

AFRICA

Tropic of Cancer

Equator

Tropic of Cancer

N
E
S
W

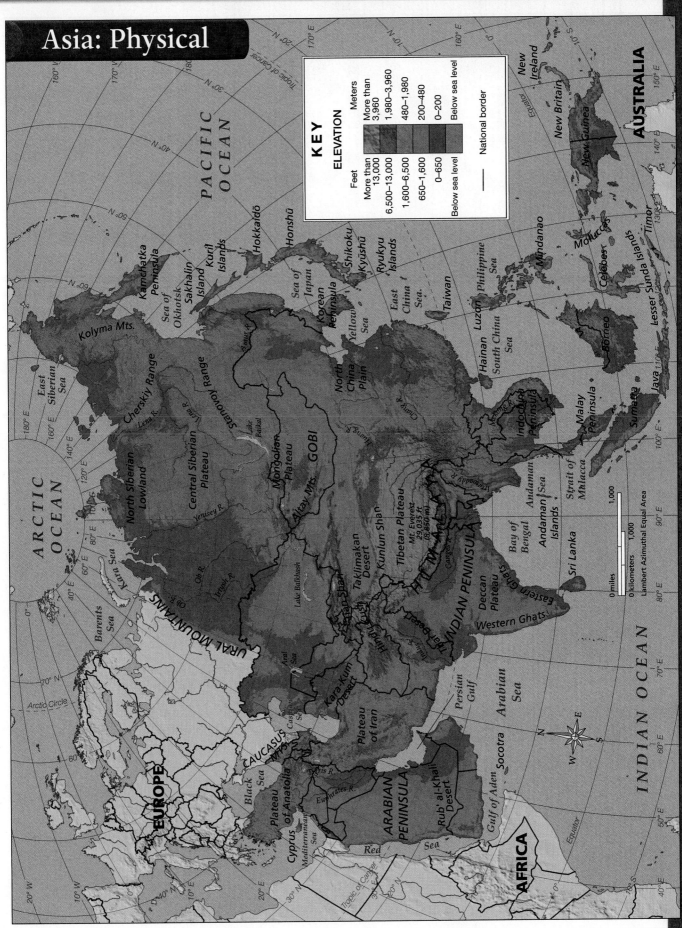

# Asia: Physical

**KEY**

**ELEVATION**

| Feet | Meters |
|------|--------|
| More than 13,000 | More than 3,960 |
| 6,500–13,000 | 1,980–3,960 |
| 1,600–6,500 | 480–1,980 |
| 650–1,600 | 200–480 |
| 0–650 | 0–200 |
| Below sea level | Below sea level |

— National border

**PACIFIC OCEAN**

**ARCTIC OCEAN**

**INDIAN OCEAN**

**EUROPE**

**AFRICA**

**AUSTRALIA**

Tropic of Cancer

East Siberian Sea

Kolyma Mts.

Kamchatka Peninsula

Sea of Okhotsk

Sakhalin Island

Kuril Islands

Hokkaidō

Honshū

Sea of Japan

Shikoku

Kyūshū

Ryukyu Islands

Korean Peninsula

Yellow Sea

East China Sea

Taiwan

Luzon

Philippine Sea

Mindanao

New Ireland

New Britain

New Guinea

Moluccas

Celebes

Timor

Lesser Sunda Islands

Java

Sumatra

Borneo

Malay Peninsula

Hainan

South China Sea

North China Plain

Cherskiy Range

Chang R.

Huang R.

Amur R.

Lena R.

Stanovoy Range

Lake Baikal

Mongolian Plateau

GOBI

Altay Mts.

North Siberian Lowland

Central Siberian Plateau

Yenisey R.

Ob R.

Irtysh R.

Lake Balkhash

Tian Shan

Taklimakan Desert

Kunlun Shan

Tibetan Plateau

Mt. Everest 29,035 ft (8,850 m)

HIMALAYA

Ganges R.

Brahmaputra R.

Irrawaddy R.

Indochina Peninsula

Mekong R.

Strait of Malacca

Andaman Sea

Andaman Islands

Bay of Bengal

Sri Lanka

Eastern Ghats

Western Ghats

Deccan Plateau

INDIAN PENINSULA

Indus R.

Thar Desert

Hindu Kush

Kara-Kum Desert

Aral Sea

Plateau of Iran

Persian Gulf

Arabian Sea

Gulf of Aden

Socotra

ARABIAN PENINSULA

Rub' al-Khali Desert

Red Sea

Euphrates R.

Tigris R.

Caspian Sea

CAUCASUS MTS.

Plateau of Anatolia

Black Sea

Mediterranean Sea

Cyprus

URAL MOUNTAINS

Ob R.

Kara Sea

Barents Sea

Arctic Circle

Tropic of Cancer

Equator

Lambert Azimuthal Equal Area

0 miles 1,000

0 kilometers 1,000

N E W S

# Oceania

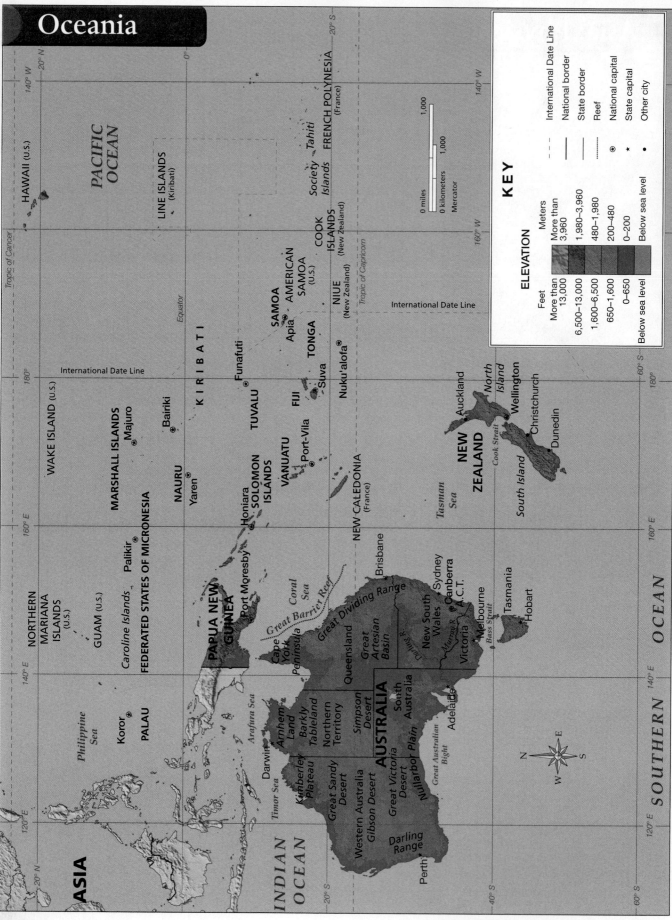

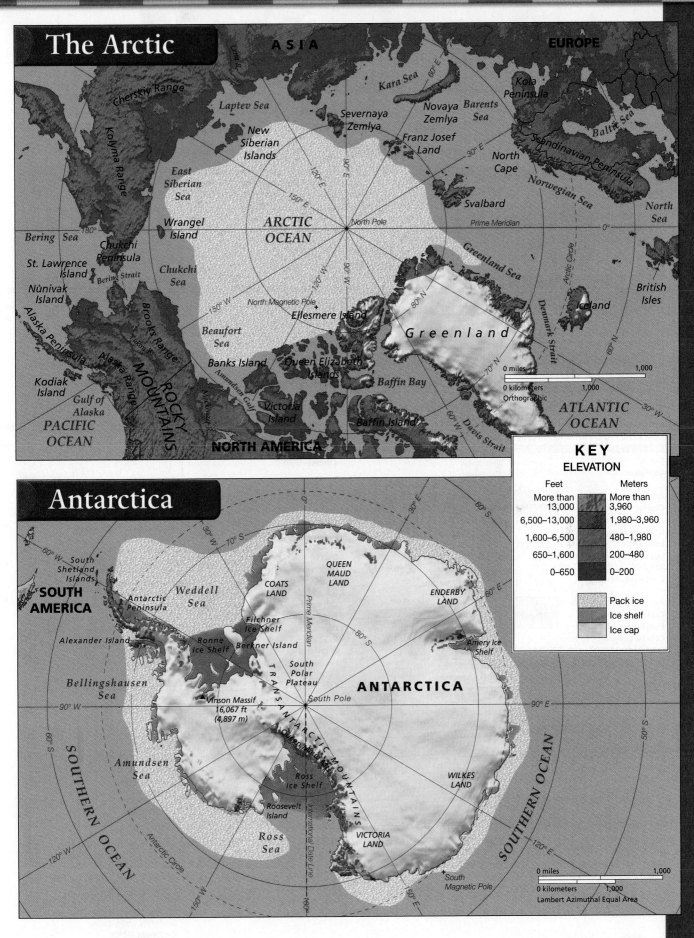

# The Arctic

ASIA   EUROPE

Cherskiy Range
Kolyma Range
Laptev Sea
New Siberian Islands
Severnaya Zemlya
Kara Sea   60° E
Novaya Zemlya
Barents Sea
Kola Peninsula
Baltic Sea
Franz Josef Land
Scandinavian Peninsula
30° E
North Cape
East Siberian Sea
Svalbard
150° E
120° E
90° E
ARCTIC OCEAN
North Pole
Norwegian Sea
Prime Meridian   0°
North Sea
Wrangel Island
Greenland Sea
Arctic Circle
Bering Sea   180°
Chukchi Peninsula
St. Lawrence Island
Chukchi Sea
Iceland
British Isles
Nùnivak Island
Bering Strait
150° W
120° W
90° W
North Magnetic Pole
Ellesmere Island
80° N
Denmark Strait
60° N
Alaska Peninsula
Brooks Range
Yukon R.
Beaufort Sea
Greenland
70° N
Kodiak Island
Alaska Range
ROCKY MOUNTAINS
Banks Island
Amundsen Gulf
Queen Elizabeth Islands
Baffin Bay
Gulf of Alaska
Mackenzie R.
Victoria Island
Baffin Island
0 miles   1,000
0 kilometers   1,000
Orthographic
PACIFIC OCEAN
Davis Strait
60° N
ATLANTIC OCEAN   30° W
NORTH AMERICA

# Antarctica

60° W
South Shetland Islands
SOUTH AMERICA
Antarctic Peninsula
Weddell Sea
30° W
COATS LAND
70° S
QUEEN MAUD LAND
Prime Meridian
30° E
60° E
ENDERBY LAND
Filchner Ice Shelf
Alexander Island
Ronne Ice Shelf
Berkner Island
80° S
Amery Ice Shelf
Bellingshausen Sea
90° W
South Polar Plateau
ANTARCTICA
90° E
Vinson Massif 16,067 ft (4,897 m)
South Pole
TRANSANTARCTIC MOUNTAINS
Amundsen Sea
Queen Maud Mts.
WILKES LAND
60° S
Ross Ice Shelf
Roosevelt Island
International Date Line
VICTORIA LAND
120° W
Ross Sea
SOUTHERN OCEAN
Antarctic Circle
South Magnetic Pole
SOUTHERN OCEAN
150° E
120° E
50° S
0 miles   1,000
0 kilometers   1,000
Lambert Azimuthal Equal Area
160°

## KEY
### ELEVATION

| Feet | | Meters |
|---|---|---|
| More than 13,000 | | More than 3,960 |
| 6,500–13,000 | | 1,980–3,960 |
| 1,600–6,500 | | 480–1,980 |
| 650–1,600 | | 200–480 |
| 0–650 | | 0–200 |

Pack ice
Ice shelf
Ice cap

# Country Databank

## Africa

### Algeria
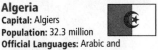
**Capital:** Algiers
**Population:** 32.3 million
**Official Languages:** Arabic and Tamazight
**Land Area:** 2,381,740 sq km; 919,590 sq mi
**Leading Exports:** petroleum, natural gas, petroleum products
**Continent:** Africa

### Angola
**Capital:** Luanda
**Population:** 10.6 million
**Official Language:** Portuguese
**Land Area:** 1,246,700 sq km; 481,551 sq mi
**Leading Exports:** crude oil, diamonds, refined petroleum products, gas, coffee, sisal, fish and fish products, timber, cotton
**Continent:** Africa

### Benin
**Capital:** Porto-Novo
**Population:** 6.9 million
**Official Language:** French
**Land Area:** 110,620 sq km; 42,710 sq mi
**Leading Exports:** cotton, crude oil, palm products, cocoa
**Continent:** Africa

### Botswana
**Capital:** Gaborone
**Population:** 1.6 million
**Official Language:** English
**Land Area:** 585,370 sq km; 226,011 sq mi
**Leading Exports:** diamonds, copper, nickel, soda ash, meat, textiles
**Continent:** Africa

### Burkina Faso
**Capital:** Ouagadougou
**Population:** 12.6 million
**Official Language:** French
**Land Area:** 273,800 sq km; 105,714 sq mi
**Leading Exports:** cotton, animal products, gold
**Continent:** Africa

### Burundi

**Capital:** Bujumbura
**Population:** 6.4 million
**Official Languages:** Kirundi and French
**Land Area:** 25,650 sq km; 9,903 sq mi
**Leading Exports:** coffee, tea, sugar, cotton, hides
**Continent:** Africa

### Cameroon
**Capital:** Yaoundé
**Population:** 16.1 million
**Official Languages:** English and French
**Land Area:** 469,440 sq km; 181,251 sqmi
**Leading Exports:** crude oil and petroleum products, lumber, cocoa, aluminum, coffee, cotton
**Continent:** Africa

### Cape Verde
**Capital:** Praia
**Population:** 408,760
**Official Language:** Portuguese
**Land Area:** 4,033 sq km; 1,557 sq mi
**Leading Exports:** fuel, shoes, garments, fish, hides
**Location:** Atlantic Ocean

### Central African Republic

**Capital:** Bangui
**Population:** 3.6 million
**Official Language:** French
**Land Area:** 622,984 sq km; 240,534 sq mi
**Leading Exports:** diamonds, timber, cotton, coffee, tobacco
**Continent:** Africa

### Chad

**Capital:** N'Djamena
**Population:** 9 million
**Official Languages:** Arabic and French
**Land Area:** 1,259,200 sq km; 486,177 sq mi
**Leading Exports:** cotton, cattle, gum arabic
**Continent:** Africa

### Comoros

**Capital:** Moroni
**Population:** 614,382
**Official Languages:** Arabic, Comoran, and French
**Land Area:** 2,170 sq km; 838 sq mi
**Leading Exports:** vanilla, ylang-ylang, cloves, perfume oil, copra
**Location:** Indian Ocean

### Congo, Democratic Republic of the

**Capital:** Kinshasa
**Population:** 55.2 million
**Official Language:** French
**Land Area:** 2,267,600 sq km; 875,520 sq mi
**Leading Exports:** diamonds, copper, coffee, cobalt, crude oil
**Continent:** Africa

### Congo, Republic of the

**Capital:** Brazzaville
**Population:** 3.3 million
**Official Language:** French
**Land Area:** 341,500 sq km; 131,853 sq mi
**Leading Exports:** petroleum, lumber, sugar, cocoa, coffee, diamonds
**Continent:** Africa

### Djibouti

**Capital:** Djibouti
**Population:** 472,810
**Official Languages:** Arabic and French
**Land Area:** 22,980 sq km; 8,873 sq mi
**Leading Exports:** reexports, hides and skins, coffee (in transit)
**Continent:** Africa

### Egypt

**Capital:** Cairo
**Population:** 70.7 million
**Official Language:** Arabic
**Land Area:** 995,450 sq km; 384,343 sq mi
**Leading Exports:** crude oil and petroleum products, cotton, textiles, metal products, chemicals
**Continent:** Africa

### Equatorial Guinea
**Capital:** Malabo
**Population:** 498,144
**Official Languages:** Spanish and French
**Land Area:** 28,050 sq km; 10,830 sq mi
**Leading Exports:** petroleum, timber, cocoa
**Continent:** Africa

### Eritrea
**Capital:** Asmara
**Population:** 4.5 million
**Official Language:** Tigrinya
**Land Area:** 121,320 sq km; 46,842 sq mi
**Leading Exports:** livestock, sorghum, textiles, food, small manufactured goods
**Continent:** Africa

### Ethiopia

**Capital:** Addis Ababa
**Population:** 67.7 million
**Official Language:** Amharic
**Land Area:** 1,119,683 sq km; 432,310 sq mi
**Leading Exports:** coffee, qat, gold, leather products, oilseeds
**Continent:** Africa

### Gabon
**Capital:** Libreville
**Population:** 1.2 million
**Official Language:** French
**Land Area:** 257,667 sq km; 99,489 sq mi
**Leading Exports:** crude oil, timber, manganese, uranium
**Continent:** Africa

### Gambia
**Capital:** Banjul
**Population:** 1.5 million
**Official Language:** English
**Land Area:** 10,000 sq km; 3,861 sq mi
**Leading Exports:** peanuts and peanut products, fish, cotton lint, palm kernels
**Continent:** Africa

### Ghana
**Capital:** Accra
**Population:** 20.2 million
**Official Language:** English
**Land Area:** 230,940 sq km; 89,166 sq mi
**Leading Exports:** gold, cocoa, timber, tuna, bauxite, aluminum, manganese ore, diamonds
**Continent:** Africa

### Guinea
**Capital:** Conakry
**Population:** 7.8 million
**Official Language:** French
**Land Area:** 245,857 sq km; 94,925 sq mi
**Leading Exports:** bauxite, alumina, gold, diamonds, coffee, fish, agricultural products
**Continent:** Africa

### Guinea-Bissau

**Capital:** Bissau
**Population:** 1.4 million
**Official Language:** Portuguese
**Land Area:** 28,000 sq km; 10,811 sq mi
**Leading Exports:** cashew nuts, shrimp, peanuts, palm kernels, lumber
**Continent:** Africa

### Ivory Coast
**Capital:** Yamoussoukro
**Population:** 16.8 million
**Official Language:** French
**Land Area:** 318,000 sq km; 122,780 sq mi
**Leading Exports:** cocoa, coffee, timber, petroleum, cotton, bananas, pineapples, palm oil, cotton, fish
**Continent:** Africa

### Kenya

**Capital:** Nairobi
**Population:** 31.3 million
**Official Languages:** Swahili and English
**Land Area:** 569,250 sq km; 219,787 sq mi
**Leading Exports:** tea, horticultural products, coffee, petroleum products, fish, cement
**Continent:** Africa

### Lesotho
**Capital:** Maseru
**Population:** 2.2 million
**Official Languages:** Sesotho and English
**Land Area:** 30,355 sq km; 11,720 sq mi
**Leading Exports:** manufactured goods (clothing, footwear, road vehicles), wool and mohair, food and live animals
**Continent:** Africa

### Liberia

**Capital:** Monrovia
**Population:** 3.3 million
**Official Language:** English
**Land Area:** 96,320 sq km; 37,189 sq mi
**Leading Exports:** rubber, timber, iron, diamonds, cocoa, coffee
**Continent:** Africa

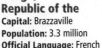

## Libya
**Capital:** Tripoli
**Population:** 5.4 million
**Official Language:** Arabic
**Land Area:** 1,759,540 sq km; 679,358 sq mi
**Leading Exports:** crude oil, refined petroleum products
**Location:** Indian

## Madagascar

**Capital:** Antananarivo
**Population:** 16.5 million
**Official Languages:** French and Malagasy
**Land Area:** 581,540 sq km; 224,533 sq mi
**Leading Exports:** coffee, vanilla, shellfish, sugar, cotton cloth, chromite, petroleum products
**Location:** Indian Ocean

## Malawi

**Capital:** Lilongwe
**Population:** 10.7 million
**Official Languages:** English and Chichewa
**Land Area:** 94,080 sq km; 36,324 sq mi
**Leading Exports:** tobacco, tea, sugar, cotton, coffee, peanuts, wood products, apparel
**Continent:** Africa

## Mali
**Capital:** Bamako
**Population:** 11.3 million
**Official Language:** French
**Land Area:** 1,220,000 sq km; 471,042 sq mi
**Leading Exports:** cotton, gold, livestock
**Continent:** Africa

## Mauritania
**Capital:** Nouakchott
**Population:** 2.8 million
**Official Language:** Arabic
**Land Area:** 1,030,400 sq km; 397,837 sq mi
**Leading Exports:** iron ore, fish and fish products, gold
**Continent:** Africa

## Mauritius
**Capital:** Port Louis
**Population:** 1.2 million
**Official Language:** English
**Land Area:** 2,030 sq km; 784 sq mi
**Leading Exports:** clothing and textiles, sugar, cut flowers, molasses
**Location:** Indian Ocean

## Morocco
**Capital:** Rabat
**Population:** 31.2 million
**Official Language:** Arabic
**Land Area:** 446,300 sq km; 172,316 sq mi
**Leading Exports:** phosphates and fertilizers, food and beverages, minerals
**Continent:** Africa

## Mozambique

**Capital:** Maputo
**Population:** 19.6 million
**Official Language:** Portuguese
**Land Area:** 784,090 sq km; 302,737 sq mi
**Leading Exports:** prawns, cashews, cotton, sugar, citrus, timber, bulk electricity
**Continent:** Africa

## Namibia

**Capital:** Windhoek
**Population:** 1.8 million
**Official Language:** English
**Land Area:** 825,418 sq km; 318,694 sq mi
**Leading Exports:** diamonds, copper, gold, zinc, lead, uranium, cattle, processed fish, karakul skins
**Continent:** Africa

## Niger
**Capital:** Niamey
**Population:** 11.3 million
**Official Language:** French
**Land Area:** 1,226,700 sq km; 489,073 sq mi
**Leading Exports:** uranium ore, livestock products, cowpeas, onions
**Continent:** Africa

## Nigeria
**Capital:** Abuja
**Population:** 129.9 million
**Official Language:** English
**Land Area:** 910,768 sq km; 351,648 sq mi
**Leading Exports:** petroleum and petroleum products, cocoa, rubber
**Continent:** Africa

## Rwanda
**Capital:** Kigali
**Population:** 7.4 million
**Official Languages:** Kinyarwanda, French, and English
**Land Area:** 24,948 sq km; 9,632 sq mi
**Leading Exports:** coffee, tea, hides, tin ore
**Continent:** Africa

## São Tomé and Príncipe

**Capital:** São Tomé
**Population:** 170,372
**Official Language:** Portuguese
**Land Area:** 1,001 sq km; 386 sq mi
**Leading Exports:** cocoa, copra, coffee, palm oil
**Location:** Atlantic Ocean

## Senegal
**Capital:** Dakar
**Population:** 10.6 million
**Official Language:** French
**Land Area:** 192,000 sq km; 74,131 sq mi
**Leading Exports:** fish, groundnuts (peanuts), petroleum products, phosphates, cotton
**Continent:** Africa

## Seychelles

**Capital:** Victoria
**Population:** 80,098
**Official Languages:** English and French
**Land Area:** 455 sq km; 176 sq mi
**Leading Exports:** canned tuna, cinnamon bark, copra, petroleum products (reexports)
**Location:** Indian Ocean

## Sierra Leone
**Capital:** Freetown
**Population:** 5.6 million
**Official Language:** English
**Land Area:** 71,620 sq km; 27,652 sq mi
**Leading Exports:** diamonds, rutile, cocoa, coffee, fish
**Continent:** Africa

## Somalia

**Capital:** Mogadishu
**Population:** 7.8 million
**Official Languages:** Somali and Arabic
**Land Area:** 627,337 sq km; 242,215 sq mi
**Leading Exports:** livestock, bananas, hides, fish, charcoal, scrap metal
**Continent:** Africa

## South Africa
**Capital:** Cape Town, Pretoria, and Bloemfontein
**Population:** 43.6 million
**Official Languages:** Eleven official languages: Afrikaans, English, Ndebele, Pedi, Sotho, Swazi, Tsonga, Tswana, Venda, Xhosa, and Zulu
**Land Area:** 1,219,912 sq km; 471,008 sq mi
**Leading Exports:** gold, diamonds, platinum, other metals and minerals, machinery and equipment
**Continent:** Africa

## Sudan

**Capital:** Khartoum
**Population:** 37.1 million
**Official Language:** Arabic
**Land Area:** 2,376,000 sq km; 917,374 sq mi
**Leading Exports:** oil and petroleum products, cotton, sesame, livestock, groundnuts, gum arabic, sugar
**Continent:** Africa

## Swaziland

**Capital:** Mbabane
**Population:** 1.1 million
**Official Languages:** English and siSwati
**Land Area:** 17,20 sq km; 6,642 sq mi
**Leading Exports:** soft drink concentrates, sugar, wood pulp, cotton yarn, refrigerators, citrus and canned fruit
**Continent:** Africa

## Tanzania

**Capital:** Dar es Salaam and Dodoma
**Population:** 37.2 million
**Official Languages:** Swahili and English
**Land Area:** 886,037 sq km; 342,099 sq mi
**Leading Exports:** gold, coffee, cashew nuts, manufactured goods, cotton
**Continent:** Africa

## Togo

**Capital:** Lomé
**Population:** 5.2 million
**Official Language:** French
**Land Area:** 54,385 sq km; 20,998 sq mi
**Leading Exports:** cotton, phosphates, coffee, cocoa
**Continent:** Africa

## Tunisia
**Capital:** Tunis
**Population:** 9.8 million
**Official Language:** Arabic
**Land Area:** 155,360 sq km; 59,984 sq mi
**Leading Exports:** textiles, mechanical goods, phosphates and chemicals, agricultural products, hydrocarbons
**Continent:** Africa

## Uganda
**Capital:** Kampala
**Population:** 24.7 million
**Official Language:** English
**Land Area:** 199,710 sq km; 77,108 sq mi
**Leading Exports:** coffee, fish and fish products, tea, gold, cotton, flowers, horticultural products
**Continent:** Africa

## Zambia

**Capital:** Lusaka
**Population:** 10.1 million
**Official Language:** English
**Land Area:** 740,724 sq km; 285,994 sq mi
**Leading Exports:** copper, cobalt, electricity, tobacco, flowers, cotton
**Continent:** Africa

## Zimbabwe
**Capital:** Harare
**Population:** 11.3 million
**Official Language:** English
**Land Area:** 386,670 sq km; 149,293 sq mi
**Leading Exports:** tobacco, gold, iron alloys, textiles and clothing
**Continent:** Africa

# Asia and the Pacific

## Afghanistan

**Capital:** Kabul
**Population:** 27.8 million
**Official Languages:** Pashtu and Dari
**Land Area:** 647,500 sq km;
250,000 sq mi
**Leading Exports:** agricultural products, hand-woven carpets, wool, cotton, hides and pelts, precious and semiprecious gems
**Continent:** Asia

## Armenia
**Capital:** Yerevan
**Population:** 3.3 million
**Official Language:** Armenian
**Land Area:** 29,400 sq km; 10,965 sq mi
**Leading Exports:** diamonds, scrap metal, machinery and equipment, brandy, copper ore
**Continent:** Asia

## Australia
**Capital:** Canberra
**Population:** 19.6 million
**Official Language:** English
**Land Area:** 7,617,930 sq km;
2,941,283 sq mi
**Leading Exports:** coal, gold, meat, wool, alumina, iron ore, wheat, machinery and transport equipment
**Continent:** Australia

## Azerbaijan
**Capital:** Baku
**Population:** 7.8 million
**Official Language:** Azerbaijani
**Land Area:** 86,100 sq km; 33,243 sq mi
**Leading Exports:** oil and gas, machinery, cotton, foodstuffs
**Continent:** Asia

## Bahrain
**Capital:** Manama
**Population:** 656,397
**Official Language:** Arabic
**Land Area:** 665 sq km; 257 sq mi
**Leading Exports:** petroleum and petroleum products, aluminum, textiles
**Continent:** Asia

## Bangladesh
**Capital:** Dhaka
**Population:** 133.4 million
**Official Language:** Bengali
**Land Area:** 133,910 sq km; 51,705 sq mi
**Leading Exports:** garments, jute and jute goods, leather, frozen fish and seafood
**Continent:** Asia

## Bhutan

**Capital:** Thimphu
**Population:** 2.1 million
**Official Language:** Dzongkha
**Land Area:** 47,000 sq km; 18,147 sq mi
**Leading Exports:** electricity, cardamom, gypsum, timber, handicrafts, cement, fruit, precious stones, spices
**Continent:** Asia

## Brunei
**Capital:** Bandar Seri Begawan
**Population:** 350,898
**Official Language:** Malay
**Land Area:** 5,270 sq km; 2,035 sq mi
**Leading Exports:** crude oil, natural gas, refined products
**Continent:** Asia

## Cambodia
**Capital:** Phnom Penh
**Population:** 12.8 million
**Official Language:** Khmer
**Land Area:** 176,520 sq km; 68,154 sq mi
**Leading Exports:** timber, garments, rubber, rice, fish
**Continent:** Asia

## China
**Capital:** Beijing
**Population:** 1.29 billion
**Official Languages:** Mandarin and Chinese
**Land Area:** 9,326,410 sq km;
3,600,927 sq mi
**Leading Exports:** machinery and equipment, textiles and clothing, footwear, toys and sports goods, mineral fuels
**Continent:** Asia

## Cyprus

**Capital:** Nicosia
**Population:** 767,314
**Official Languages:** Greek and Turkish
**Land Area:** 9,240 sq km; 3,568 sq mi
**Leading Exports:** citrus, potatoes, grapes, wine, cement, clothing and shoes
**Location:** Mediterranean Sea

## East Timor

**Capital:** Dili
**Population:** 952,618
**Official Languages:** Tetum and Portuguese
**Land Area:** 15,007 sq km; 5,794 sq mi
**Leading Exports:** coffee, sandalwood, marble
**Continent:** Asia

## Fiji

**Capital:** Suva
**Population:** 856,346
**Official Language:** English
**Land Area:** 18,270 sq km; 7,054 sq mi
**Leading Exports:** sugar, garments, gold, timber, fish, molasses, coconut oil
**Location:** Pacific Ocean

## Georgia

**Capital:** Tbilisi
**Population:** 5 million
**Official Languages:** Georgian and Abkhazian
**Land Area:** 69,700 sq km; 26,911 sq mi
**Leading Exports:** scrap metal, machinery, chemicals, fuel reexports, citrus fruits, tea, wine, other agricultural products
**Continent:** Asia

## India

**Capital:** New Delhi
**Population:** 1.05 billion
**Official Languages:** Hindi and English
**Land Area:** 2,973,190 sq km;
1,147,949 sq mi
**Leading Exports:** textile goods, gems and jewelry, engineering goods, chemicals, leather manufactured goods
**Continent:** Asia

## Indonesia

**Capital:** Jakarta
**Population:** 231.3 million
**Official Language:** Bahasa Indonesia
**Land Area:** 1,826,440 sq km;
705,188 sq mi
**Leading Exports:** oil and gas, electrical appliances, plywood, textiles, rubber
**Continent:** Asia

## Iran

**Capital:** Tehran
**Population:** 66.6 million
**Official Language:** Farsi
**Land Area:** 1,636,000 sq km;
631,660 sq mi
**Leading Exports:** petroleum, carpets, fruits and nuts, iron and steel, chemicals
**Continent:** Asia

## Iraq

**Capital:** Baghdad
**Population:** 24.7 million
**Official Language:** Arabic
**Land Area:** 432,162 sq km;
166,858 sq mi
**Leading Exports:** crude oil
**Continent:** Asia

## Israel
**Capital:** Jerusalem
**Population:** 6.0 million
**Official Language:** Hebrew, Arabic
**Land Area:** 20,330 sq km; 7,849 sq mi
**Leading Exports:** machinery and equipment, software, cut diamonds, agricultural products, chemicals, textiles and apparel
**Continent:** Asia

## Japan
**Capital:** Tokyo
**Population:** 127 million
**Official Language:** Japanese
**Land Area:** 374,744 sq km;
144,689 sq mi
**Leading Exports:** motor vehicles, semiconductors, office machinery, chemicals
**Continent:** Asia

## Jordan
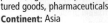
**Capital:** Amman
**Population:** 5.3 million
**Official Language:** Arabic
**Land Area:** 91,971 sq km; 35,510 sq mi
**Leading Exports:** phosphates, fertilizers, potash, agricultural products, manufactured goods, pharmaceuticals
**Continent:** Asia

## Kazakhstan

**Capital:** Astana
**Population:** 16.7 million
**Official Language:** Kazakh
**Land Area:** 2,669,800 sq km;
1,030,810 sq mi
**Leading Exports:** oil and oil products, ferrous metals, machinery, chemicals, grain, wool, meat, coal
**Continent:** Asia

## Kiribati

**Capital:** Bairiki (Tarawa Atoll)
**Population:** 96,335
**Official Language:** English
**Land Area:** 811 sq km; 313 sq mi
**Leading Exports:** copra, coconuts, seaweed, fish
**Location:** Pacific Ocean

## Korea, North

**Capital:** Pyongyang
**Population:** 22.3 million
**Official Language:** Korean
**Land Area:** 120,410 sq km; 46,490 sq mi
**Leading Exports:** minerals, metallurgical products, manufactured goods (including armaments), agricultural and fishery products
**Continent:** Asia

## Korea, South
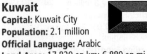
**Capital:** Seoul
**Population:** 48.3 million
**Official Language:** Korean
**Land Area:** 98,190 sq km; 37,911 sq mi
**Leading Exports:** electronic products, machinery and equipment, motor vehicles, steel, ships, textiles, clothing, footwear, fish
**Continent:** Asia

## Kuwait

**Capital:** Kuwait City
**Population:** 2.1 million
**Official Language:** Arabic
**Land Area:** 17,820 sq km; 6,880 sq mi
**Leading Exports:** oil and refined products, fertilizers
**Continent:** Asia

## Kyrgyzstan

**Capital:** Bishkek
**Population:** 4.8 million
**Official Languages:** Kyrgyz and Russian
**Land Area:** 191,300 sq km; 73,861 sq mi
**Leading Exports:** cotton, wool, meat, tobacco, gold, mercury, uranium, hydropower, machinery, shoes
**Continent:** Asia

## Laos

**Capital:** Vientiane
**Population:** 5.8 million
**Official Language:** Lao
**Land Area:** 230,800 sq km;
89,112 sq mi
**Leading Exports:** wood products, garments, electricity, coffee, tin
**Continent:** Asia

## Lebanon

**Capital:** Beirut
**Population:** 3.7 million
**Official Language:** Arabic
**Land Area:** 10,230 sq km; 3,950 sq mi
**Leading Exports:** foodstuffs and tobacco, textile, chemicals, precious stones, metal and metal products, electrical equipment and products, jewelry, paper and paper products
**Continent:** Asia

## Malaysia

**Capital:** Kuala Lumpur and Putrajaya
**Population:** 22.7 million
**Official Language:** Bahasa Malaysia
**Land Area:** 328,550 sq km; 126,853 sq mi
**Leading Exports:** electronic equipment, petroleum and liquefied natural gas, wood and wood products, palm oil, rubber, textiles, chemicals
**Continent:** Asia

## Maldives

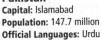

**Capital:** Malé
**Population:** 320,165
**Official Language:** Dhivehi (Maldivian)
**Land Area:** 300 sq km; 116 sq mi
**Leading Exports:** fish, clothing
**Location:** Indian Ocean

## Marshall Islands

**Capital:** Majuro
**Population:** 73,360
**Official Languages:** Marshallese and English
**Land Area:** 181.3 sq km; 70 sq mi
**Leading Exports:** copra cake, coconut oil, handicrafts
**Location:** Pacific Ocean

## Micronesia, Federated States of

**Capital:** Palikir (Pohnpei Island)
**Population:** 135,869
**Official Language:** English
**Land Area:** 702 sq km; 271 sq mi
**Leading Exports:** fish, garments, bananas, black pepper
**Location:** Pacific Ocean

## Mongolia

**Capital:** Ulaanbaatar
**Population:** 2.6 million
**Official Language:** Khalkha Mongolian
**Land Area:** 1,555,400 sq km; 600,540 sq mi
**Leading Exports:** copper, livestock, animal products, cashmere, wool, hides, fluorspar, other nonferrous metals
**Continent:** Asia

## Myanmar (Burma)

**Capital:** Rangoon (Yangon)
**Population:** 42.2 million
**Official Language:** Burmese (Myanmar)
**Land Area:** 657,740 sq km; 253,953 sq mi
**Leading Exports:** apparel, foodstuffs, wood products, precious stones
**Continent:** Asia

## Nauru

**Capital:** Yaren District
**Population:** 12,329
**Official Language:** Nauruan
**Land Area:** 21 sq km; 8 sq mi
**Leading Exports:** phosphates
**Location:** Pacific Ocean

## Nepal

**Capital:** Kathmandu
**Population:** 25.9 million
**Official Language:** Nepali
**Land Area:** 136,800 sq km; 52,818 sq mi
**Leading Exports:** carpets, clothing, leather goods, jute goods, grain
**Continent:** Asia

## New Zealand

**Capital:** Wellington
**Population:** 3.8 million
**Official Languages:** English and Maori
**Land Area:** 268,680 sq km; 103,737 sq mi
**Leading Exports:** dairy products, meat, wood and wood products, fish, machinery
**Location:** Pacific Ocean

## Oman

**Capital:** Muscat
**Population:** 2.7 million
**Official Language:** Arabic
**Land Area:** 212,460 sq km; 82,030 sq mi
**Leading Exports:** petroleum, reexports, fish, metals, textiles
**Continent:** Asia

## Pakistan

**Capital:** Islamabad
**Population:** 147.7 million
**Official Languages:** Urdu and English
**Land Area:** 778,720 sq km; 300,664 sq mi
**Leading Exports:** textiles (garments, cotton cloth, and yarn), rice, other agricultural products
**Continent:** Asia

## Palau

**Capital:** Koror
**Population:** 19,409
**Official Languages:** English and Palauan
**Land Area:** 458 sq km; 177 sq mi
**Leading Exports:** shellfish, tuna, copra, garments
**Location:** Pacific Ocean

## Papua New Guinea

**Capital:** Port Moresby
**Population:** 5.2 million
**Official Language:** English
**Land Area:** 452,860 sq km; 174,849 sq mi
**Leading Exports:** oil, gold, copper ore, logs, palm oil, coffee, cocoa, crayfish, prawns
**Location:** Pacific Ocean

## Philippines

**Capital:** Manila
**Population:** 84.5 million
**Official Languages:** Filipino and English
**Land Area:** 298,170 sq km; 115,123 sq mi
**Leading Exports:** electronic equipment, machinery and transport equipment, garments, coconut products
**Continent:** Asia

## Qatar

**Capital:** Doha
**Population:** 793,341
**Official Language:** Arabic
**Land Area:** 11,437 sq km; 4,416 sq mi
**Leading Exports:** petroleum products, fertilizers, steel
**Continent:** Asia

## Samoa

**Capital:** Apia
**Population:** 178,631
**Official Languages:** Samoan and English
**Land Area:** 2,934 sq km; 1,133 sq mi
**Leading Exports:** fish, coconut oil cream, copra, taro, garments, beer
**Location:** Pacific Ocean

## Saudi Arabia

**Capital:** Riyadh and Jiddah
**Population:** 23.5 million
**Official Language:** Arabic
**Land Area:** 1,960,582 sq km; 756,981 sq mi
**Leading Exports:** petroleum and petroleum products
**Continent:** Asia

## Singapore

**Capital:** Singapore
**Population:** 4.5 million
**Official Languages:** Malay, English, Mandarin, Chinese, and Tamil
**Land Area:** 683 sq km; 264 sq mi
**Leading Exports:** machinery and equipment (including electronics), consumer goods, chemicals, mineral fuels
**Continent:** Asia

## Solomon Islands

**Capital:** Honiara
**Population:** 494,786
**Official Language:** English
**Land Area:** 27,540 sq km; 10,633 sq mi
**Leading Exports:** timber, fish, copra, palm oil, cocoa
**Location:** Pacific Ocean

## Sri Lanka

**Capital:** Colombo
**Population:** 19.6 million
**Official Language:** Sinhala, Tamil, and English
**Land Area:** 64,740 sq km; 24,996 sq mi
**Leading Exports:** textiles and apparel, tea, diamonds, coconut products, petroleum products
**Continent:** Asia

## Syria

**Capital:** Damascus
**Population:** 17.2 million
**Official Language:** Arabic
**Land Area:** 184,050 sq km; 71,062 sq mi
**Leading Exports:** crude oil, textiles, fruits and vegetables, raw cotton
**Continent:** Asia

## Taiwan

**Capital:** Taipei
**Population:** 22.5 million
**Official Language:** Mandarin Chinese
**Land Area:** 32,260 sq km; 12,456 sq mi
**Leading Exports:** machinery and electrical equipment, metals, textiles, plastics, chemicals
**Continent:** Asia

## Tajikistan

**Capital:** Dushanbe
**Population:** 6.7 million
**Official Language:** Tajik
**Land Area:** 142,700 sq km; 55,096 sq mi
**Leading Exports:** aluminum, electricity, cotton, fruits, vegetables, oil, textiles
**Continent:** Asia

## Thailand

**Capital:** Bangkok
**Population:** 62.5 million
**Official Language:** Thai
**Land Area:** 511,770 sq km; 197,564 sq mi
**Leading Exports:** computers, transistors, seafood, clothing, rice
**Continent:** Asia

## Tonga

**Capital:** Nuku'alofa
**Population:** 106,137
**Official Languages:** Tongan and English
**Land Area:** 718 sq km; 277 sq mi
**Leading Exports:** squash, fish, vanilla beans, root crops
**Location:** Pacific Ocean

## Turkey

**Capital:** Ankara
**Population:** 67.3 million
**Official Language:** Turkish
**Land Area:** 770,760 sq km; 297,590 sq mi
**Leading Exports:** apparel, foodstuffs, textiles, metal manufactured goods, transport equipment
**Continent:** Asia

## Turkmenistan

**Capital:** Ashgabat
**Population:** 4.7 million
**Official Language:** Turkmen
**Land Area:** 488,100 sq km; 188,455 sq mi
**Leading Exports:** gas, oil, cotton fiber, textiles
**Continent:** Asia

### Tuvalu

**Capital:** Fongafale
**Population:** 10,800
**Official Language:** English
**Land Area:** 26 sq km; 10 sq mi
**Leading Exports:** copra, fish
**Location:** Pacific Ocean

### United Arab Emirates
**Capital:** Abu Dhabi
**Population:** 2.4 million
**Official Language:** Arabic
**Land Area:** 82,880 sq km; 32,000 sq mi
**Leading Exports:** crude oil, natural gas, reexports, dried fish, dates
**Continent:** Asia

### Uzbekistan

**Capital:** Tashkent
**Population:** 25.5 million
**Official Language:** Uzbek
**Land Area:** 425,400 sq km; 164,247 sq mi
**Leading Exports:** cotton, gold, energy products, mineral fertilizers, ferrous metals, textiles, food products, automobiles
**Continent:** Asia

### Vanuatu
**Capital:** Port-Vila
**Population:** 196,178
**Official Languages:** English, French, and Bislama
**Land Area:** 12,200 sq km; 4,710 sq mi
**Leading Exports:** copra, kava, beef, cocoa, timber, coffee
**Location:** Pacific Ocean

### Vietnam
**Capital:** Hanoi
**Population:** 81.1 million
**Official Language:** Vietnamese
**Land Area:** 325,320 sq km; 125,621 sq mi
**Leading Exports:** crude oil, marine products, rice, coffee, rubber, tea, garments, shoes
**Continent:** Asia

### Yemen
**Capital:** Sanaa
**Population:** 18.7 million
**Official Language:** Arabic
**Land Area:** 527,970 sq km; 203,849 sq mi
**Leading Exports:** crude oil, coffee, dried and salted fish
**Continent:** Asia

# Europe and Russia

### Albania
**Capital:** Tiranë
**Population:** 3.5 million
**Official Language:** Albanian
**Land Area:** 27,398 sq km; 10,578 sq mi
**Leading Exports:** textiles and footwear, asphalt, metals and metallic ores, crude oil, vegetables, fruits, tobacco
**Continent:** Europe

### Andorra
**Capital:** Andorra la Vella
**Population:** 68,403
**Official Language:** Catalan
**Land Area:** 468 sq km; 181 sq mi
**Leading Exports:** tobacco products, furniture
**Continent:** Europe

### Austria
**Capital:** Vienna
**Population:** 8.2 million
**Official Language:** German
**Land Area:** 82,738 sq km; 31,945 sq mi
**Leading Exports:** machinery and equipment, motor vehicles and parts, paper and paperboard, metal goods, chemicals, iron and steel, textiles, foodstuffs
**Continent:** Europe

### Belarus

**Capital:** Minsk
**Population:** 10.3 million
**Official Languages:** Belarussian and Russian
**Land Area:** 207,600 sq km; 80,154 sq mi
**Leading Exports:** machinery and equipment, mineral products, chemicals, textiles, food stuffs, metals
**Continent:** Europe

### Belgium
**Capital:** Brussels
**Population:** 10.3 million
**Official Languages:** Dutch and French
**Land Area:** 30,230 sq km; 11,172 sq mi
**Leading Exports:** machinery and equipment, chemicals, metals and metal products
**Continent:** Europe

### Bosnia and Herzegovina

**Capital:** Sarajevo
**Population:** 4.0 million
**Official Language:** Serbo-Croat
**Land Area:** 51,129 sq km; 19,741 sq mi
**Leading Exports:** miscellaneous manufactured goods, crude materials
**Continent:** Europe

### Bulgaria

**Capital:** Sofía
**Population:** 7.6 million
**Official Language:** Bulgarian
**Land Area:** 110,550 sq km; 42,683 sq mi
**Leading Exports:** clothing, footwear, iron and steel, machinery and equipment, fuels
**Continent:** Europe

### Croatia

**Capital:** Zagreb
**Population:** 4.4 million
**Official Language:** Croatian
**Land Area:** 56,414 km; 21,781 sq mi
**Leading Exports:** transport equipment, textiles, chemicals, foodstuffs, fuels
**Continent:** Europe

### Czech Republic

**Capital:** Prague
**Population:** 10.3 million
**Official Language:** Czech
**Land Area:** 78,276 sq km; 29,836 sq mi
**Leading Exports:** machinery and transport equipment, intermediate manufactured goods, chemicals, raw materials and fuel
**Continent:** Europe

### Denmark

**Capital:** Copenhagen
**Population:** 5.4 million
**Official Language:** Danish
**Land Area:** 42,394 sq km; 16,368 sq mi
**Leading Exports:** machinery and instruments, meat and meat products, dairy products, fish, chemicals, furniture, ships, windmills
**Continent:** Europe

### Estonia
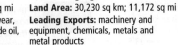
**Capital:** Tallinn
**Population:** 1.4 million
**Official Language:** Estonian
**Land Area:** 43,211 sq km; 16,684 sq mi
**Leading Exports:** machinery and equipment, wood products, textiles, food products, metals, chemical products
**Continent:** Europe

### Finland

**Capital:** Helsinki
**Population:** 5.2 million
**Official Languages:** Finnish and Swedish
**Land Area:** 305,470 sq km; 117,942 sq mi
**Leading Exports:** machinery and equipment, chemicals, metals, timber, paper, pulp
**Continent:** Europe

### France
**Capital:** Paris
**Population:** 59.8 million
**Official Language:** French
**Land Area:** 545,630 sq km; 310,668 sq mi
**Leading Exports:** machinery and transportation equipment, aircraft, plastics, chemicals, pharmaceutical products, iron and steel, beverages
**Continent:** Europe

### Germany

**Capital:** Berlin
**Population:** 83 million
**Official Language:** German
**Land Area:** 349,223 sq km; 134,835 sq mi
**Leading Exports:** machinery, vehicles, chemicals, metals and manufactured goods, foodstuffs, textiles
**Continent:** Europe

### Greece

**Capital:** Athens
**Population:** 10.6 million
**Official Language:** Greek
**Land Area:** 130,800 sq km; 50,502 sq mi
**Leading Exports:** food and beverages, manufactured goods, petroleum products, chemicals, textiles
**Continent:** Europe

### Holy See (Vatican City)

**Capital:** Vatican City
**Population:** 900
**Official Languages:** Latin and Italian
**Land Area:** 0.44 sq km; 0.17 sq mi
**Leading Exports:** no information available
**Continent:** Europe

## Hungary

**Capital:** Budapest
**Population:** 10.1 million
**Official Language:** Hungarian
**Land Area:** 92,340 sq km; 35,652 sq mi
**Leading Exports:** machinery and equipment, other manufactured goods, food products, raw materials, fuels and electricity
**Continent:** Europe

## Iceland

**Capital:** Reykjavík
**Population:** 279,384
**Official Language:** Icelandic
**Land Area:** 100,250 sq km; 38,707 sq mi
**Leading Exports:** fish and fish products, animal products, aluminum, diatomite, ferrosilicon
**Location:** Atlantic Ocean

## Ireland
**Capital:** Dublin
**Population:** 3.9 million
**Official Languages:** Irish Gaelic and English
**Land Area:** 68,890 sq km; 26,598 sq mi
**Leading Exports:** machinery and equipment, computers, chemicals, pharmaceuticals, live animals, animal products
**Continent:** Europe

## Italy
**Capital:** Rome
**Population:** 57.7 million
**Official Language:** Italian
**Land Area:** 294,020 sq km; 113,521 sq mi
**Leading Exports:** fruits, vegetables, grapes, potatoes, sugar beets, soybeans, grain, olives, beef, diary products, fish
**Continent:** Europe

## Latvia

**Capital:** Riga
**Population:** 2.4 million
**Official Language:** Latvian
**Land Area:** 63,589 sq km; 24,552 sq mi
**Leading Exports:** wood and wood products, machinery and equipment, metals, textiles, foodstuffs
**Continent:** Europe

## Liechtenstein

**Capital:** Vaduz
**Population:** 32,842
**Official Language:** German
**Land Area:** 160 sq km; 62 sq mi
**Leading Exports:** small specialty machinery, dental products, stamps, hardware, pottery
**Continent:** Europe

## Lithuania

**Capital:** Vilnius
**Population:** 3.6 million
**Official Language:** Lithuanian
**Land Area:** 65,200 sq km; 25,174 sq mi
**Leading Exports:** mineral products, textiles and clothing, machinery and equipment, chemicals, wood and wood products, foodstuffs
**Continent:** Europe

## Luxembourg

**Capital:** Luxembourg
**Population:** 448,569
**Official Languages:** Luxembourgish, French, and German
**Land Area:** 2,586 sq km; 998 sq mi
**Leading Exports:** machinery and equipment, steel products, chemicals, rubber products, glass
**Continent:** Europe

## Macedonia, The Former Yugoslav Republic of

**Capital:** Skopje
**Population:** 2.1 million
**Official Languages:** Macedonian and Albanian
**Land Area:** 24,856 sq km; 9,597 sq mi
**Leading Exports:** food, beverages, tobacco, miscellaneous manufactured goods, iron and steel
**Continent:** Europe

## Malta

**Capital:** Valletta
**Population:** 397,499
**Official Languages:** Maltese and English
**Land Area:** 316 sq km; 122 sq mi
**Leading Exports:** machinery and transport equipment, manufactured goods
**Location:** Mediterranean Sea

## Moldova

**Capital:** Chişinău
**Population:** 4.4 million
**Official Language:** Moldovan
**Land Area:** 33,371 sq km; 12,885 sq mi
**Leading Exports:** foodstuffs, textiles and footwear, machinery
**Continent:** Europe

## Monaco
**Capital:** Monaco
**Population:** 31,987
**Official Language:** French
**Land Area:** 1.95 sq km; 0.75 sq mi
**Leading Exports:** no information available
**Continent:** Europe

## Montenegro

**Capital:** Podgorica
**Population:** 620,145
**Official Language:** Serbian
**Land Area:** 13,812 sq km; 5,333 sq mi
**Leading Exports:** food products
**Continent:** Europe

## Netherlands
**Capital:** Amsterdam and The Hague
**Population:** 16.1 million
**Official Language:** Dutch
**Land Area:** 33,883 sq km; 13,082 sq mi
**Leading Exports:** machinery and equipment, chemicals, fuels, foodstuffs
**Continent:** Europe

## Norway
**Capital:** Oslo
**Population:** 4.5 million
**Official Language:** Norwegian
**Land Area:** 307,860 sq km; 118,865 sq mi
**Leading Exports:** petroleum and petroleum products, machinery and equipment, metals, chemicals, ships, fish
**Continent:** Europe

## Poland
**Capital:** Warsaw
**Population:** 38.6 million
**Official Language:** Polish
**Land Area:** 304,465 sq km; 117,554 sq mi
**Leading Exports:** machinery and transport equipment, intermediate manufactured goods, miscellaneous manufactured goods, food and live animals
**Continent:** Europe

## Portugal

**Capital:** Lisbon
**Population:** 10.1 million
**Official Language:** Portuguese
**Land Area:** 91,951 sq km; 35,502 sq mi
**Leading Exports:** clothing and footwear, machinery, chemicals, cork and paper products, hides
**Continent:** Europe

## Romania
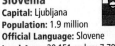
**Capital:** Bucharest
**Population:** 22.3 million
**Official Language:** Romanian
**Land Area:** 230,340 sq km; 88,934 sq mi
**Leading Exports:** textiles and footwear, metals and metal products, machinery and equipment, minerals and fuels
**Continent:** Europe

## Russia

**Capital:** Moscow
**Population:** 145 million
**Official Language:** Russian
**Land Area:** 16,995,800 sq km; 6,592,100 sq mi
**Leading Exports:** petroleum and petroleum products, natural gas, wood and wood products, metals, chemicals, and a wide variety of civilian and military manufactured goods
**Continents:** Europe and Asia

## San Marino

**Capital:** San Marino
**Population:** 27,730
**Official Language:** Italian
**Land Area:** 61 sq km; 24 sq mi
**Leading Exports:** building stone, lime, wood, chestnuts, wheat, wine, baked goods, hides, ceramics
**Continent:** Europe

## Serbia

**Capital:** Belgrade
**Population:** 9.4 million
**Official Language:** Serbian
**Land Area:** 88,361 sq km; 34,116 sq mi
**Leading Exports:** food and live animals, manufactured goods, raw materials
**Continent:** Europe

## Slovakia
**Capital:** Bratislava
**Population:** 5.4 million
**Official Language:** Slovak
**Land Area:** 48,800 sq km; 18,842 sq mi
**Leading Exports:** machinery and transport equipment, intermediate manufactured goods, miscellaneous manufactured goods, chemicals
**Continent:** Europe

## Slovenia
**Capital:** Ljubljana
**Population:** 1.9 million
**Official Language:** Slovene
**Land Area:** 20,151 sq km; 7,780 sq mi
**Leading Exports:** manufactured goods, machinery and transport equipment, chemicals, food
**Continent:** Europe

## Spain
**Capital:** Madrid
**Population:** 40.1 million
**Official Languages:** Spanish, Galician, Basque, and Catalan
**Land Area:** 499,542 sq km; 192,873 sq mi
**Leading Exports:** machinery, motor vehicles, foodstuffs, other consumer goods
**Continent:** Europe

# Europe and Russia (continued)

## Sweden
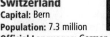
**Capital:** Stockholm
**Population:** 8.9 million
**Official Language:** Swedish
**Land Area:** 410,934 sq km; 158,662 sq mi
**Leading Exports:** machinery, motor vehicles, paper products, pulp and wood, iron and steel products, chemicals
**Continent:** Europe

## Switzerland

**Capital:** Bern
**Population:** 7.3 million
**Official Languages:** German, French, and Italian
**Land Area:** 39,770 sq km; 15,355 sq mi
**Leading Exports:** machinery, chemicals, metals, watches, agricultural products
**Continent:** Europe

## Ukraine
**Capital:** Kiev
**Population:** 48.4 million
**Official Language:** Ukrainian
**Land Area:** 603,700 sq km; 233,090 sq mi
**Leading Exports:** ferrous and nonferrous metals, fuel and petroleum products, machinery and transport equipment, food products
**Continent:** Europe

## United Kingdom

**Capital:** London
**Population:** 59.8 million
**Official Languages:** English and Welsh
**Land Area:** 241,590 sq km; 93,278 sq mi
**Leading Exports:** manufactured goods, fuels, chemicals, food, beverages, tobacco
**Continent:** Europe

# Latin America

## Antigua and Barbuda

**Capital:** Saint John's
**Population:** 67,448
**Official Language:** English
**Land Area:** 442 sq km; 171 sq mi
**Leading Exports:** petroleum products, manufactured goods, machinery and transport equipment, food and live animals
**Location:** Caribbean Sea

## Argentina

**Capital:** Buenos Aires
**Population:** 37.8 million
**Official Language:** Spanish
**Land Area:** 2,736,690 sq km; 1,056,636 sq mi
**Leading Exports:** edible oils, fuels and energy, cereals, feed, motor vehicles
**Continent:** South America

## Bahamas
**Capital:** Nassau
**Population:** 300,529
**Official Language:** English
**Land Area:** 10,070 sq km; 3,888 sq mi
**Leading Exports:** fish and crawfish, rum, salt, chemicals, fruit and vegetables
**Location:** Caribbean Sea

## Barbados
**Capital:** Bridgetown
**Population:** 276,607
**Official Language:** English
**Land Area:** 431 sq km; 166 sq mi
**Leading Exports:** sugar and molasses, rum, other foods and beverages, chemicals, electrical components, clothing
**Location:** Caribbean Sea

## Belize
**Capital:** Belmopan
**Population:** 262,999
**Official Language:** English
**Land Area:** 22,806 sq km; 8,805 sq mi
**Leading Exports:** sugar, bananas, citrus, clothing, fish products, molasses, wood
**Continent:** North America

## Bolivia
**Capital:** La Paz and Sucre
**Population:** 8.5 million
**Official Language:** Spanish, Quechua, and Aymara
**Land Area:** 1,084,390 sq km; 418,683 sq mi
**Leading Exports:** soybeans, natural gas, zinc, gold, wood
**Continent:** South America

## Brazil

**Capital:** Brasília
**Population:** 176 million
**Official Language:** Portuguese
**Land Area:** 8,456,510 sq km; 3,265,059 sq mi
**Leading Exports:** manufactured goods, iron ore, soybeans, footwear, coffee, autos
**Continent:** South America

## Chile

**Capital:** Santiago
**Population:** 15.5 million
**Official Language:** Spanish
**Land Area:** 748,800 sq km; 289,112 sq mi
**Leading Exports:** copper, fish, fruits, paper and pulp, chemicals
**Continent:** South America

## Colombia

**Capital:** Bogotá
**Population:** 41 million
**Official Language:** Spanish
**Land Area:** 1,038,700 sq km; 401,042 sq mi
**Leading Exports:** petroleum, coffee, coal, apparel, bananas, cut flowers
**Continent:** South America

## Costa Rica

**Capital:** San José
**Population:** 3.8 million
**Official Language:** Spanish
**Land Area:** 51,660 sq km; 19,560 sq mi
**Leading Exports:** coffee, bananas, sugar, pineapples, textiles, electronic components, medical equipment
**Continent:** North America

## Cuba

**Capital:** Havana
**Population:** 11.2 million
**Official Language:** Spanish
**Land Area:** 110,860 sq km; 42,803 sq mi
**Leading Exports:** sugar, nickel, tobacco, fish, medical products, citrus, coffee
**Location:** Caribbean Sea

## Dominica
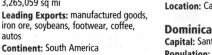
**Capital:** Roseau
**Population:** 73,000
**Official Language:** English
**Land Area:** 754 sq km; 291 sq mi
**Leading Exports:** bananas, soap, bay oil, vegetables, grapefruit, oranges
**Location:** Caribbean Sea

## Dominican Republic

**Capital:** Santo Domingo
**Population:** 8.7 million
**Official Language:** Spanish
**Land Area:** 48,380 sq km; 18,679 sq mi
**Leading Exports:** ferronickel, sugar, gold, silver, coffee, cocoa, tobacco, meats, consumer goods
**Location:** Caribbean Sea

## Ecuador

**Capital:** Quito
**Population:** 13.5 million
**Official Language:** Spanish
**Land Area:** 276,840 sq km; 106,888 sq mi
**Leading Exports:** petroleum, bananas, shrimp, coffee, cocoa, cut flowers, fish
**Continent:** South America

## El Salvador

**Capital:** San Salvador
**Population:** 6.4 million
**Official Language:** Spanish
**Land Area:** 20,720 sq km; 8,000 sq mi
**Leading Exports:** offshore assembly exports, coffee, sugar, shrimp, textiles, chemicals, electricity
**Continent:** North America

## Grenada

**Capital:** Saint George's
**Population:** 89,211
**Official Language:** English
**Land Area:** 344 sq km; 133 sq mi
**Leading Exports:** bananas, cocoa, nutmeg, fruit and vegetables, clothing, mace
**Location:** Caribbean Sea

## Guatemala

**Capital:** Guatemala City
**Population:** 13.3 million
**Official Language:** Spanish
**Land Area:** 108,430 sq km; 41,865 sq mi
**Leading Exports:** coffee, sugar, bananas, fruits and vegetables, cardamom, meat, apparel, petroleum, electricity
**Continent:** North America

## Guyana

**Capital:** Georgetown
**Population:** 698,209
**Official Language:** English
**Land Area:** 196,850 sq km; 76,004 sq mi
**Leading Exports:** sugar, gold, bauxite/alumina, rice, shrimp, molasses, rum, timber
**Continent:** South America

## Haiti

**Capital:** Port-au-Prince
**Population:** 7.1 million
**Official Language:** French and French Creole
**Land Area:** 27,560 sq km; 10,641 sq mi
**Leading Exports:** manufactured goods, coffee, oils, cocoa
**Location:** Caribbean Sea

## Honduras
**Capital:** Tegucigalpa
**Population:** 6.6 million
**Official Language:** Spanish
**Land Area:** 111,890 sq km; 43,201 sq mi
**Leading Exports:** coffee, bananas, shrimp, lobster, meat, zinc, lumber
**Continent:** North America

### Jamaica

**Capital:** Kingston
**Population:** 2.7 million
**Official Language:** English
**Land Area:** 10,831 sq km; 4,182 sq mi
**Leading Exports:** alumina, bauxite, sugar, bananas, rum
**Location:** Caribbean Sea

### Mexico

**Capital:** Mexico City
**Population:** 103.4 million
**Official Language:** Spanish
**Land Area:** 1,923,040 sq km; 742,486 sq mi
**Leading Exports:** manufactured goods, oil and oil products, silver, fruits, vegetables, coffee, cotton
**Continent:** North America

### Nicaragua

**Capital:** Managua
**Population:** 5 million
**Official Language:** Spanish
**Land Area:** 120,254 sq km; 46,430 sq mi
**Leading Exports:** coffee, shrimp and lobster, cotton, tobacco, beef, sugar, bananas, gold
**Continent:** North America

### Panama

**Capital:** Panama City
**Population:** 2.9 million
**Official Language:** Spanish
**Land Area:** 75,990 sq km; 29,340 sq mi
**Leading Exports:** bananas, shrimp, sugar, coffee, clothing
**Continent:** North America

### Paraguay

**Capital:** Asunción
**Population:** 5.9 million
**Official Language:** Spanish
**Land Area:** 397,300 sq km; 153,398 sq mi
**Leading Exports:** electricity, soybeans, feed, cotton, meat, edible oils
**Continent:** South America

### Peru

**Capital:** Lima
**Population:** 28 million
**Official Languages:** Spanish and Quechua
**Land Area:** 1,280,000 sq km; 494,208 sq mi
**Leading Exports:** fish and fish products, gold, copper, zinc, crude petroleum and byproducts, lead, coffee, sugar, cotton
**Continent:** South America

### Saint Kitts and Nevis

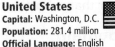

**Capital:** Basseterre
**Population:** 38,736
**Official Language:** English
**Land Area:** 261 sq km; 101 sq mi
**Leading Exports:** machinery, food, electronics, beverages, tobacco
**Location:** Caribbean Sea

### Saint Lucia

**Capital:** Castries
**Population:** 160,145
**Official Language:** English
**Land Area:** 606 sq km; 234 sq mi
**Leading Exports:** bananas, clothing, cocoa, vegetables, fruits, coconut oil
**Location:** Caribbean Sea

### Saint Vincent and the Grenadines

**Capital:** Kingstown
**Population:** 116,394
**Official Language:** English
**Land Area:** 389 sq km; 150 sq mi
**Leading Exports:** bananas, eddoes and dasheen, arrowroot starch, tennis racquets
**Location:** Caribbean Sea

### Suriname

**Capital:** Paramaribo
**Population:** 436,494
**Official Language:** Dutch
**Land Area:** 161,470 sq km; 62,344 sq mi
**Leading Exports:** alumina, crude oil, lumber, shrimp and fish, rice, bananas
**Continent:** South America

### Trinidad and Tobago

**Capital:** Port-of-Spain
**Population:** 1.2 million
**Official Language:** English
**Land Area:** 5,128 sq km; 1,980 sq mi
**Leading Exports:** petroleum and petroleum products, chemicals, steel products, fertilizer, sugar, cocoa, coffee, citrus, flowers
**Location:** Caribbean Sea

### Uruguay

**Capital:** Montevideo
**Population:** 3.4 million
**Official Language:** Spanish
**Land Area:** 173,620 sq km; 67,100 sq mi
**Leading Exports:** meat, rice, leather products, wool, vehicles, dairy products
**Continent:** South America

### Venezuela

**Capital:** Caracas
**Population:** 24.3 million
**Official Language:** Spanish
**Land Area:** 882,050 sq km; 340,560 sq mi
**Leading Exports:** petroleum, bauxite and aluminum, steel, chemicals, agricultural products, basic manufactured goods
**Continent:** South America

# United States and Canada

### Canada

**Capital:** Ottawa
**Population:** 31.9 million
**Official Languages:** English and French
**Land Area:** 9,220,970 sq km; 3,560,217 sq mi
**Leading Exports:** motor vehicles and parts, industrial machinery, aircraft, telecommunications equipment, chemicals, plastics, fertilizers, wood pulp, timber, crude petroleum, natural gas, electricity, aluminum
**Continent:** North America

### United States

**Capital:** Washington, D.C.
**Population:** 281.4 million
**Official Language:** English
**Land Area:** 9,158,960 sq km; 3,536,274 sq mi
**Leading Exports:** capital goods, automobiles, industrial supplies and raw materials, consumer goods, agricultural products
**Continent:** North America

SOURCE: CIA World Factbook Online, 2002 and 2006

# Glossary of Geographic Terms

**basin**
an area that is lower than surrounding land areas; some basins are filled with water

**bay**
a body of water that is partly surrounded by land and that is connected to a larger body of water

**butte**
a small, high, flat-topped landform with cliff-like sides

▲ butte

**canyon**
a deep, narrow valley with steep sides; often with a stream flowing through it

**cataract**
a large waterfall or steep rapids

**delta**
a plain at the mouth of a river, often triangular in shape, formed where sediment is deposited by flowing water

**flood plain**
a broad plain on either side of a river, formed where sediment settles during floods

**glacier**
a huge, slow-moving mass of snow and ice

**hill**
an area that rises above surrounding land and has a rounded top; lower and usually less steep than a mountain

**island**
an area of land completely surrounded by water

**isthmus**
a narrow strip of land that connects two larger areas of land

**mesa**
a high, flat-topped land-form with cliff-like sides; larger than a butte

**mountain**
a landform that rises steeply at least 2,000 feet (610 meters) above surrounding land; usually wide at the bottom and rising to a narrow peak or ridge

 glacier

◀ cataract

◀ **delta**

**mountain pass**
a gap between mountains

**peninsula**
an area of land almost completely surrounded by water but connected to the mainland

**plain**
a large area of flat or gently rolling land

**plateau**
a large, flat area that rises above the surrounding land; at least one side has a steep slope

**river mouth**
the point where a river enters a lake or sea

**strait**
a narrow stretch of water that connects two larger bodies of water

**tributary**
a river or stream that flows into a larger river

**valley**
a low stretch of land between mountains or hills; land that is drained by a river

**volcano**
an opening in Earth's surface through which molten rock, ashes, and gases escape from the interior

▶ **volcano**

# Gazetteer

## A

**Africa** (10° N, 22° E) the world's second-largest continent, surrounded by the Mediterranean Sea, the Atlantic Ocean, the Indian Ocean, and the Red Sea (p. 154–155)

**Antarctic Circle** (66°30′ S) line of latitude around Earth near the South Pole (p. 32)

**Antarctica** (87° S, 60° E) the continent that contains the South Pole; almost completely covered by an ice sheet (p. 35)

**Antofagasta** (23°39′ S, 70°24′ W) a coastal city in Chile (p. 43)

**Appalachian Mountains** (41° N, 77° W) a mountain system in eastern North America (p. 39)

**Arctic Circle** (66°30′ N) line of latitude around Earth near the North Pole (p. 30)

**Arctic** region located around the North Pole (p. 31)

**Asia** (50° N, 100° E) the world's largest continent, the main part of the Eurasian land-mass, surrounded by the Arctic Ocean, the Pacific Ocean, the Indian Ocean, the Red Sea, the Mediterranean Sea, and Europe (p. 54)

**Australia** (25° S, 135° E) a continent in the Southern Hemisphere, the world's smallest continent; also a country including the continent and Tasmania (p. 68)

## B

**Bangladesh** (24° N, 90° E) a country in South Asia (p. 66)

**Brazil** (10° S, 55° W) a large country in South America (p. 71)

## C

**Canada** (60° N, 95° W) a large country in North America (p. 31)

**Central America** the part of Latin America between Mexico and South America; an area including the seven republics of Guatemala, Honduras, El Salvador, Nicaragua, Costa Rica, Panama, and Belize (p. 103)

**China** (35° N, 105° E) a large country in East Asia, officially the People's Republic of China (p. 20)

**Cuba** (22° N, 80° W) the largest island country in the Caribbean Sea (p. 160)

## D

**Denmark** (56° N, 10° E) a country in northern Europe (p. 118)

## E

**Egypt** (27° N, 30° E) a country in North Africa (p. 60)

**Equator** (0°) a line of latitude that circles Earth at the center of the tropics, midway between the North and South poles, along which days and nights are always equal in length (p. 11)

**Europe** (50° N, 28° E) the world's second-smallest continent; a peninsula of the Eurasian landmass bounded by the Arctic Ocean, the Atlantic Ocean, the Mediterranean Sea, and Asia (p. 158–159)

## F

**Florida** (28° N, 82° W) a state in the United States that is largely a peninsula (p. 12)

## G

**Genoa** (44°25′ N, 8°57′ E) a seaport city of Italy (p. 104)

**Georgia** (33° N, 83° W) a state in the southeastern United States (p. 12); also a nation of southwestern Asia (p. 156)

**Germany** (51° N, 10° E) a country in central Europe (p. 97)

**Great Plains** (42° N, 100° W) a semiarid plain located in North America, stretching from the Rio Grande at the U.S.-Mexico border in the south to the Mackenzie River Delta in the north, and from the Canadian Shield in the east to the Rocky Mountains in the west (p. 128)

**Greece** (39° N, 22° E) a country in southeastern Europe (p. 93)

**Greenland** (70° N, 40° W) a self-governing island in the northern Atlantic Ocean, Earth's largest island; a possession of Denmark (p. 18)

**Greenwich** (51°28′ N, 0°) a borough of London, England, and location of the Royal Greenwich Observatory, whose location serves as the basis for longitude and for setting standard time (p. 12)

**Gulf Stream** a warm ocean current in the North Atlantic, flowing northeastward off the North American coast (p. 43)

# I

**India** (20° N, 77° E) a large country occupying most of the Indian subcontinent in South Asia (p. 13)

**Indonesia** (5° S, 120° E) a country in Southeast Asia consisting of many islands (p. 93)

**Iran** (32° N, 53° W) a country in Southwest Asia (p. 118)

**Italy** (43° N, 13° E) a boot-shaped country in southern Europe (p. 104)

# J

**Jakarta** (6°10′ S, 106°48′ E) the capital and largest city of Indonesia (p. 71)

**Japan** (36° N, 138° E) an island country in the Pacific Ocean off the east coast of Asia, consisting of four main islands (p. 156)

# L

**Libya** (27° N, 17° E) a country in North Africa (p. 82)

**London** (51°30′ N, 0°10′ W) the capital and largest city of the United Kingdom (p. 22)

# M

**Mexico** (23° N, 102° W) a country in North America (p. 67)

**Miami** (25°46′ N, 80°11′ W) a coastal city in Florida (p. 12)

**Milky Way** a galaxy consisting of several billion stars, including the sun (p. 28)

**Mount Everest** (27°59′ N, 86°56′ E) highest point on Earth, located in the Himalayas on the border between Nepal and China (p. 54)

**Myanmar** (22° N, 98° E) a country in Southeast Asia, also known as Burma (p. 82)

# N

**Nepal** (28° N, 83° E) a country in South Asia (p. 54)

**New York** (43° N, 75° W) a state in the northeastern United States (p. 132)

**New York City** (40°43′ N, 74°1′ W) a coastal city in New York State; the largest city in the United States (p. 84)

**New Zealand** (41° S, 174° E) an island country in the Pacific Ocean (p. 122)

**Nile Valley** the fertile land located on both sides of the Nile River in northeastern Africa; site of one of the earliest civilizations (p. 63)

**North America** (45° N, 100° W) the world's third-largest continent, consisting of Canada, the United States, Mexico, Central America, and many islands (p. 17)

**North Atlantic Current** a warm ocean current in the North Atlantic, flowing eastward toward western and northern Europe (p. 43)

**North Korea** (40° N, 127° E) a country in East Asia, officially the Democratic People's Republic of Korea (p. 82)

**North Pole** (90° N) the northernmost end of Earth's axis, located in the Arctic Ocean (p. 11)

**Norway** (62° N, 10° E) a country in northern Europe (p. 118)

# P

**Pangaea** according to scientific theory, a single landmass that broke apart to form today's separate continents; thought to have existed about 200 million years ago (p. 38)

**Peru Current** a cold-water current of the southeast Pacific Ocean; flowing northward between 40° S and 4° S (p. 43)

**Philippines** (13° N, 122° E) an island country in Southeast Asia (p. 67)

# R

**Ring of Fire** a circle of volcanic mountains that surrounds the Pacific Ocean, including those on the islands of Japan and Indonesia, the Cascades of North America, and the Andes of South America (p. 33)

**Rocky Mountains** the major mountain range in western North America, extending south from western Canada, through the western United States, to Mexico (p. 12)

**Rotterdam** (51°55′ N, 4°28′ E) a seaport city in the Netherlands (p. 131)

**Russia** (60° N, 80° E) a country stretching across eastern Europe and northern Asia; the largest country in the world (p. 159)

# S

**Sahara** the largest desert in the world, covering almost all of North Africa (p. 53)

**St. Louis** (38°37′ N, 90°11′ W) a city in Missouri (p. 45)

**San Francisco** (37°46′ N, 122°25′ W) a coastal city in California (p. 45)

**São Paulo** (23°32′ S, 46°37′ W) the largest city in Brazil (p. 48)

**Saudi Arabia** (25° N, 45° E) a country in Southwest Asia (p. 101)

**South Africa** (30° S, 26° E) a country in southern Africa (p. 70)

**South America** (15° S, 60° W) the world's fourth-largest continent, bounded by the Caribbean Sea, the Atlantic Ocean, and the Pacific Ocean, and linked to North America by the Isthmus of Panama (p. 17)

**A cloud forest in the mountains of Ecuador, a country in South America**

**South Korea** (37° N, 128° E) a country in East Asia (p. 67)

**South Pole** (90° S) the southernmost end of Earth's axis, located in Antarctica (p. 12)

**Switzerland** (47° N, 8° E) a country in central Europe (p. 78)

# T

**Texas** (32° N, 99° W) a state in the south central United States (p. 15)

**Tokyo** (35°42′ N, 139°46′ E) the capital and largest city of Japan; the largest city in the world (p. 63)

**Tropic of Cancer** (23°30′ N) the northern boundary of the tropics; the band of Earth, on either side of the Equator, that receives the most direct light and heat energy from the sun (p. 30)

**Tropic of Capricorn** (23°30′ S) the southern boundary of the tropics (p. 31). *See* **Tropic of Cancer.**

# U

**United States** (38° N, 97° W) a large country in North America (p. 12)

# V

**Vatican City** (41°54′ N, 12°27′ E) a nation-state of southern Europe; the smallest nation-state in the world, completely surrounded by the city of Rome, Italy (p. 81)

**Venezuela** (8° N, 66° W) a country in northern South America (p. 135)

**Vietnam** (16° N, 108° E) a country located in Southeast Asia (p. 67)

# Glossary

## A

**absolute location** (AB suh loot loh KAY shun) *n.* the exact position of a place on Earth (p. 12)

**absolute monarchy** (AB suh loot MAHN ur kee) *n.* a system of complete control by a king or queen who inherits the throne by birth (p. 82)

**acculturation** (uh kul chur AY shun) *n.* the process of accepting new ideas from one culture and fitting them into another culture (p. 106)

**aerial photograph** (EHR ee ul FOHT uh graf) *n.* a photographic image of Earth's surface taken from the air (p. 17)

**agriculture** (AG rih kul chur) *n.* farming; including growing crops and raising livestock (p. 94)

**arid** (A rid) *adj.* dry (p. 44)

**atmosphere** (AT muh sfeer) *n.* a layer of gases surrounding a planet (p. 35)

**axis** (AK sis) *n.* an imaginary line around which a planet turns. Earth's axis runs through the center of the planet from the North to the South Pole. (p. 29)

## B

**barometer** (buh RAHM uh tur) *n.* an instrument for forecasting changes in the weather; anything that indicates a change (p. 89)

**biodiversity** (by oh duh VUR suh tee) *n.* a large variety of living things in a region (p. 129)

**birthrate** (BURTH rayt) *n.* the number of live births each year per 1,000 people (p. 64)

**blizzard** (BLIZ urd) *n.* a heavy snowstorm with strong winds (p. 47)

**A blizzard in Bavaria, Germany**

# C

**canopy** (KAN uh pea) *n.* the layer formed by the uppermost branches of the rain forest (p. 52)

**capitalism** (KAP ut ul iz um) *n.* an economic system in which private individuals or groups of people own most businesses (p. 75)

**cardinal directions** (KAHR duh nul duh REK shunz) *n.* north, east, south, and west (p. 11)

**city-state** (SIH tee stayt) *n.* a small city-centered state (p. 81)

**civil engineering** (SIV ul en juh NIHR ing) *n.* technology for building structures that alter the landscape, such as dams, roads, and bridges (p. 131)

**civilization** (sih vuh luh ZAY shun) *n.* an advanced culture with cities and the use of writing (p. 94)

**climate** (KLY mut) *n.* the average weather of a place over many years (p. 40)

**colonization** (kahl uh nih ZAY shun) *n.* movement of settlers and their culture to a new country (p. 125)

**commercial farmers** (kuh MUR shul FAHR murz) *n.* farmers who grow most of their food for sale rather than for their own needs (p. 76)

**communism** (KAHM yoo niz um) *n.* an economic system in which the central government owns farms, factories, and offices (p. 75)

**compass rose** (KUM pus rohz) *n.* a diagram of a compass showing direction on a map (p. 21)

**conformal map** (kun FAWR mul map) *n.* a flat map of the entire planet Earth, which shows correct shapes but not true distances or sizes; also known as a Mercator projection after geographer Gerardus Mercator (p. 18)

**coniferous trees** (koh NIF ur us treez) *n.* trees that produce cones to carry seeds (p. 52)

**constitution** (kahn stuh TOO shun) *n.* a set of laws that defines and limits a government's power (p. 83)

**constitutional monarchy** (kahn stuh TOO shun ul MAHN ur kee) *n.* a government in which the power of the king or queen is limited by law (p. 83)

**consumer** (kun SOO mur) *n.* a person who buys and uses goods and services (p. 74)

**copse** (kahps) *n.* a thicket of small trees or shrubs (p. 89)

**core** (kawr) *n.* the ball of very hot metal at the center of Earth (p. 34)

**crust** (krust) *n.* the thin layer of rocks and minerals that surrounds Earth's mantle (p. 34)

**cultural diffusion** (KUL chur ul dih FYOO zhun) *n.* the movement of customs and ideas from one culture to another (p. 106)

**cultural landscape** (KUL chur ul LAND skayp) *n.* the parts of a people's environment that they have shaped and that reflect their culture (p. 93)

**cultural trait** (KUL chur ul trayt) *n.* a skill, custom, idea, or way of doing things that forms part of a culture (p. 92)

**culture** (KUL chur) *n.* the way of life of a people, including their language, beliefs, customs, and practices (p. 92)

# D

**death rate** (deth rayt) *n.* the number of deaths each year per 1,000 people (p. 64)

**deciduous trees** (dih SIJ oo us treez) *n.* trees that lose their leaves in the fall (p. 52)

**deforestation** (dee fawr uh STAY shun) *n.* a loss of forest cover in a region (p. 129)

**degrees** (dih GREEZ) *n.* units that measure angles (p. 11)

**demography** (dih MAH gruh fee) *n.* the scientific study of population change and population distribution (p. 60)

**dependency** (dee PEN dun see) *n.* a region that belongs to another state (p. 81)

**desert** (DEZ urt) *n.* a hot, dry region with little vegetation (p. 52)

**desert scrub** (DEZ urt skrub) *n.* desert vegetation that needs little water (p. 52)

**developed nations** (dih VEL upt NAY shunz) *n.* nations with many industries and advanced technology (p. 76)

**developing nations** (dih VEL up ing NAY shunz) *n.* nations with few industries and simple technology (p. 76)

**dictator** (DIK tay tur) *n.* a leader who has almost total power over an entire country (p. 82)

**direct democracy** (duh REKT dih MAHK ruh see) *n.* a form of government in which all adults take part in decisions (p. 82)

**distortion** (dih STAWR shun) *n.* loss of accuracy. Every map projection causes some distortion of shape. (p. 17)

# E

**economy** (ih KAHN uh mee) *n.* a system in which people make, exchange, and use things that have value (p. 74)

**empire** (EM pyr) *n.* a state containing several countries (p. 81)

**energy** (EN ur jee) *n.* usable heat or power; capacity for doing work (p. 115)

**environment** (en VY run munt) *n.* natural surroundings (p. 120)

**equal-area map** (EEK wul EHR ee uh map) *n.* a map showing the correct size of landmasses but with altered shapes (p. 19)

**Equator** (ee KWAYT ur) *n.* the line of latitude around the middle of the globe (p. 11)

**equinox** (EE kwih nahks) *n.* one of two days in the year when the sun is directly over the Equator and the days are almost exactly as long as the nights; known as spring and fall equinoxes (p. 30)

**erosion** (ee ROH zhun) *n.* a process in which water, ice, or wind remove small pieces of rock (p. 39)

**ethics** (ETH iks) *n.* the standards or code of moral behavior distinguishing between right and wrong (p. 101)

**extended family** (ek STEN did FAM uh lee) *n.* a family that includes several generations (p. 97)

# F

**faults** (fawlts) *n.* cracks in Earth's crust (p. 37)

**fossil fuels** (FAHS ul FYOO ulz) *n.* fuels created over millions of years from the remains of prehistoric living things (p. 117)

# G

**geographic information systems** (jee uh GRAF ik in fur MAY shun SIS tumz) *n.* computer-based systems that store and use information linked to geographic locations (p. 17)

**geography** (jee AHG ruh fee) *n.* the study of Earth (p. 10)

**globe** (glohb) *n.* a model of Earth with the same round shape as Earth itself (p. 16)

**goods** (gudz) *n.* physical products (p. 75)

**government** (GUV urn munt) *n.* a system that creates and enforces laws and institutions in a region (p. 80)

**Green Revolution** (green rev uh LOO shun) *n.* the increased use of chemicals, machinery, and new crop varieties in agriculture since the 1950s that has greatly increased the world's food supply. It has also created environmental challenges. (p. 65)

**A hill in northern England**

# H

**hemisphere** (HEM ih sfeer) *n.* one half of Earth (p. 11)

**hemlock** (HEM lahk) *n.* an evergreen tree with drooping branches and short needles (p. 89)

**high latitudes** (hy LAT uh toodz) *n.* the areas north of the Arctic Circle and south of the Antarctic Circle (p. 32)

**hill** (hil) *n.* a landform with a rounded top that rises above the surrounding land but is lower and less steep than a mountain (p. 35)

**human-environment interaction** (HYOO mun en VY run munt in tur AK shun) *n.* how people affect the environment and the physical characteristics of their surroundings and how the environment affects them (p. 13)

**humid continental climate** (HYOO mid kahn tuh NENT ul KLY mut) *n.* climate with moderate to hot summers but very cold winters; supporting grasslands and forests (p. 51)

**hurricane** (HUR ih kayn) *n.* a tropical cyclone, or violent storm, that forms over the Atlantic Ocean (p. 47)

# I

**immigrant** (IM uh grunt) *n.* a person who moves into one country from another (p. 67)

**industrialization** (in dus tree ul ih ZAY shun) *n.* the growth of manufacturing in an economy (p. 125)

**institution** (in stuh TOO shun) *n.* a custom or organization with social, educational, or religious purposes (p. 95)

**interdependent** (in tur dee PEN dunt) *adj.* dependent on one another (p. 79)

**international** (in tur NASH un ul) *adj.* involving more than one nation (p. 84)

**irrigation** (ih ruh GAY shun) *n.* supplying dry land with water for farming (p. 94)

# K

**key** (kee) *n.* the section of a map that explains the symbols and shading on the map (p. 21)

# L

**landform** (LAND fawrm) *n.* a shape or type of land (p. 35)

**landmass** (LAND mas) *n.* a large area of land (p. 19)

**latitude** (LAT uh tood) *n.* the distance north or south of the Equator, measured in units called degrees (p. 11)

**lichen** (LY kun) *n.* a plant that is a combination of a fungus and an alga and that grows and spreads over rocks and tree trunks (p. 39)

**life expectancy** (lyf ek SPEK tun see) *n.* the average number of years that people live (p. 65)

**longitude** (LAHN juh tood) *n.* the distance east or west of the Prime Meridian, measured in degrees (p. 11)

**low latitudes** (loh LAT uh toodz) *n.* the area between the Tropic of Cancer and the Tropic of Capricorn (p. 32)

# M

**magma** (MAG muh) *n.* soft, nearly molten rock (p. 36)

**mantle** (MAN tul) *n.* the thick, rocky layer around Earth's core (p. 34)

**manufacturing** (man yoo FAK chur ing) *n.* processing a raw material to make a finished product, (p. 123)

**marine west coast climate** (muh REEN west kohst KLY mut) *n.* moderate climate occurring in areas cooled by ocean currents; supporting forests more often than grasses (p. 51)

**Mediterranean climate** (med uh tuh RAY nee un KLY mut) *n.* moderate climate that receives most of its rain in winter and has hot and dry summers; supporting plants with leathery leaves that hold water (p. 51)

**meridian** (muh RID ee un) *n.* a line of longitude (p. 12)

**middle latitudes** (MID ul LAT uh toodz) *n.* the areas between the high and low latitudes (p. 32)

**migration** (my GRAY shun) *n.* movement from one place or region to another (p. 67)

**mineral** (MIN ur ul) *v.* a natural resource that is obtained by mining, such as gold, iron, or copper (p. 114)

**mountain** (MOWN tun) *n.* a steep landform that rises usually more than 2,000 feet (610 m) above sea level or the surrounding flatlands (p. 35)

**A mountain in British Columbia, Canada**

# N

**nation-state** (NAY shun stayt) *n.* a state that is independent of other states (p. 81)

**natural resource** (NACH ur ul REE sawrs) *n.* a useful material found in the environment (p. 114)

**nonrenewable resource** (nahn rih NOO uh bul REE sawrs) *n.* a resource that cannot be replaced (p. 116)

**nuclear family** (NOO klee ur FAM uh lee) *n.* a mother, a father, and their children (p. 97)

# O

**ocean current** (OH shun KUR unt) *n.* a fast-moving stream of water in the ocean created by uneven heating of Earth's surface (p. 42)

**oligarchy** (AHL ih gahr kee) *n.* a government controlled by a small group of people (p. 82)

**orbit** (AWR bit) *n.* the path one body makes as it circles around another (p. 28)

# P

**parallel** (PA ruh lel) *n.* in geography, a line of latitude (p. 12)

**petroleum** (puh TROH lee um) *n.* an oily substance found under Earth's crust; the source of gasoline and other fuels; an energy resource (p. 116)

**plain** (playn) *n.* a large area of flat or gently rolling land (p. 35)

**plate** (playt) *n.* in geography, a huge section of Earth's crust (p. 36)

**plateau** (pla TOH) *n.* a large, mostly flat area that rises above the surrounding land (p. 35)

**polar climate** (POH lur KLY mut) *n.* a climate of the high latitudes that is cold all year and has short summers (p. 50)

**pollution** (puh LOO shun) *n.* waste, usually made by people, that makes a place's air, water, or soil less clean (p. 132)

**population** (pahp yuh LAY shun) *n.* total number of people in an area (p. 60)

**population density** (pahp yuh LAY shun DEN suh tee) *n.* the average number of people per square mile or square kilometer (p. 62)

**population distribution** (pahp yuh LAY shun dis truh BYOO shun) *n.* the way the population is spread out over an area (p. 60)

**precipitation** (pree sip uh TAY shun) *n.* water that falls to the ground as rain, sleet, hail, or snow (p. 40)

**Prime Meridian** (prym muh RID ee un) *n.* the meridian that runs through Greenwich, England (p. 11)

**producer** (pruh DOO sur) *n.* a person who makes products that are used by other people (p. 74)

**projection** (proh JEK shun) *n.* method of mapping Earth on a flat surface (p. 18)

**push-pull theory** (push pul THEE uh ree) *n.* a theory of migration claiming that difficulties "push" people to leave their old homes, while a hope for better living conditions "pulls" them to a new country (p. 68)

**The Prime Meridian runs through the middle of the Royal Observatory in Greenwich, England.**

# R

**raw materials** (raw muh TIHR ee ulz) *n.* natural resources that must be processed to be useful (p. 114)

**region** (REE jun) *n.* an area with a unifying characteristic such as climate, land, population, or history (p. 12)

**relative location** (REL uh tiv loh KAY shun) *n.* the location of a place described in relation to places near it (p. 12)

**renewable resource** (rih NOO uh bul REE sawrs) *n.* a natural resource that can be replaced (p. 115)

**representative democracy** (rep ruh ZEN tuh tiv dih MAHK ruh see) *n.* a government run by representatives that the people choose (p. 83)

**revolution** (rev uh LOO shun) *n.* a circular journey (p. 28)

**rotation** (roh TAY shun) *n.* a complete turn (p. 29)

**rural** (ROOR ul) *adj.* located in the countryside (p. 71)

# S

**sanitation** (san uh TAY shun) *n.* disposal of sewage and waste (p. 65)

**satellite image** (SAT uh lyt IM ij) *n.* an image of Earth's surface taken from a satellite in orbit (p. 17)

**savanna** (suh VAN uh) *n.* a parklike landscape of grasslands with scattered trees that can survive dry spells (p. 52)

**scale** (skayl) *n.* relative size (p. 16)

**semiarid climate** (sem ee A rid KLY mut) *n.* hot, dry climate with little rain, supporting only shrubs and grasses (p. 44)

**services** (SUR vih siz) *n.* kinds of work that producers perform for other people (p. 123)

**social class** (SOH shul klas) *n.* a grouping of people based on rank or status (p. 97)

**social structure** (SOH shul STRUK chur) *n.* a pattern of organized relationships among groups of people within a society (p. 96)

**society** (suh SY uh tee) *n.* a group of people sharing a culture and social structure (p. 96)

**solstice** (SAHL stis) *n.* one of two days in the year when the sun is directly overhead at its farthest point from the Equator. Summer solstice, in the hemisphere where the sun is overhead, is the longest day and shortest night of the year. Winter solstice, in the opposite hemisphere, is the shortest day and longest night of the year. (p. 30)

**state** (stayt) *n.* a region that shares a government (p. 80)

**subarctic climate** (sub AHRK tik KLY mut) *n.* a continental dry climate with cool summers and cold winters (p. 51)

**subsistence farmers** (sub SIS tuns FAHR murz) *n.* farmers who raise food and animals mainly to feed their own families (p. 77)

# T

**technology** (tek NAHL uh jee) *n.* a way of putting knowledge to practical use (p. 76)

**temperature** (TEM pur uh chur) *n.* the hotness or coldness of the air or some other substance (p. 40)

**tornadoes** (tawr NAY dohz) *n.* swirling funnels of wind moving as fast as 200 miles (320 kilometers) per hour (p. 47)

**treaty** (TREE tee) *n.* a formal written agreement between states (p. 84)

**tropical cyclone** (TRAHP ih kul SY klohn) *n.* an intense wind and rain storm that forms over oceans in the tropics or low latitudes (p. 47)

**tundra** (TUN druh) *n.* an area of cold climate and low-lying vegetation (p. 51)

# U

**urban** (UR bun) *adj.* located in cities and nearby towns (p. 71)

**urbanization** (ur ban ih ZAY shun) *n.* the movement of people to cities (p. 70)

# V

**vegetation** (vej uh TAY shun) *n.* plants that grow in a region, (p. 50)

**vertical climate** (VUR tih kul KLY mut) *n.* the overall weather patterns of a region as influenced by elevation; the higher the elevation, the colder the climate (p. 54)

# W

**weather** (WETH ur) *n.* the condition of the air and sky from day to day (p. 40)

**weathering** (WETH ur ing) *n.* a process that breaks rocks down into tiny pieces (p. 39)

# Index

The *italicized* page numbers refer to illustrations. The italic letter preceding some numbers refers to maps *(m)*, charts *(c)*, graphs *(g)*, and pictures *(p)*.

## A

**Aborigines,** *p108*
**absolute location,** 12, 168
**absolute monarchy,** 82, 168
**acculturation,** 104, 106, 168
**aerial photographs,** 17, 168
**Afghanistan,** 156
**Africa,** 154–155, 164
  developing nations 77
  plate movements *m38*
  population density *m63*
  population growth 66
  slave trade 68
  urbanization 71
  *See also* individual countries
**Agricultural Revolution,** 94
**agriculture,**
  colonization 125
  and cultural change 106
  cultural development 94, *p94*
  cultural landscape 93, *p93*
  defined 168
  developed nations 76
  developing nations 77
  early farming and modern
   industrialization *m61*
  economic activity 122, *p122*
  effect on environment 128, 129
  irrigation 121, *p121*
  land use 121
  population distribution 61, *m61*
  population growth 65
  renewable resources 116
  subsistence farmers 77, 175
**air circulation,** *p42*
**air pollution,** 132
**air pressure, tornadoes,** 47
**air temperature,** 40
**Albania,** 158
**Alexander Island,** *p35*

**Algeria,** 154
**alliances,**
  nations 84
  trade 79
**Amritsar, India,** *p101*
**Amsterdam, Netherlands,** *p72*
**Anasazi people,** 103
**Andorra,** 158
**Angola,** 154
**animals,**
  biodiversity 129
  *See also* agriculture
**Antarctic Circle,** 32, 164
**Antarctica,** 164
  ice floes *p35*
  ocean currents 43
**antibiotics,** 65
**Antigua and Barbuda,** 160
**Antofagasta, Chile,** 43, 164
**Appalachian Mountains,** 39, 164
**Arches National Park, Utah,**
  *p26–27*
**Arctic,** *p31*, 120, 164
**Arctic Circle,** *p30*, *p31*, 32, 51, 164
**Arctic Ocean,** 56
**Argentina,** 160
**arid, defined,** 168
**arid climates,** *p44*, 51
**Armenia,** 156
**Asia,** 156–58, 164
  cultural change 104
  developing nations 77
  population density *m63*
  population growth 66
  religions 100
  Silk Road 78
  urbanization 71
  *See also* South Asia; Southwest
   Asia; and individual countries
**Atlantic Ocean,** 56
  currents 43
  hurricanes 47
  slave trade 68
**atmosphere,** *p34*, 35, 168
**atomic energy,** 118
**Australia,** 156, 164
  colonization 125, *p125*
  cultural change 107, *p108*

  families 97
  immigrants 68
**Austria,** 158
**axis, Earth's,** 28, 29, 30, *p30*, 168
**Azerbaijan,** 156

## B

**Bahamas,** 160
**Bahrain,** 156
**Bali,** 93, *p93*
**balloons, weather,** 46
**Bangladesh,** *p66*, 156, 164
**banks,** 75
**Barbados,** 160
**barometers,** 89, 168
**baseball,** 106
**Beatrix, Queen of the**
  **Netherlands,** *p83*
**Belarus,** 158
**Belgium,** 158
**Belize,** 160
**Benin,** 154
**Bhutan,** 156
**biodiversity,** 128, 129, 168
**biomass energy,** 118
**birthrate,** 60, 64–65, *g64*, 168
**blizzards,** 47, 168
**Bolivia,** 160
**Bonneville Dam,** *p117*
**Bosnia and Herzegovina,** 158
**Boston, Massachusetts,** *p124*
  changes in land use *m124*
**Botswana,** 154
**Brazil,** *p52*, 71, 160, 164
**Britain,** *See* United Kingdom
**Brunei,** 156, 164
**Buddhism,** 100, *p100*
**Bulgaria,** 158
**Burkina Faso,** 154
**Burma,** *See* Myanmar
**Burundi,** 154

## C

**California,** *p53*, *p133*
**Cambodia,** 156
**Cameroon,** 154

# Index

# Index

middle 32, *m32*

seasons and 30–32, *p30–31*

winds and *p42*

zones of *m32*

**Latvia,** 159

**lava,** 36

**laws,** 80, 81, 94

**Lebanon,** 157

**legend, maps,** 21

**Lesotho,** 154

**Liberia,** 154

**Libya,** 82, 155, 165

**lichen,** 172

**Liechtenstein,** 159

**life expectancy,** 64, 65, 172

**Lithuania,** 159

**living resources,** 116

**location,** 11–12

climate and 41

*See also* place location

**locator globes, maps,** *m20*

**London, England,** *m22*, 165

**longitude,** 11–12, *p11*

defined 10, 172

global grid 12, *p12*

Mercator Projection 18

time zones and 29

**low latitudes,** 32, *m32*, 41, 172

**Luxembourg,** 159

# M

**Macedonia,** 159

**Machapuchare, Nepal** *p54*

**machines,**

and economic development 76

*See also* industrialization

**Madagascar,** 155

**Madeira,** *p46*

**magazines,** 107

**magma,** 33, 36, *p36–37*, 172

**main ideas, reading skills,**

identifying 87, 114, 135

implied main ideas 128

**Maine,** *p30*

**Malawi,** 155

**Malaysia,** *p103*, 157

**Maldives,** 157

**Mali,** 155

**Malta,** 159

**mantle, Earth's,** 33, 34, *p34*, *p36*, 172

**manufacturing,** 120, 123, 172

*See also* industrialization

**maps and globes,** 16–22

distortion in 16, 17, 18–19

equal-area projections 19, *p19*, 170

keys 16, *m20*, 21, 57, 172

latitude and longitude in 11–12, *p11*, *p12*

mental maps 25

Mercator projection 18, *p18*

parts of a map 21

physical maps 20, *m20*, 136

population density 72–73, *m73*, 86

reading maps 20–22

Robinson projection 19, *p19*

scale in 16, 21, *m22*, 174

weather forecasting *p46*

**marine west coast climate,** 51, 172

**markets,** *p74*

**Marshall Islands,** 157

**materials,** *See* resources

**math,**

links 29, 129

population bar graphs 86

predictions 110

writing activities 86, 110

**Mauritania,** 155

**Mauritius,** 155

**Maya,** 103

**medicine, and population growth,** 65

**Mediterranean climate,** 51, 172

**Mediterranean Sea,** 56

**Mediterranean vegetation,** 51, 52

**Mercator, Gerardus,** 18

**Mercator projection,** 18, *p18*

**meridians,** 10, 12, 170

**metals, natural resources,** 116

**Mexico,** 135, 161, 165

migration 67

energy resources 118

Maya 103

trade 79

**Miami, Florida,** *p42*, 43, 165

**Micronesia,** 157

**Middle East, irrigation,** 121, *p121*

**middle latitudes,** 32, *m32*, 173

**migration,** 67–71

defined 173

in South Asia *m69*

urbanization 67, 70–71, *c70*

**Milky Way Galaxy,** 28, *p28*, 165

**minerals,** 116, 173

**Mississippi Valley,** 68

**mixed forests,** 52, *p53*

**mixed ownership,** 75

**Mojave Desert,** 12

**Moldova,** 159

**Monaco,** 159

**monarchy,** 82, 83

**money, capitalism,** 75

**Mongolia,** 157

**Montenegro,** 159

**Morocco,** 155

**Mount Everest,** 54, 165

**mountains,** 35

Appalachian 39

climate and 41

defined 173

formation *p36*

Rocky 12, 39

vertical climate zones 54

water cycle *g41*

**movement,** 13

**Mozambique,** 155

**music,**

link 107

**Muslims,** *See* Islam and Muslims

**Myanmar (Burma),** 82, 156, 165

# N

**Namibia,** 155

**nation-states,** 80, 81, 173

**natural resources,** 114–119, *m115*, *m134*, 173

**Nauru,** 157

# Index

# Index

# Acknowledgments

## Cover Design

Pronk&Associates

## Staff Credits

The people who made up the *World Studies* team—representing design services, editorial, editorial services, educational technology, marketing, market research, photo research and art development, production services, project office, publishing processes, and rights & permissions—are listed below. Bold type indicates core team members.

Greg Abrom, Ernie Albanese, Rob Aleman, Susan Andariese, **Rachel Avenia-Prol,** Leann Davis Alspaugh, Penny Baker, Barbara Bertell, **Peter Brooks,** Rui Camarinha, John, Carle, **Lisa Del Gatto,** Paul Delsignore, Kathy Dempsey, Anne Drowns, Deborah Dukeshire, Marlies Dwyer, **Frederick Fellows,** Paula C. Foye, Lara Fox, Julia Gecha, **Mary Hanisco,** Salena Hastings, Lance Hatch, Kerri Hoar, **Beth Hyslip,** Katharine Ingram, Nancy Jones, John Kingston, Deborah Levheim, Constance J. McCarty, **Kathleen Mercandetti,** Art Mkrtchyan, Ken Myett, **Mark O'Malley,** Jen Paley, Ray Parenteau, **Gabriela Pérez Fiato,** Linda Punskovsky, Kirsten Richert, **Lynn Robbins,** Nancy Rogier, Bruce Rolff, Robin Samper, Mildred Schulte, **Malti Sharma,** Lisa Smith-Ruvalcaba, Roberta Warshaw, Sarah Yezzi

## Additional Credits

Jonathan Ambar, Tom Benfatti, Lisa D. Ferrari, Paul Foster, Florrie Gadson, Phil Gagler, Ella Hanna, Jeffrey LaFountain, Karen Mancinelli, Michael McLaughlin, Lesley Pierson, Debi Taffet, Linda Westerhoff

**DK** The DK Designs team who contributed to *World Studies* were as follows: Hilary Bird, Samantha Borland, Marian Broderick, Richard Czapnik, Nigel Duffield, Heather Dunleavy, Cynthia Frazer, James A. Hall, Lucy Heaver, Rose Horridge, Paul Jackson, Heather Jones, Ian Midson, Marie Ortu, Marie Osborn, Leyla Ostovar, Ralph Pitchford, Ilana Sallick, Pamela Shiels, Andrew Szudek, Amber Tokeley.

**DK** ## Maps

Maps and globes were created by **DK Cartography**. The team consisted of Tony Chambers, Damien Demaj, Julia Lunn, Ed Merritt, David Roberts, Ann Stephenson, Gail Townsley, Iorwerth Watkins.

## Illustrations

31, 34, 36, 41, 43, DK images; 140, Kevin Jones Associates

## Photos

**Cover Photos**

**tl,** Alec Pytlowany/Masterfile; **tm,** David Muir/Masterfile; **tr,** Gordon Wiltsie; **b,** Royalty Free/CORBIS/MAGMA/Artbase, Inc.

**Title Page**

Royalty Free/CORBIS/MAGMA/Artbase, Inc.

**Table of Contents**

**iv-v,** Philip Blenkinsop/DK Images; **vi-vii,** Brenda Tharp/Corbis; **viii,** sun, DK Images; globes, Planetary Visions

**Learning With Technology**

**xiii,** Discovery Channel School

**Reading and Writing Handbook**

**RW,** Michael Newman/PhotoEdit; **RWl,** Walter Hodges/Getty Images, Inc.; **RW2,** Digital Vision/Getty Images, Inc.; **RW3,** Will Hart/PhotoEdit; **RW5,** Jose Luis Pelaez, Inc./Corbis

**Guiding Questions**

**1,** Christine Osborne/World Religions Photo Library

**World Overview**

**2 l, 2 t,** DK Images; **3 l,** Daniel Laine/Corbis; **3 tr,** DK Images; **3 br,** Sipa/Rex Features; **4 bl,** Layne Kennedy/Corbis; **4 tr,** DK Images; **5 t,** Royalty Free Images/Corbis; **6 t,** Roger Ressmeyer/Corbis; **7 br,** Amet Jean Pierre/Sygma/Corbis; **7 tr,** DK Images

**Chapter One**

**8–9,** Johnson Space Center/NASA; **10,** Steve Gorton/DK Images; **13,** M. Balan/DK Images; **14,** Will & Deni McIntyre/Corbis; **15 b,** Richard Powers/Corbis; **15 t,** DK Images; **16,** Peter Wilson/DK Images; **17,** MSFC/NASA; **23,** Johnson Space Center/NASA

**Chapter Two**

**26–27,** George H. Huey/Corbis; **28,** Daniel Pyne/DK Images; **30 bl,** Alan Briere/DK Images; **30–31,** sun, DK Images; globes, Planetary Visions; **31 tr,** Barnabas Kindersley/DK Images; **33,** Brenda Tharp/Corbis; **35,** C. M. Leask/Eye Ubiquitous; **36 bl,** James Balog/Getty Images; **37 tr,** James A. Sugar/Corbis; **39,** Alan Hills/DK Images; **40,** Galen Rowell/Corbis; **41 tr,** Hutchison Library; **43 tr,** Royalty Free Images/Corbis; **44 b,** Demetrio Carrasco/DK Images; **45 bl,** Chris Stowers/DK Images; **46 m,** DK Images; **46 bl,** NASA; **46 tr,** N.H.P.A.; **46 mr,** Lelan Statom, meteorologist; Mark Martin, photojournalist/network operations manager, WTVF-Newschannel 5 Network, Nashville, Tenn.; **47,** Chris Graythen/Getty Images; **48 t,** Michael S. Yamashita/Corbis; **50,** Liu Liqun/Corbis; **51 br,** Terry W. Eggers/Corbis; **51 tr,** Denver Museum of Nature and Science; **52,** Alan Watson/DK Images; **53 t,** Photo-wood Inc./Corbis; **53 bl,** Neil Lukas; **53 br,** Stephen Hayward/DK Images; **54,** Galen Rowell/Corbis; **55,** George H. Huey/Corbis

**Chapter Three**

**58–59,** Keren Su/Corbis; **60,** James Strachan/Getty Images; **61 t,** Royalty Free Images/Corbis; **62 bl,** Wolfgang Kaehler/Corbis; **63 br,** Peter Wilson/DK Images; **64 t,** Howard Davies/Corbis; **65 b,** Patricia Aithie/Ffotograff; **66,** Dirk R. Frans/Hutchison Library; **67,** Bettmann Corbis; **68,** Dave King/DK Images; **69 bl,** Bettmann/Corbis; **70 bl,** Hulton-Deutsch Collection/Corbis; **70 br,** Paul Almasy/Corbis; **71,** Stephanie Maze/Corbis; **72,** Bill Ross/Corbis; **74,** Rob Reichenfeld/DK Images; **75 t,** Corbis; **76,** Philip Blenkinsop/DK Images; **77 b,** Tom Wagner/Corbis; **78 l,** Mark E. Gibson/Corbis; **78 b,** Annebicque Bernard/Sygma/Corbis; **78 r,** Mary Ann McDonald/Corbis; **79,** Peter Blakely/SABA/Corbis; **80,** Patrick Durand/Sygma/Corbis; **81,** Franz-Marc Frei/Corbis; **82,** Tom Haskell/Sygma/Corbis; **83 t,** Pa Photos; **83 b,** Ron Sachs/Rex Features; **84,** Joseph Sohm/Chromosohm Inc./Corbis; **85,** Keren Su/Corbis; **88,** Peter Finger/Corbis

**Chapter Four**

**90–91,** Bryan Colton/Assignments Photographers/Corbis; **92,** Royalty Free Images/Corbis; **93 b,** Dennis Degnan/Corbis; **94 tl,** Geoff Brightling/DK Images; **94 b,** Richard Leeney/DK Images; **94 ml,** Museum of English Rural Life; **95,** Kim Sayer/DK Images; **96,** DK Images; **97,** Rob Lewine/Corbis; **98 t,** Richard T. Nowitz/Corbis; **98 b,** Barnabas Kindersley/DK Images; **99 b,** Demetrio Carrasco/DK Images; **100 t,** Barnabas Kindersley/DK Images; **100 b,** Peter Wilson/DK Images; **101,** B.P.S. Walia/

DK Images; **102,** Foodpix/Getty Images; **103 l,** Christine Osborne/World Religions Photo Library; **104,** DK Images; **105 b,** Dallas and John Heaton/Corbis; **105 t,** Royalty Free Images/Corbis; **106,** DK Images; **107 mr,** Tom Wagner/Corbis; **107 tr,** Sony/Newscast; **108,** Penny Tweedy/Panos Pictures; **109,** Bryan Colton/Assignments photographers/Corbis

**Chapter Five**

**112–113,** M. L. Sinibaldi/Corbis; **114,** Liba Taylor/Corbis; **116 t, 116–117,** Chinch Gryniewitz/Ecoscene/Corbis; **117 t,** Royalty Free Images/Corbis; **118,** Corbis; **119,** Bob Krist/Corbis; **120,** Holt Studios International; **121 t,** Bob Rowan; Progressive Image/Corbis; **121 b,** Hutchison Library; **122 l,** Paul A. Souders/Corbis; **122 r,** DK Images; **123 l,** James L. Amos/Corbis; **123 m, r,** DK Images; **124,** David Noble/Pictures Colour Library; **125,** Oliver Strewe/Getty Images; **126,** Dennis O'Clair/Getty Images; **127,** DK Images; **128,** Paul A. Souders/Corbis; **129 t,** Wayne Lawler; Ecoscene/Corbis; **129 b,** Martin Wyness/Still Pictures; **130 t,** Benjamin Rondel/Corbis; **130 b,** DK Images; **131,** Frans Lemmens/Getty Images; **132,** Syracuse Newspapers/David Lassman/The Image Works/Topfoto; **133,** M. L. Sinibaldi/Corbis

**Glossary of Geographic Terms**

**162t,** A & L Sinibaldi/Getty Images, Inc.; **162b,** John Beatty/Getty Images, Inc.; **162–163 b,** Spencer Swanger/Tom Stack & Associates; **163 t,** Hans Strand/Getty Images, Inc.; **163 m,** Paul Chesley/Getty Images, Inc.

**Gazetteer**

**166,** DK Images; **167,** Alan Watson/DK Images

**Glossary**

**168,** Bob Krist/Corbis; **171,** Patrick Ward/Corbis; **173,** Gunter Marx/Corbis; **174,** James A. Hall/DK Images

## Text
**Chapter Three**

Page 88–89, Excerpt from *My Side of the Mountain* by Jean Craighead George. Copyright © 1959 by Jean Craighead George.

Note: Every effort has been made to locate the copyright owner of material reprinted in this book. Omissions brought to our attention will be corrected in subsequent editions.